THE BIG PHOTO

OF CATS, KITTENS, AND KITTIES

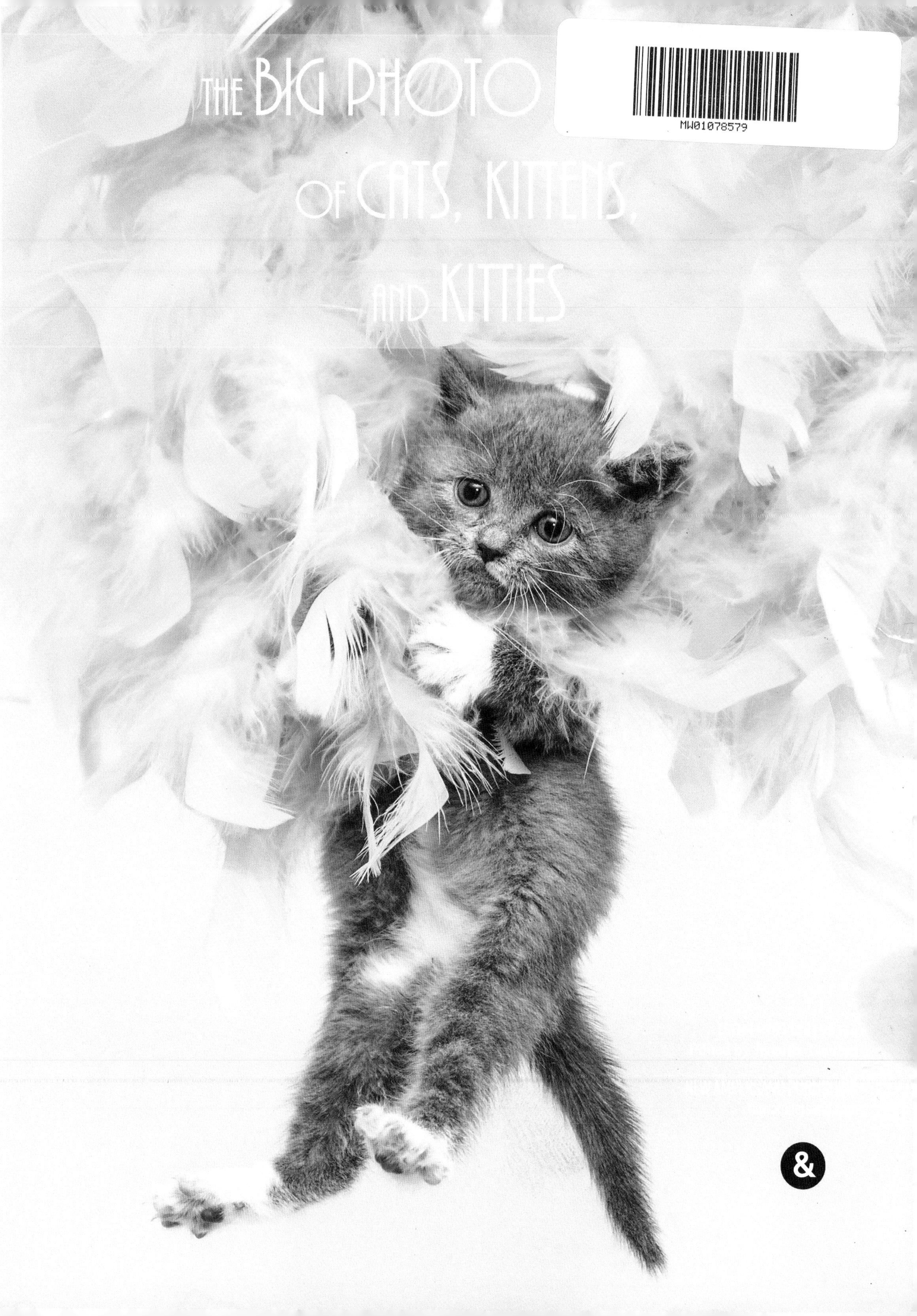

&

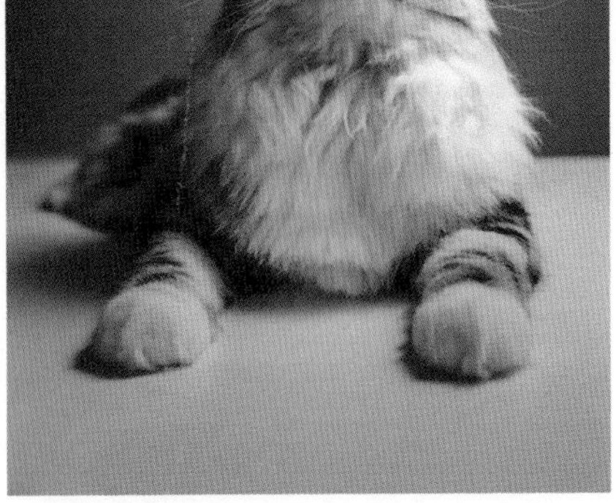
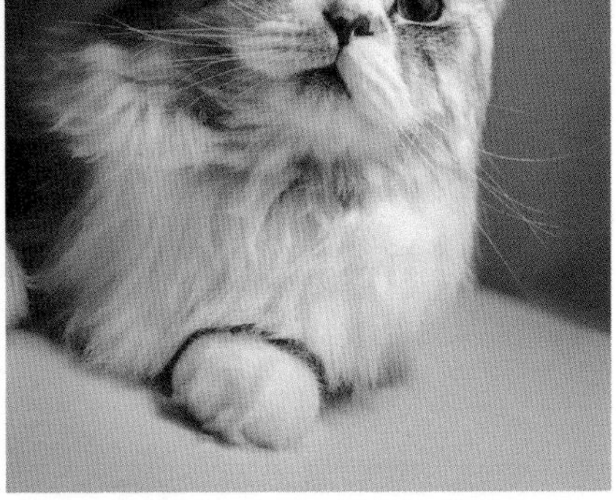
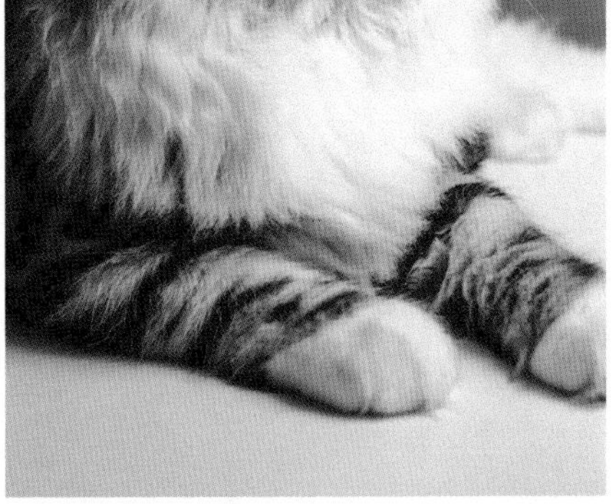
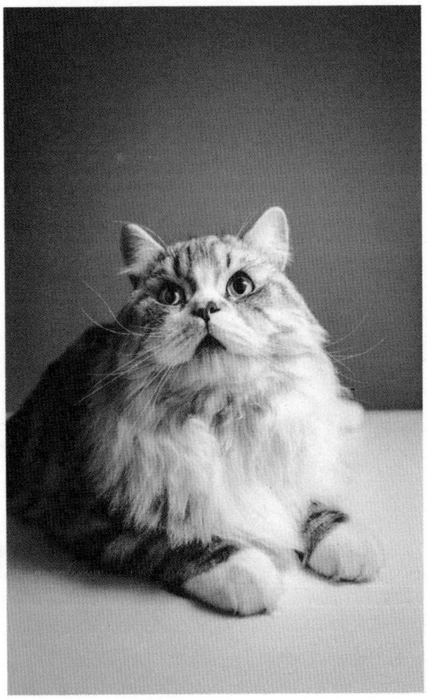
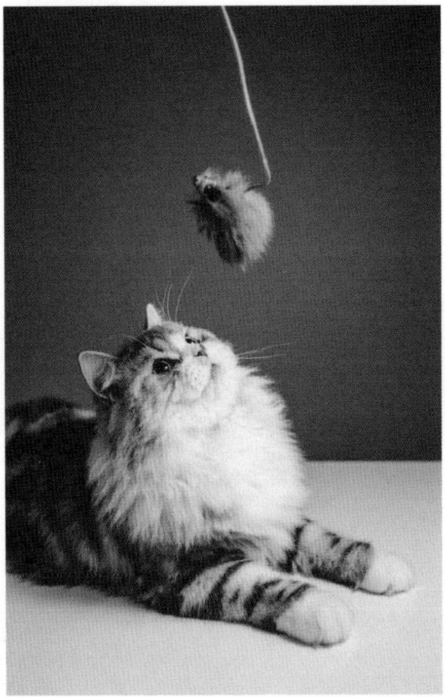
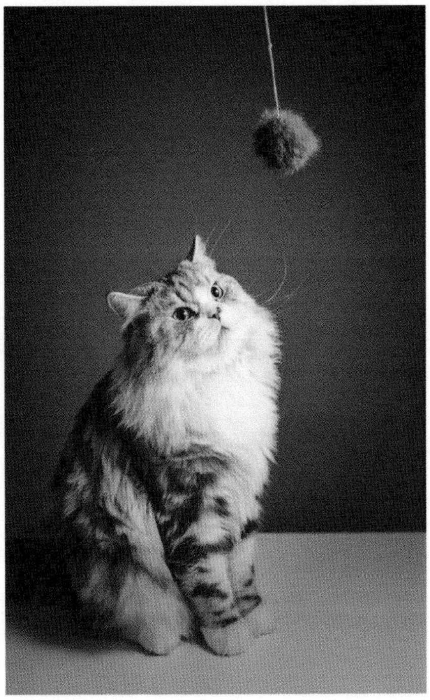

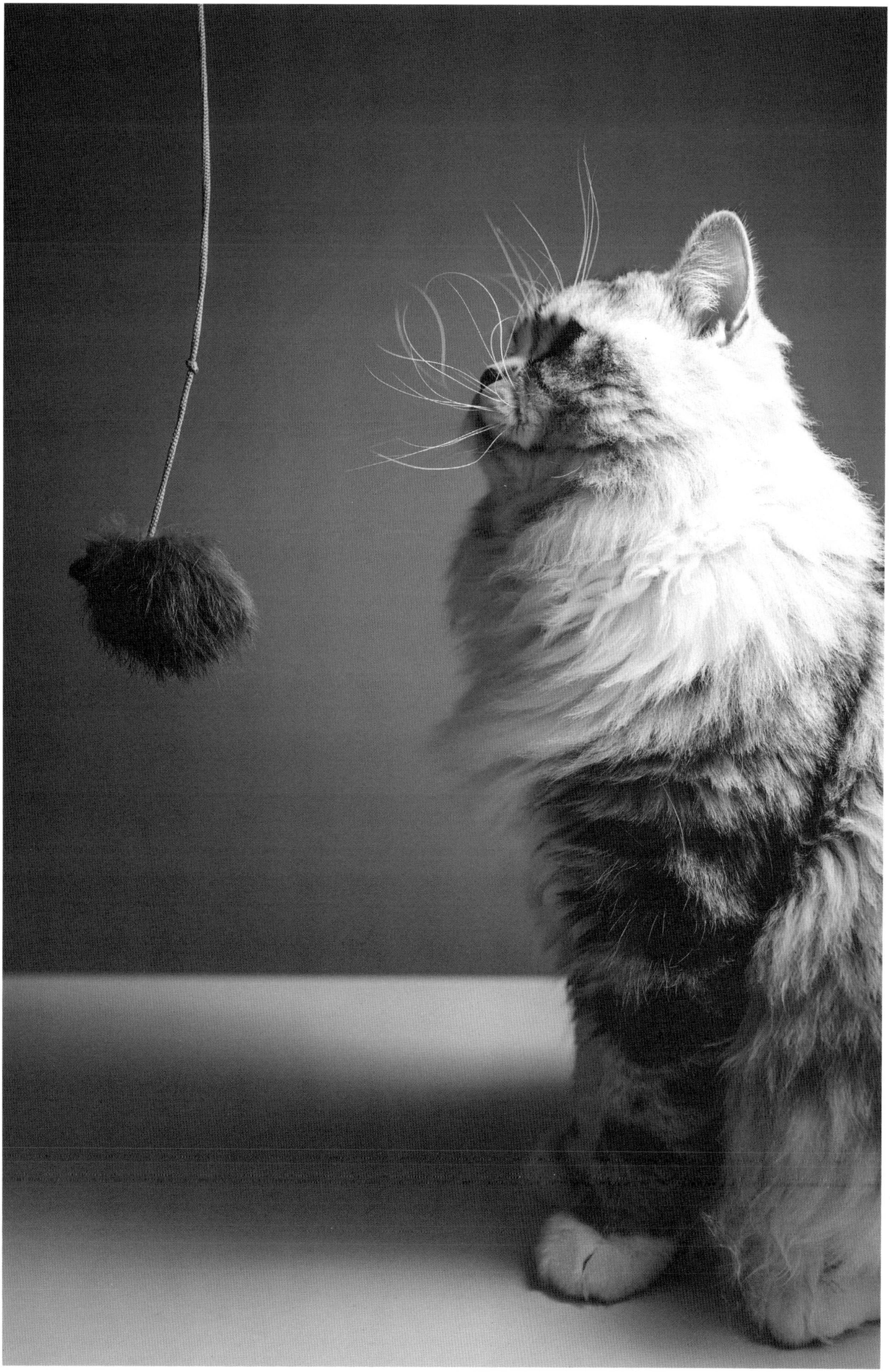

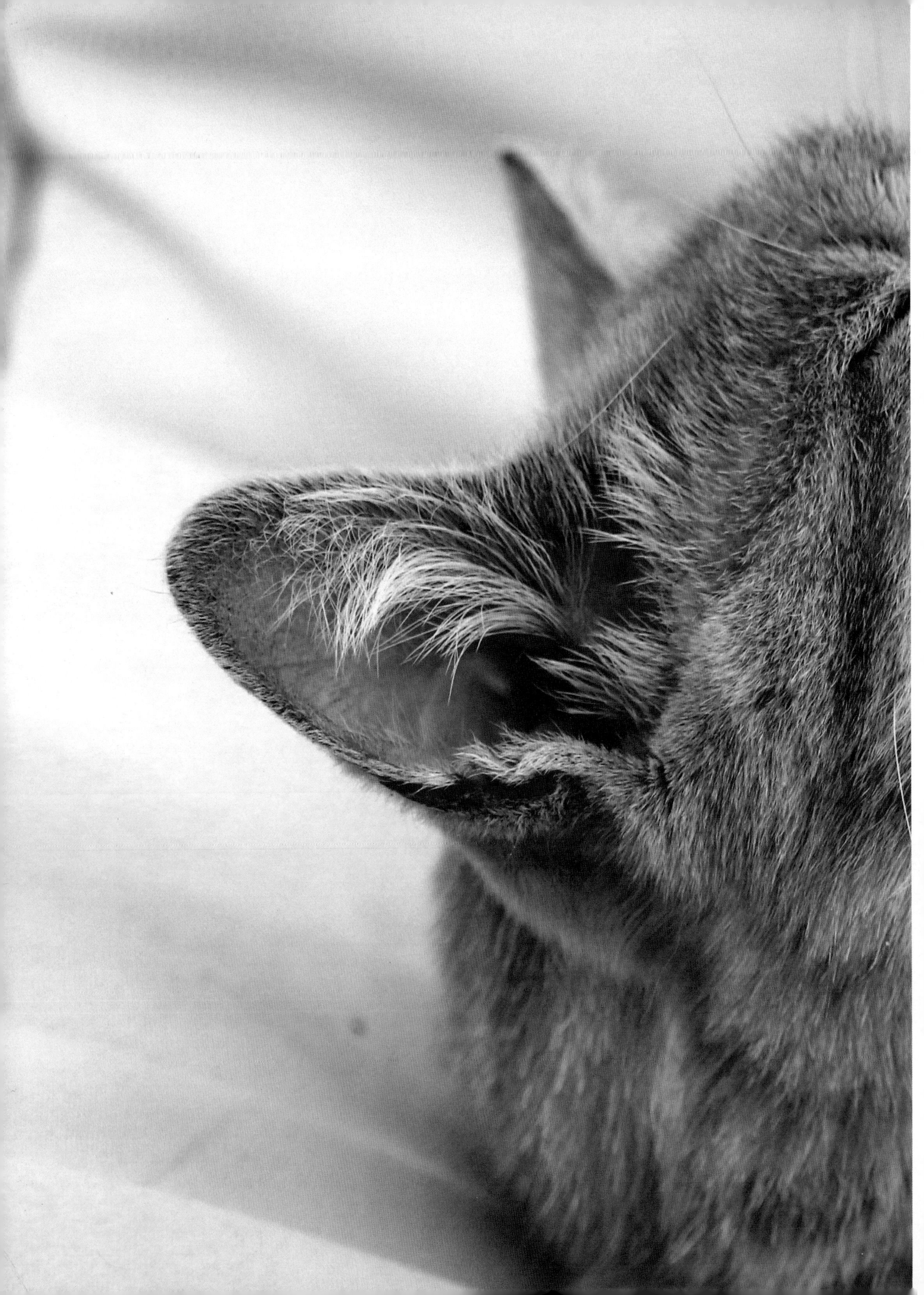

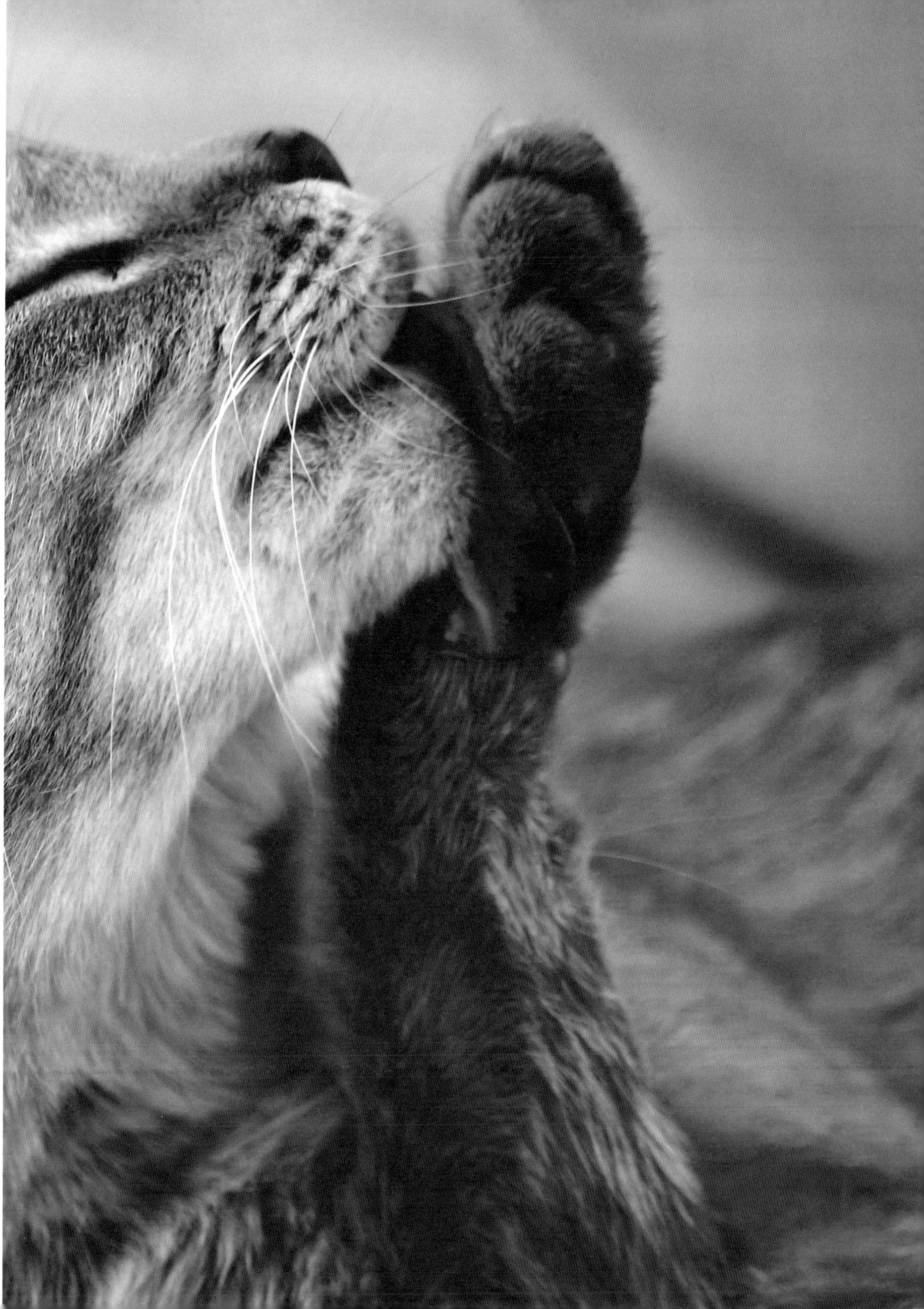

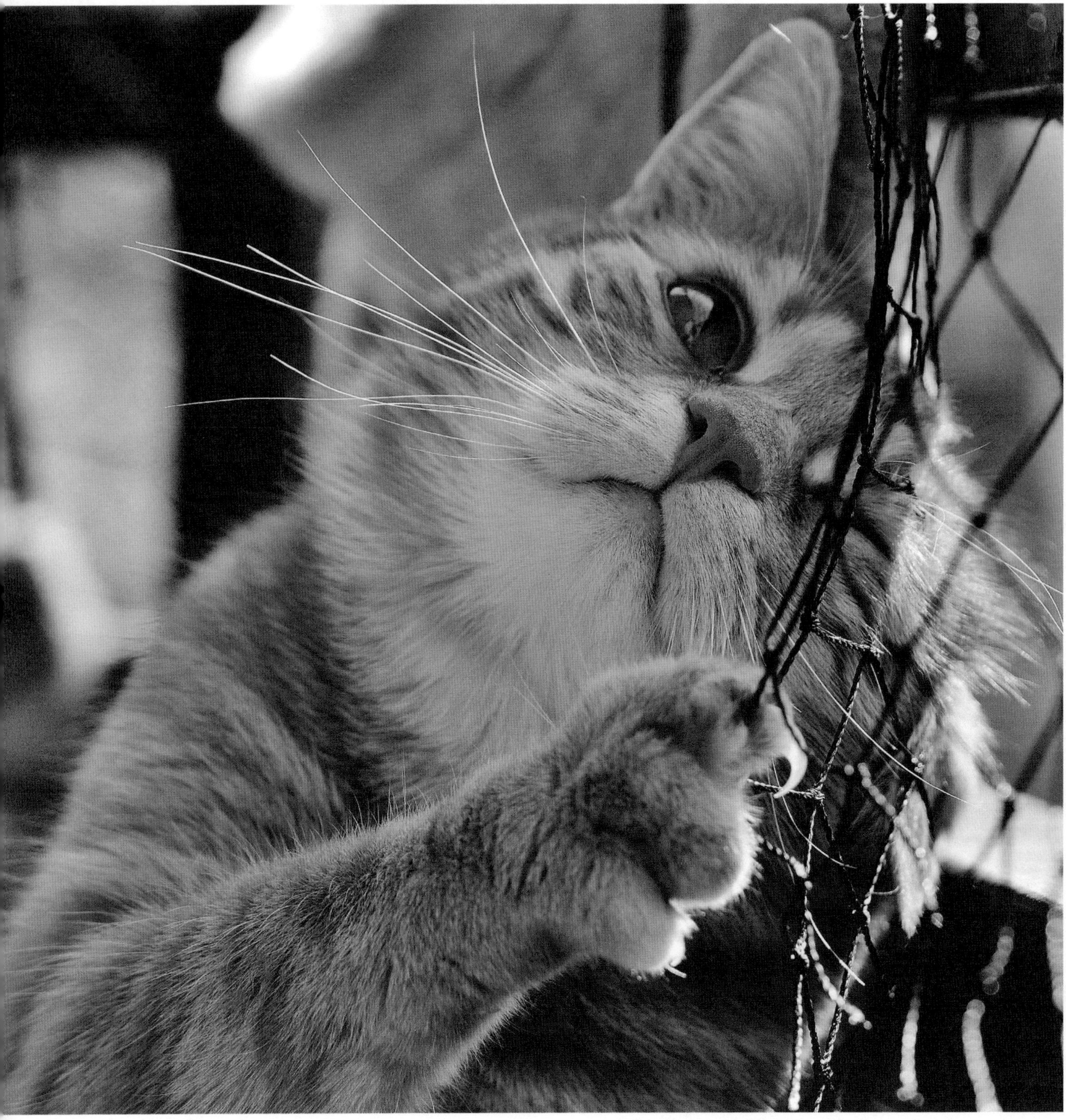

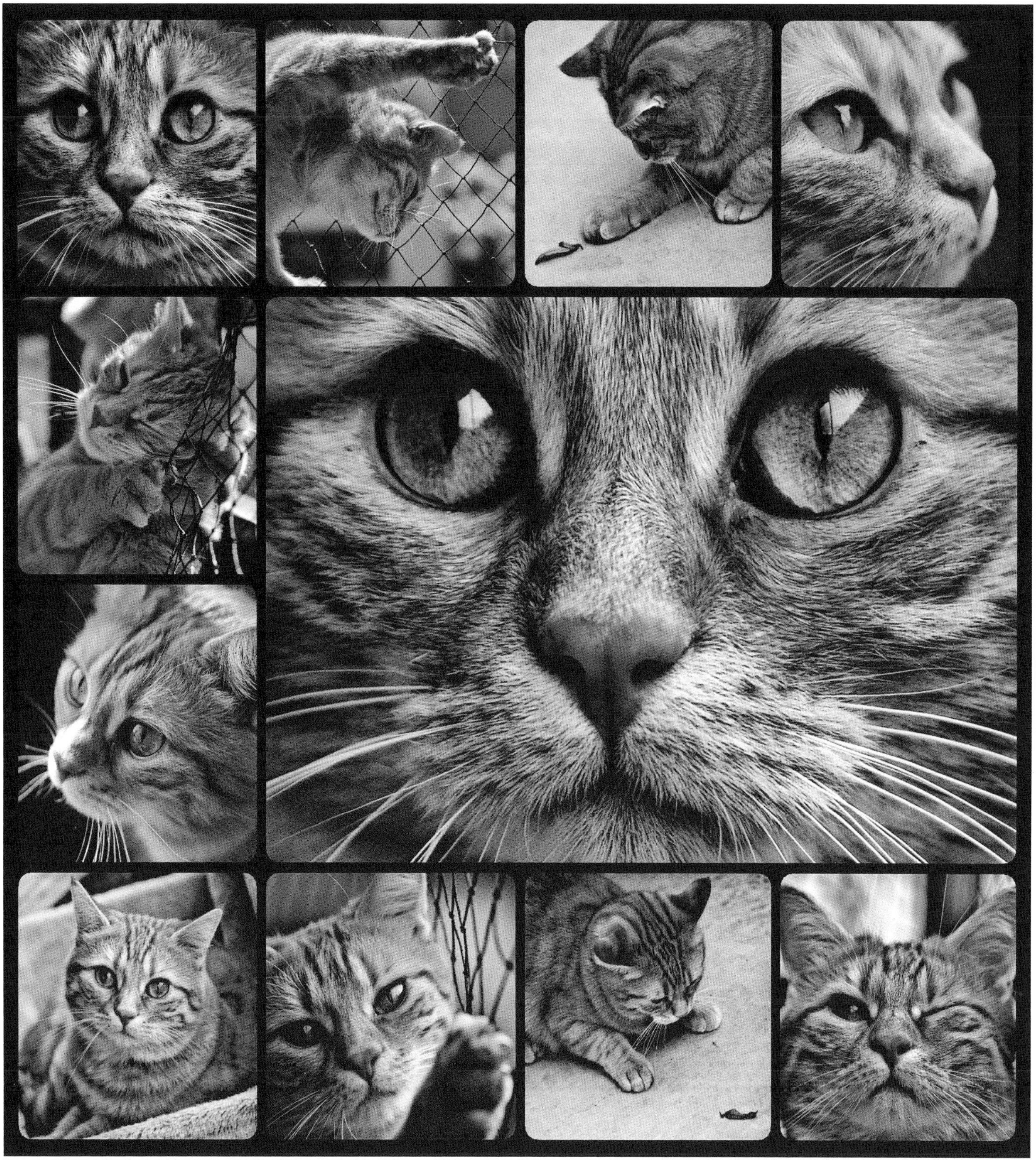

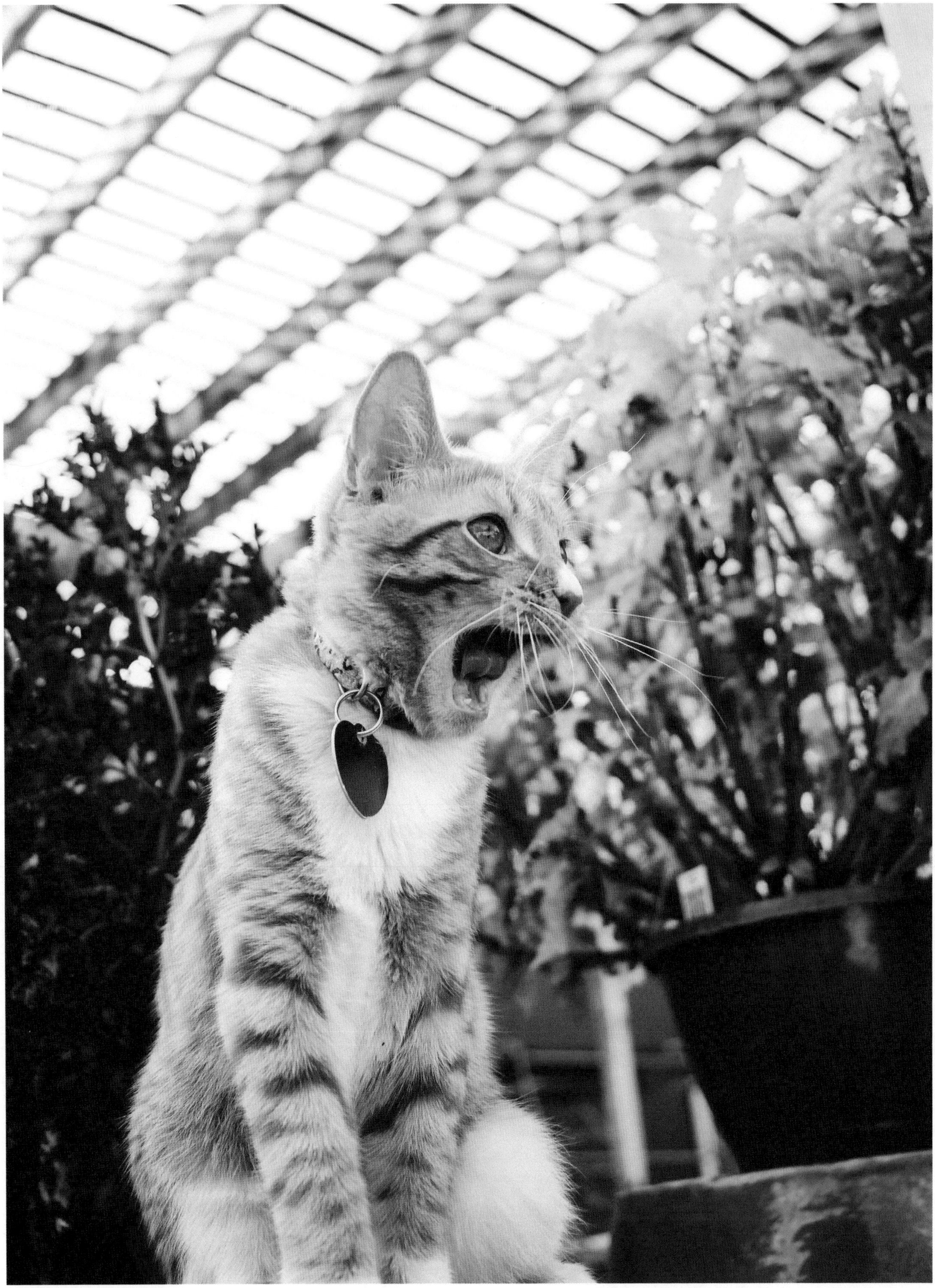

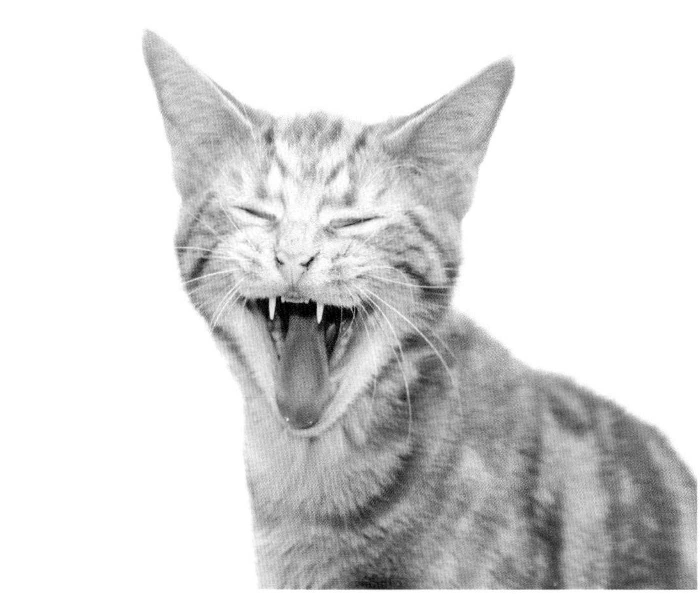
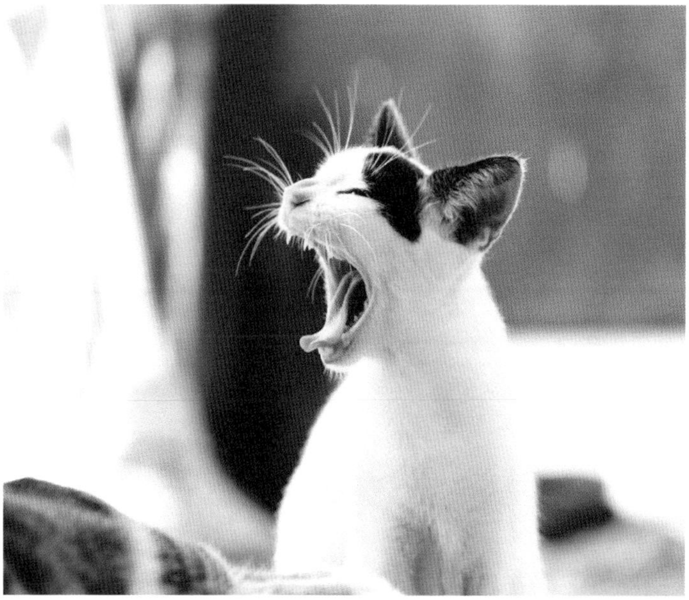
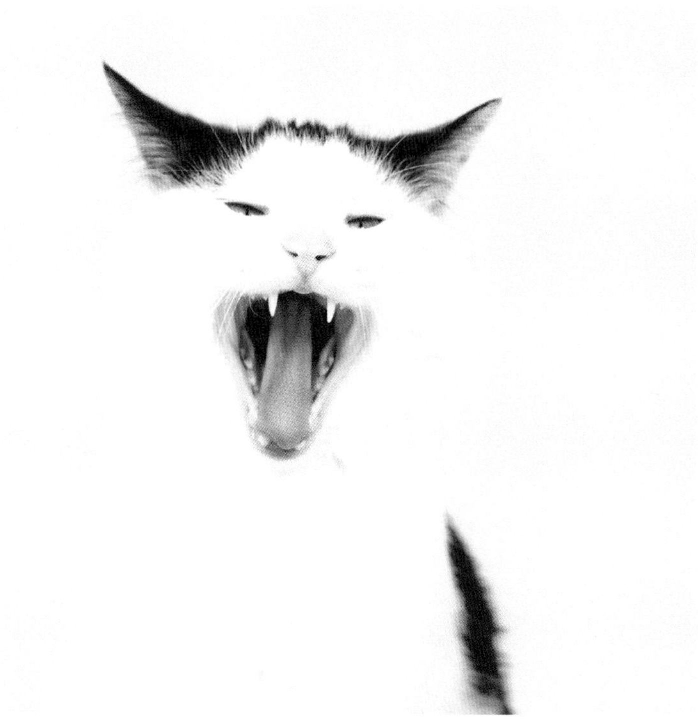
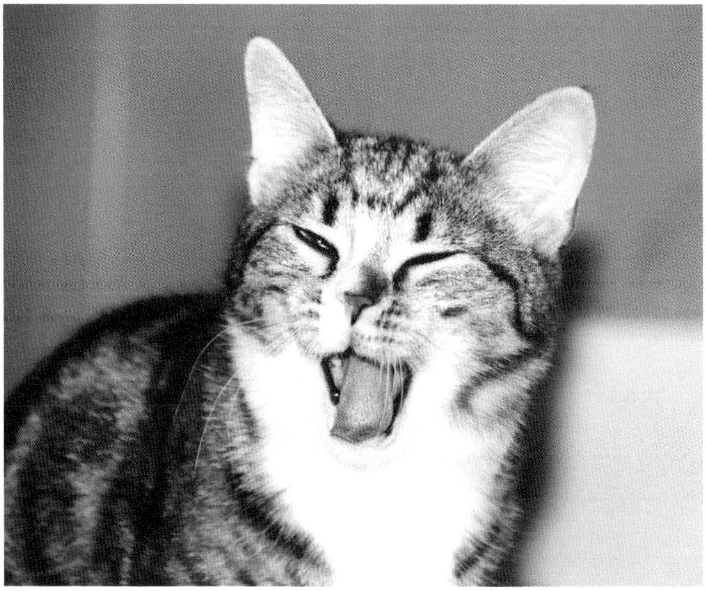
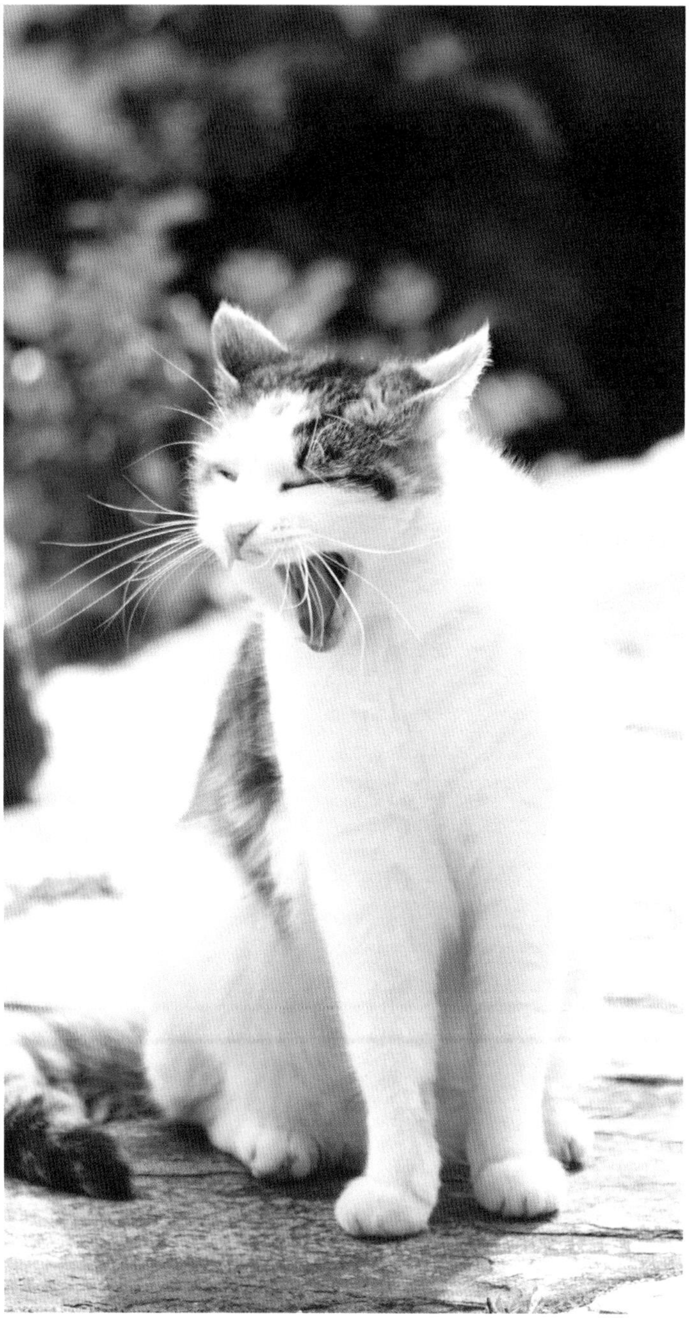

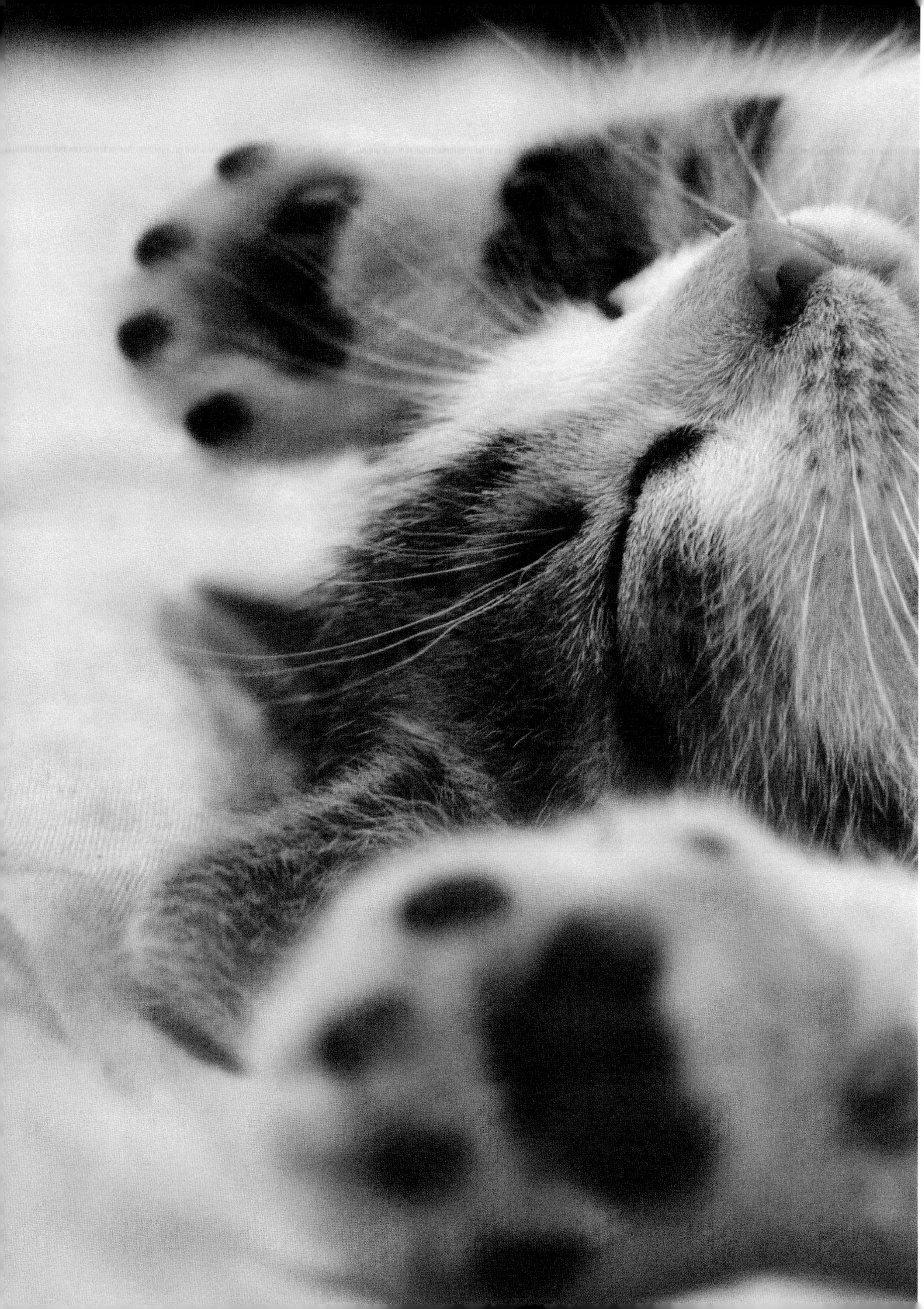

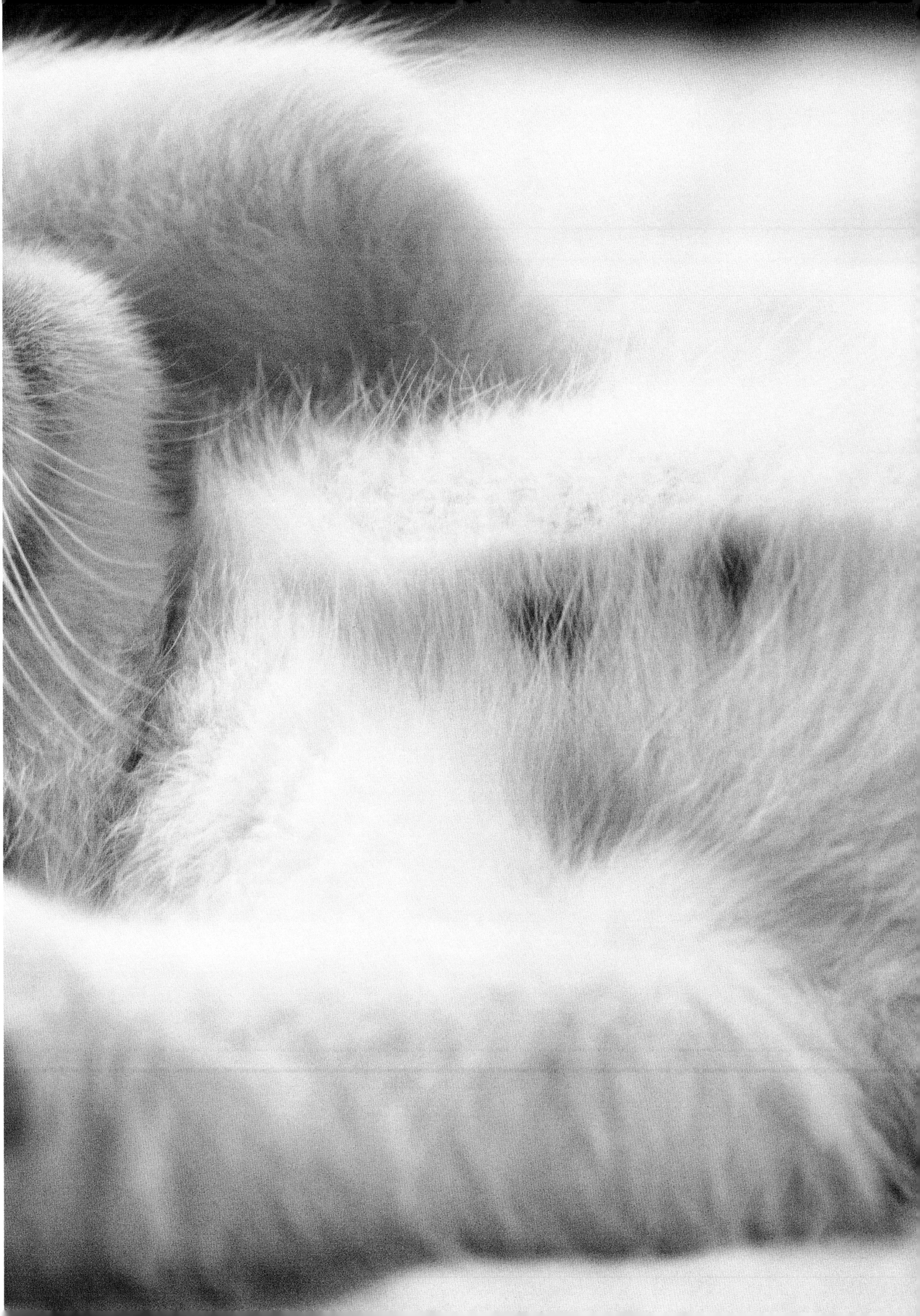

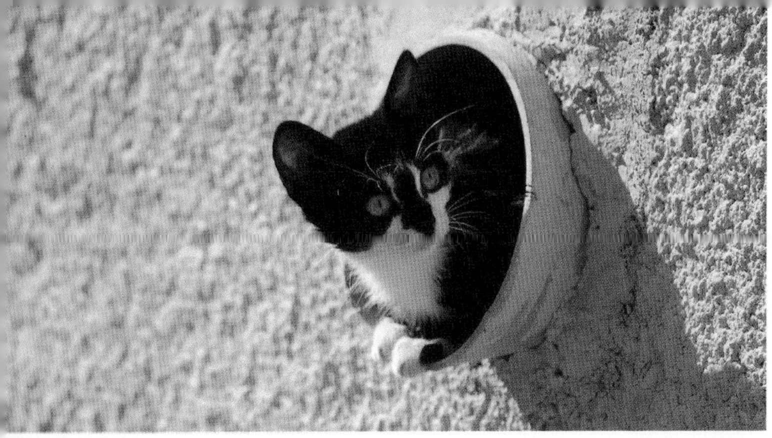
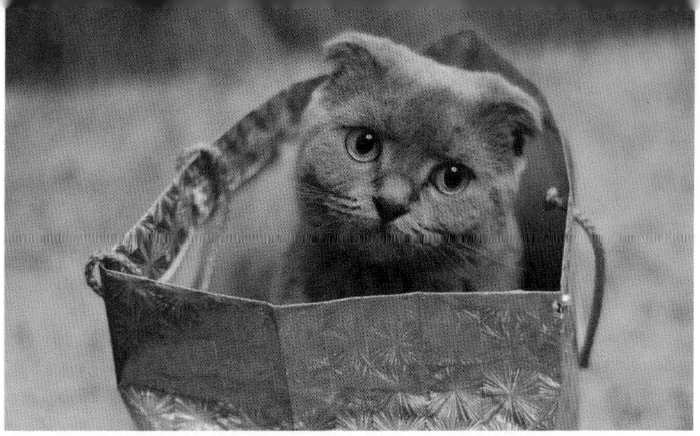
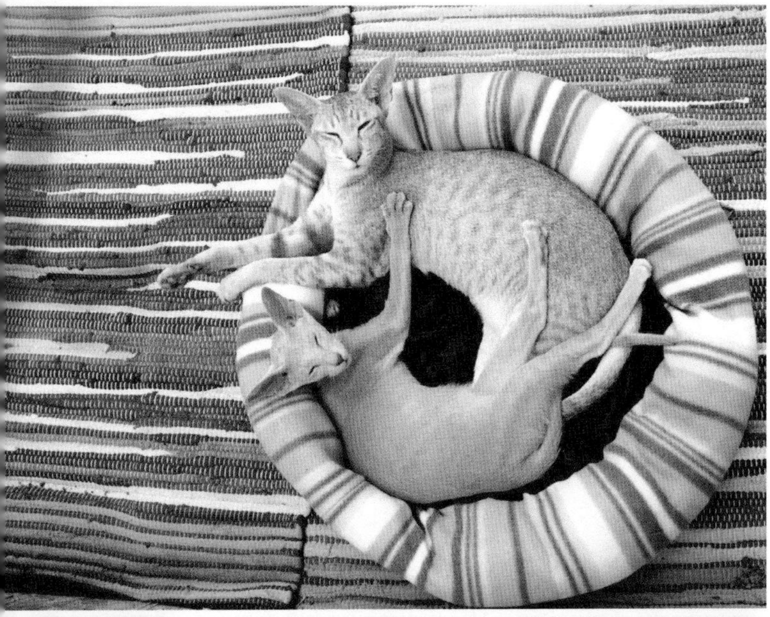
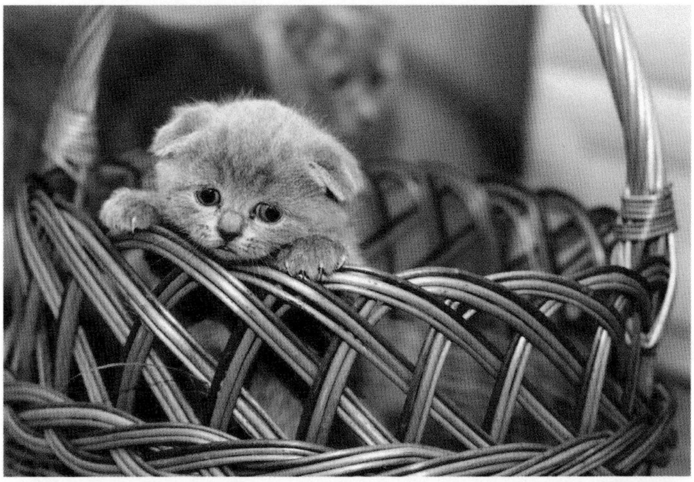
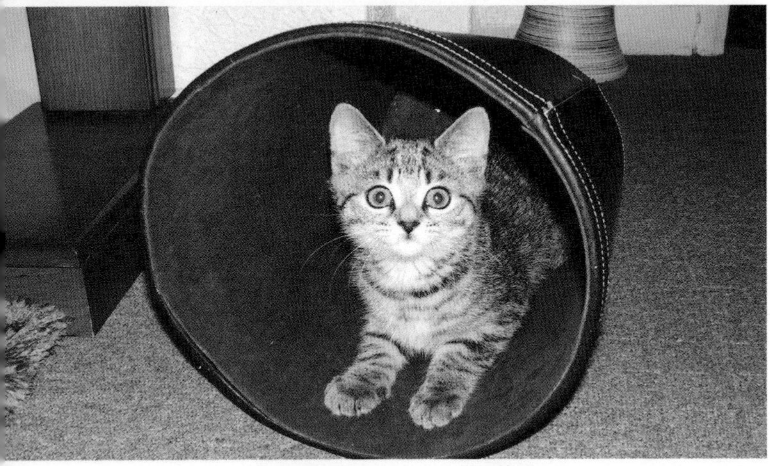
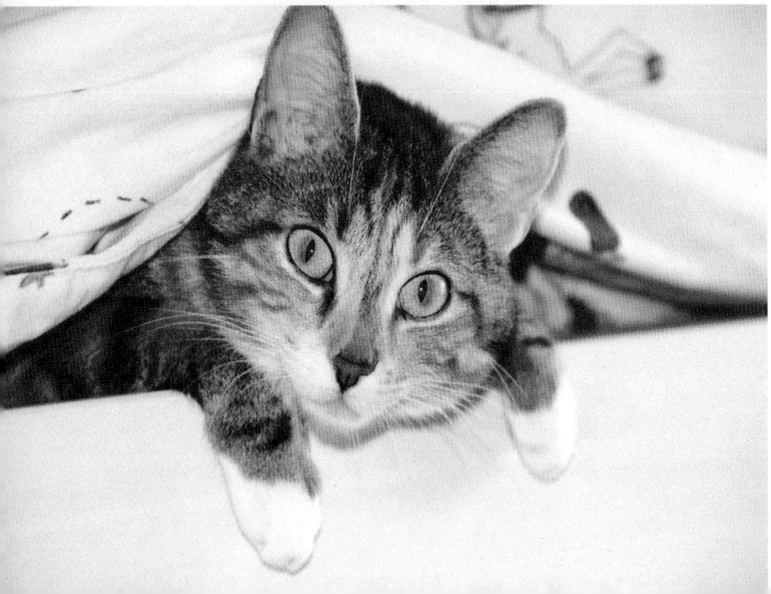
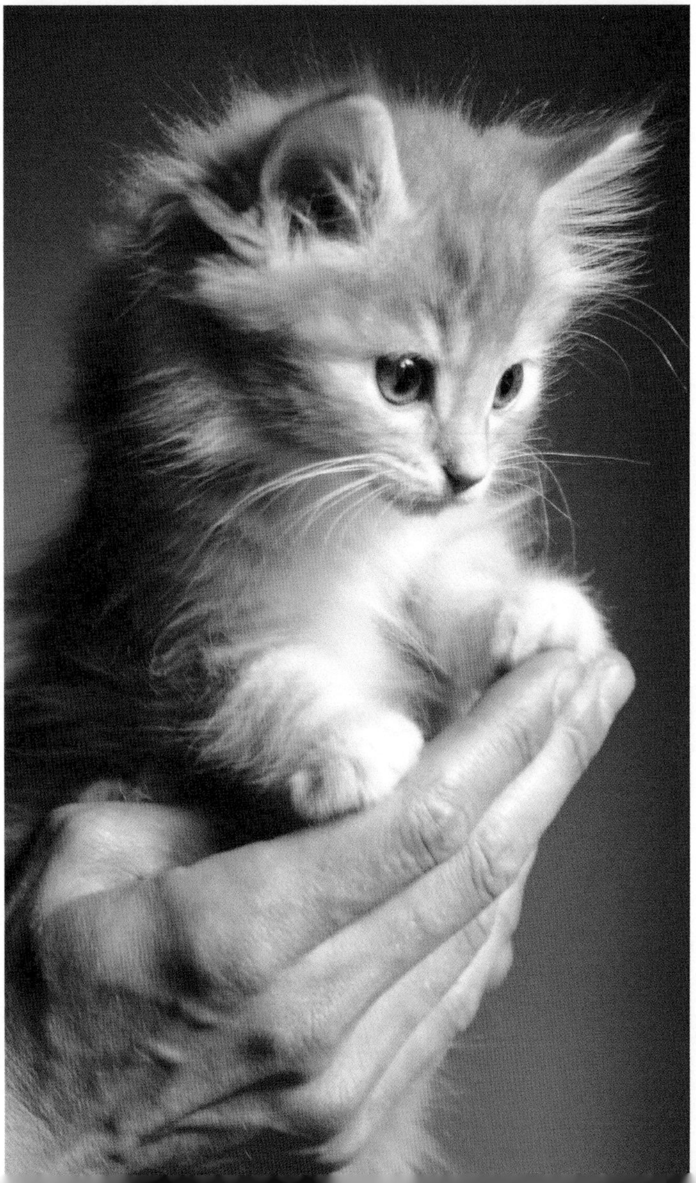

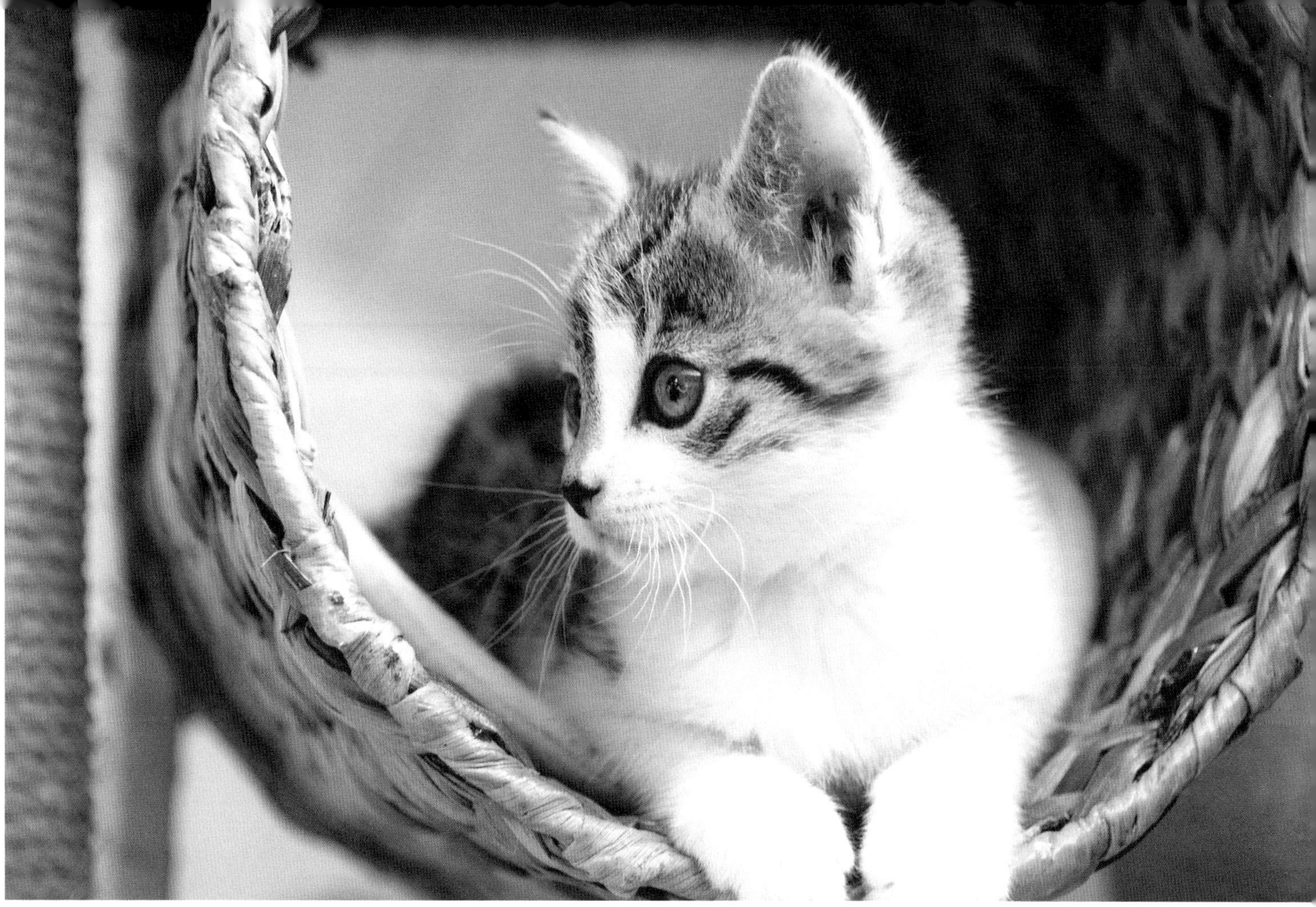

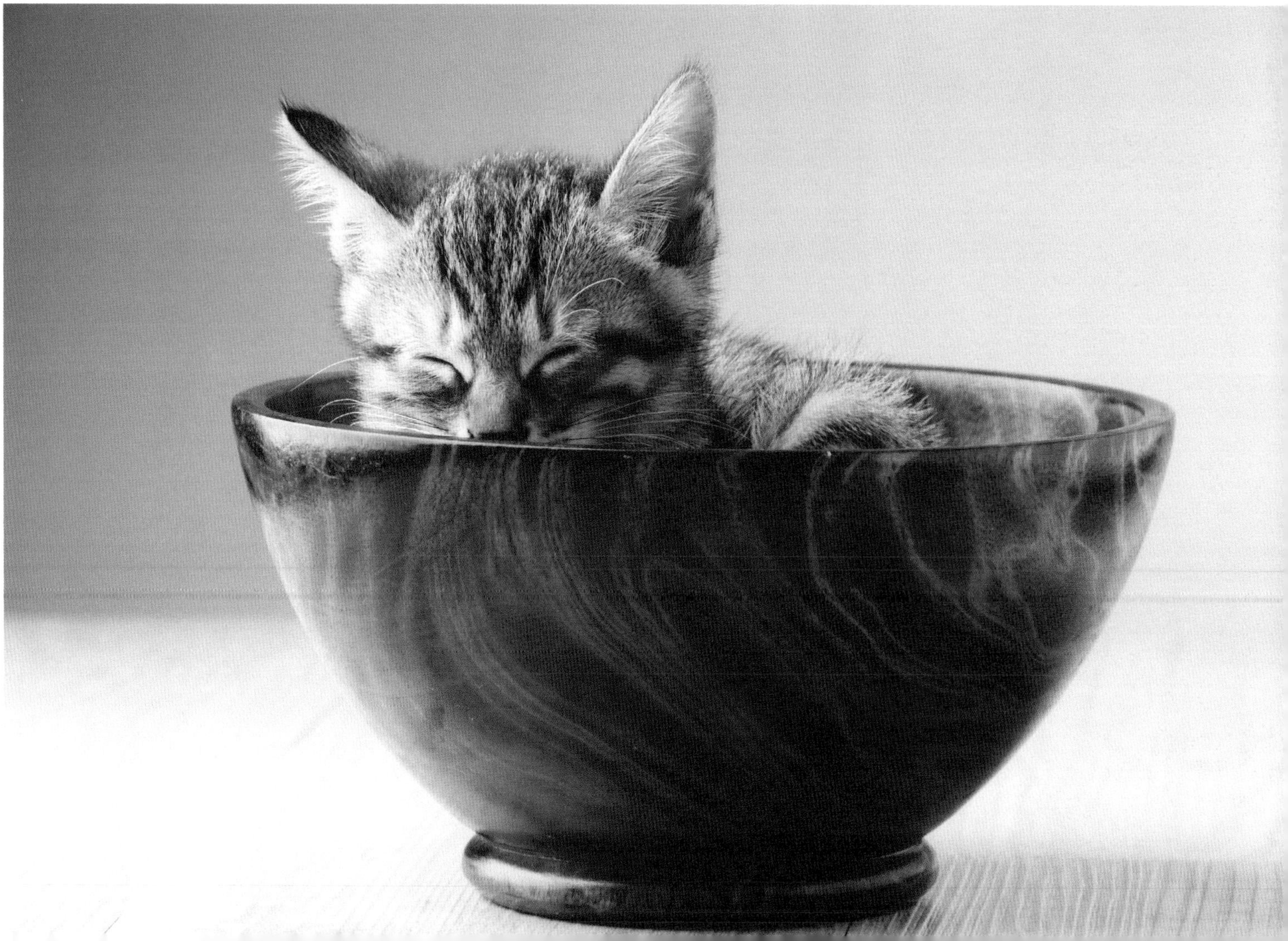

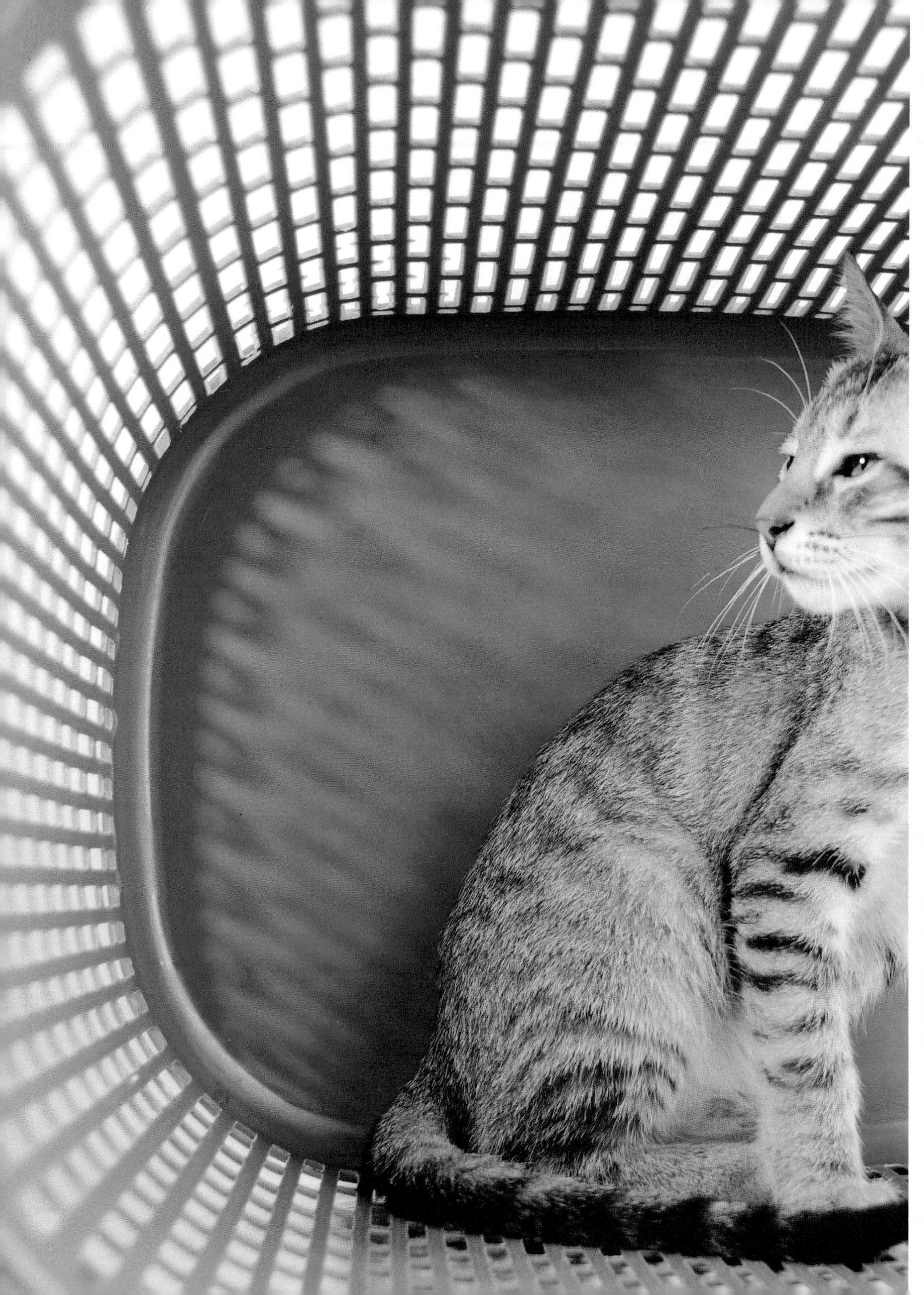

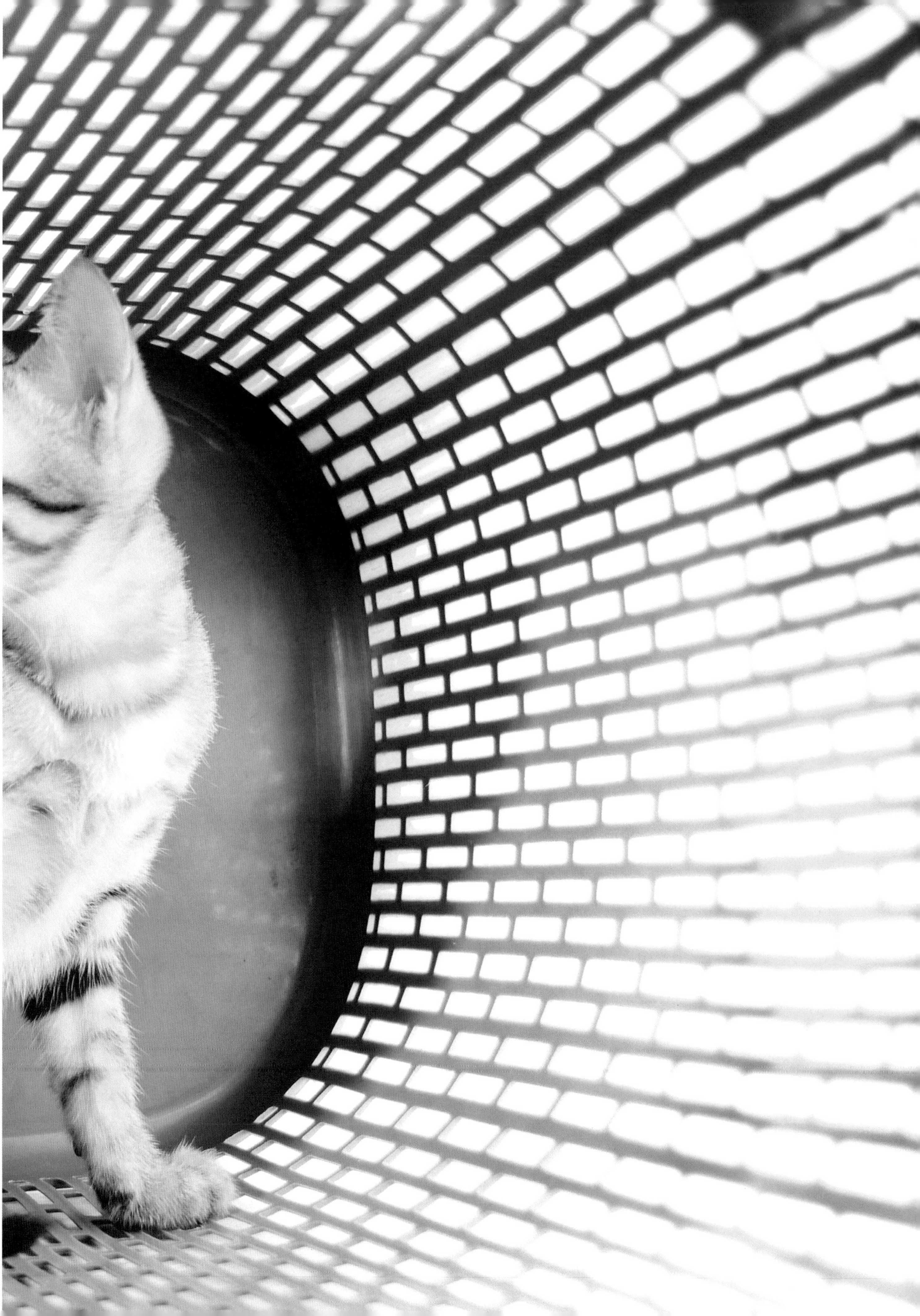

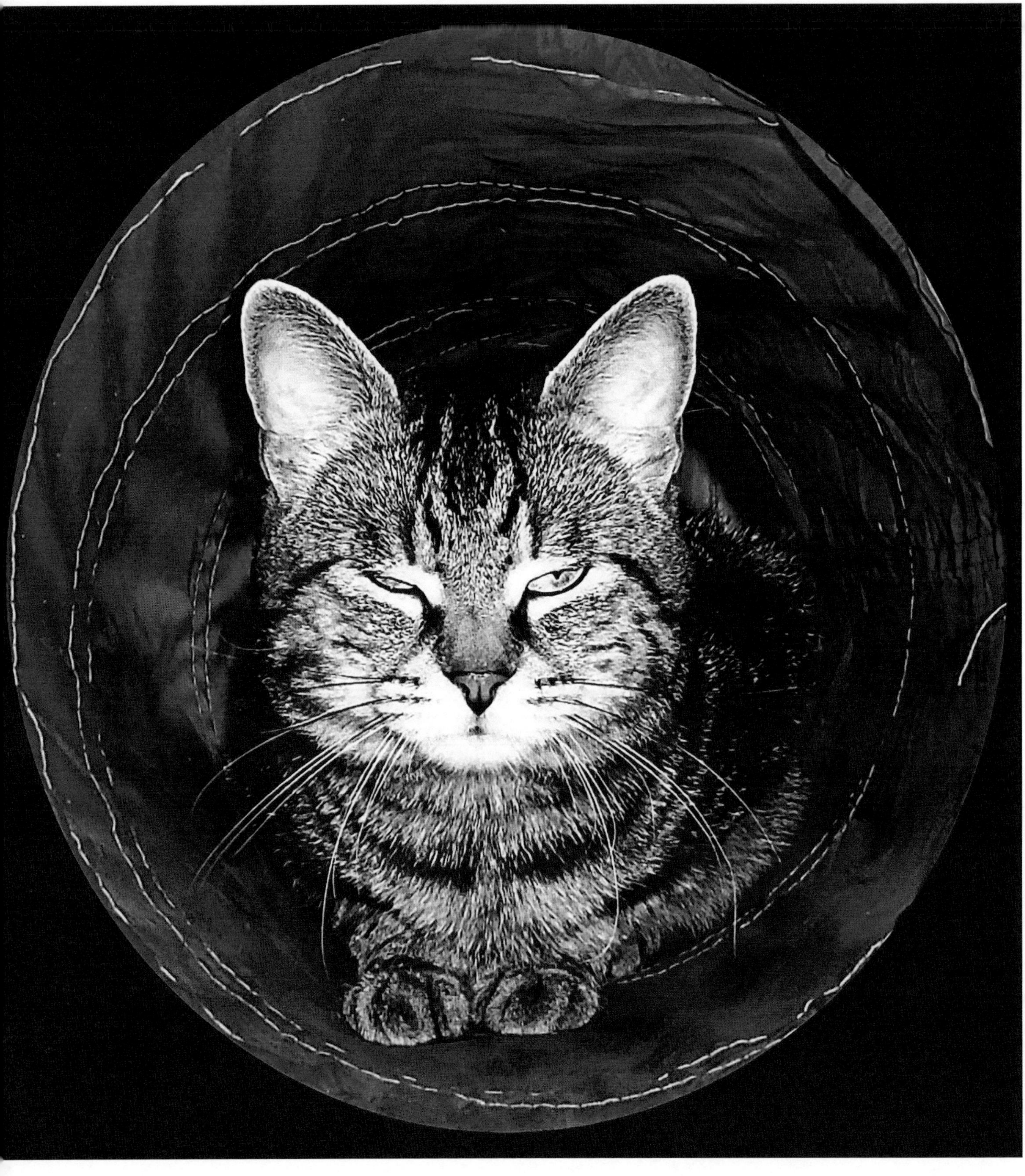

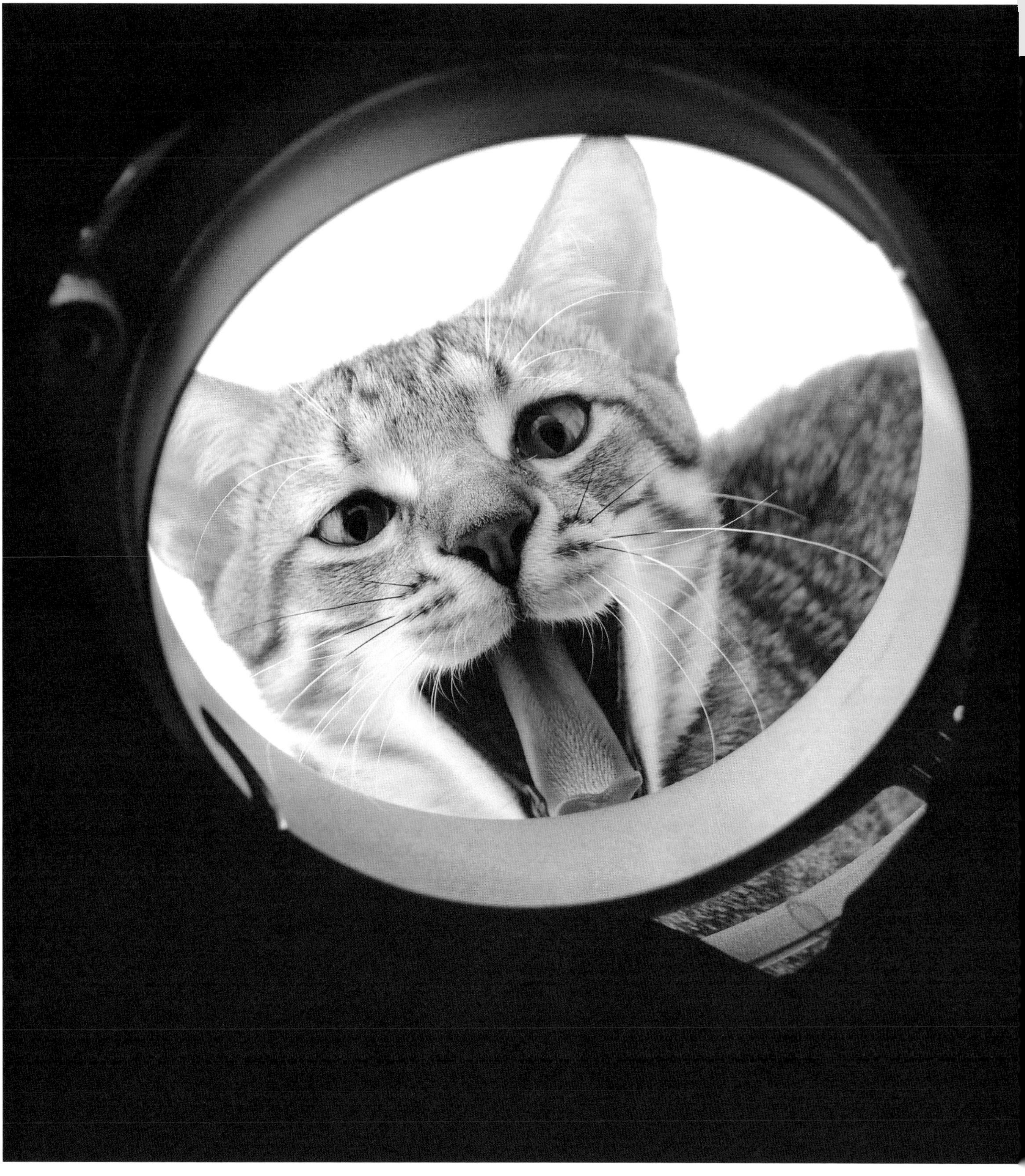

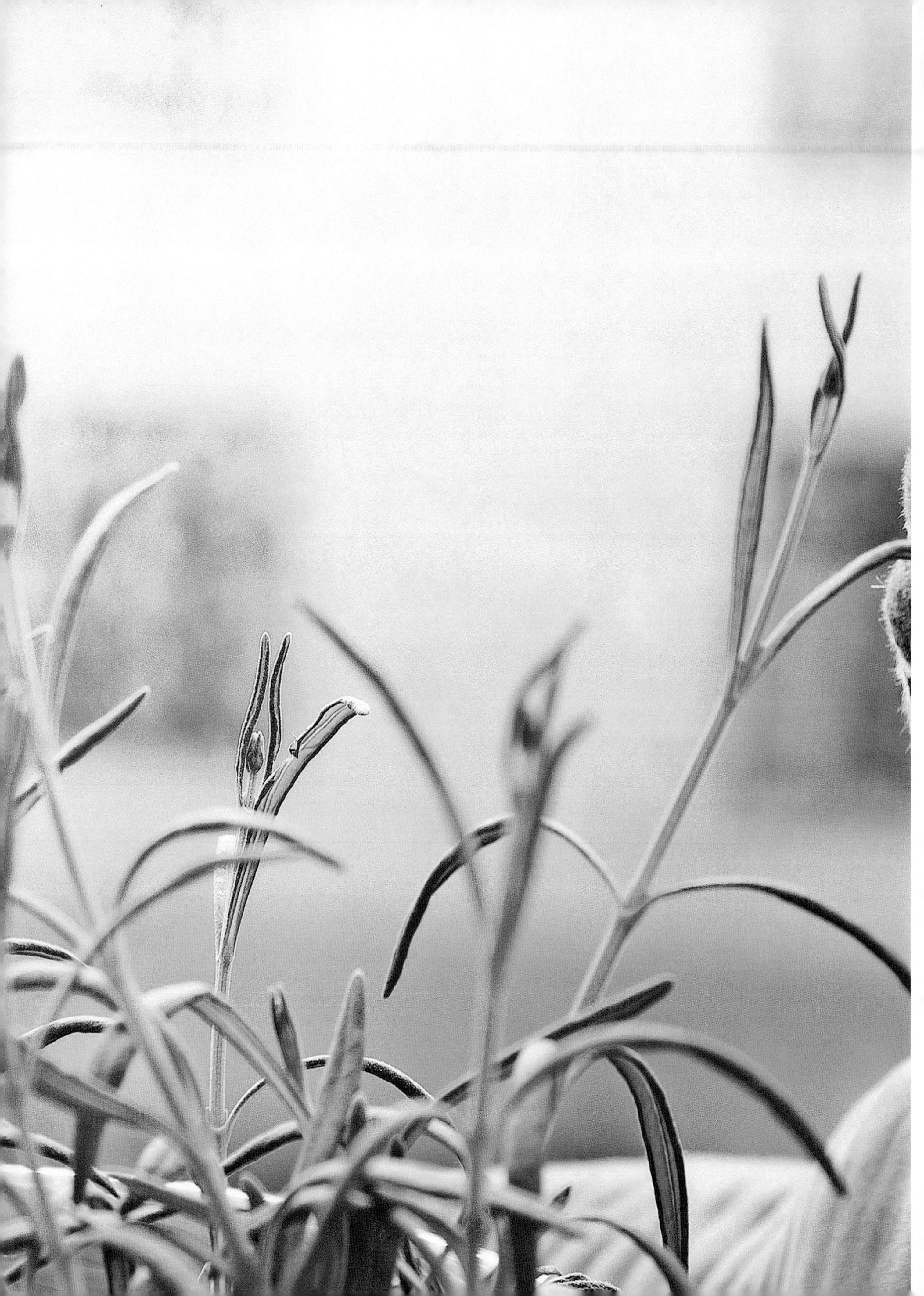

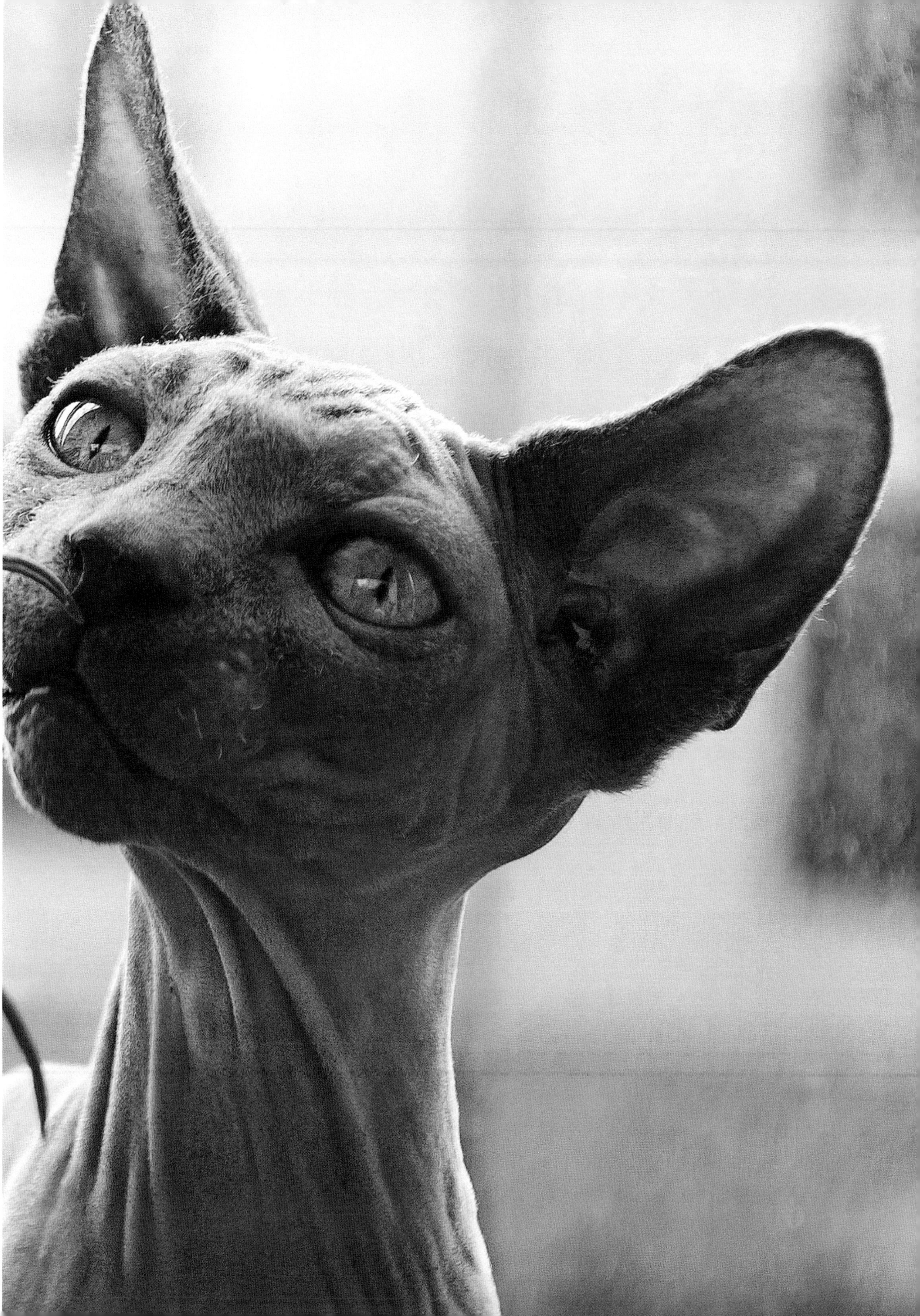

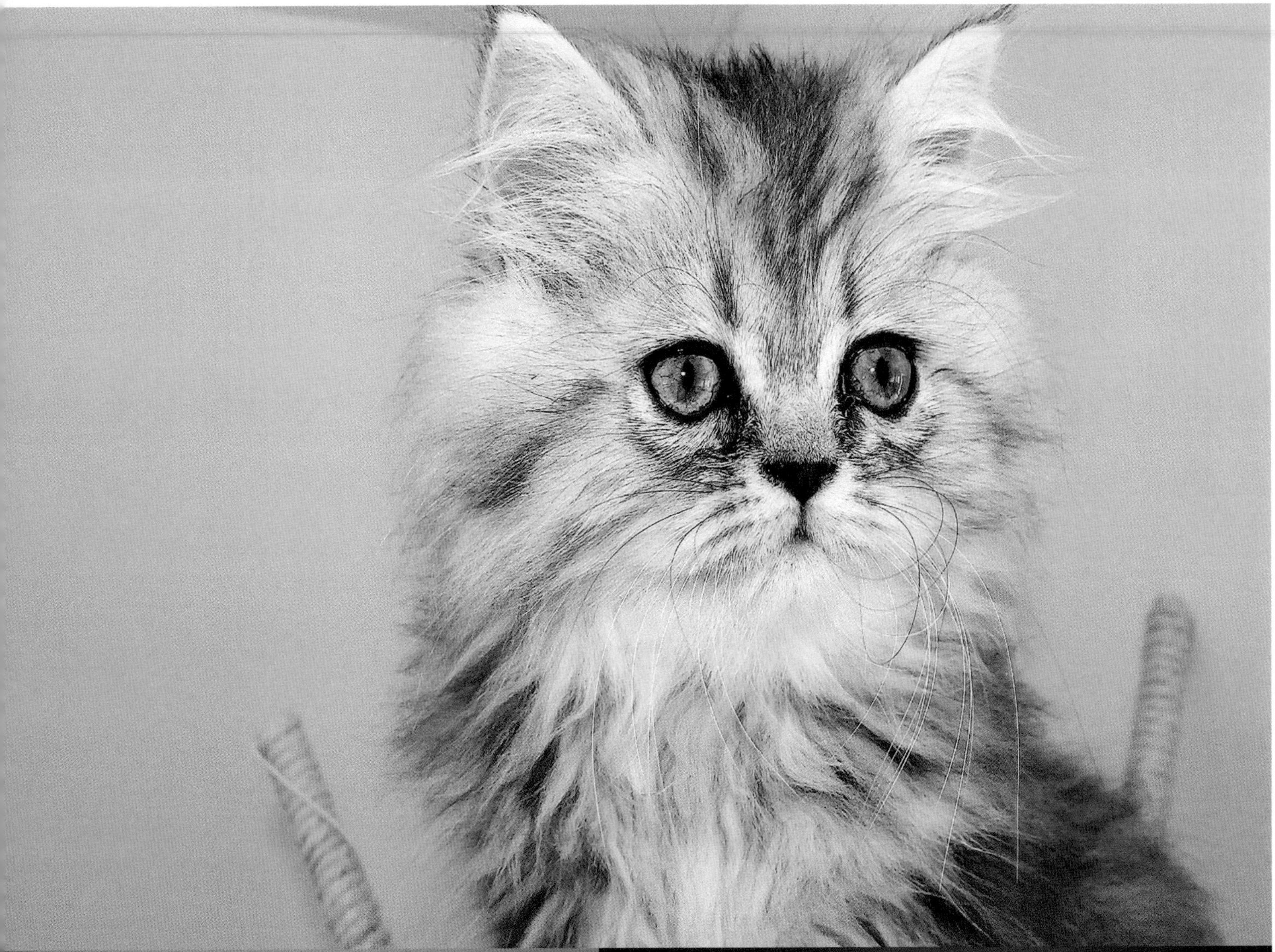
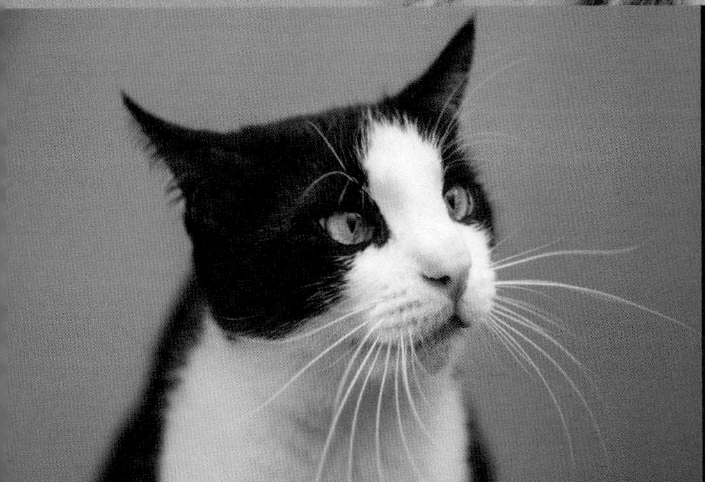
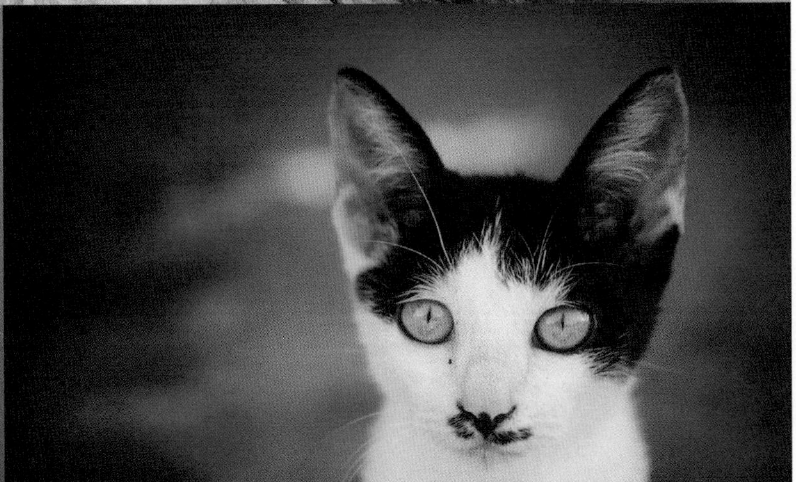

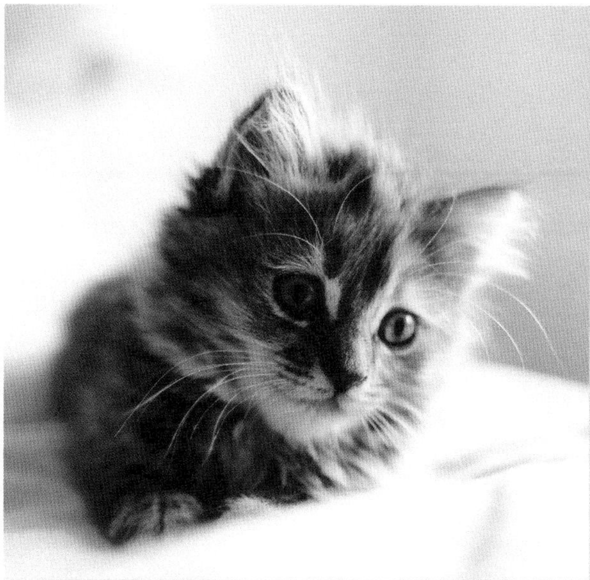
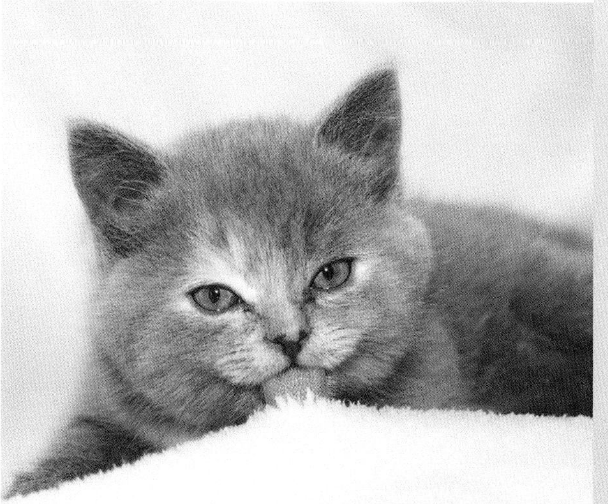
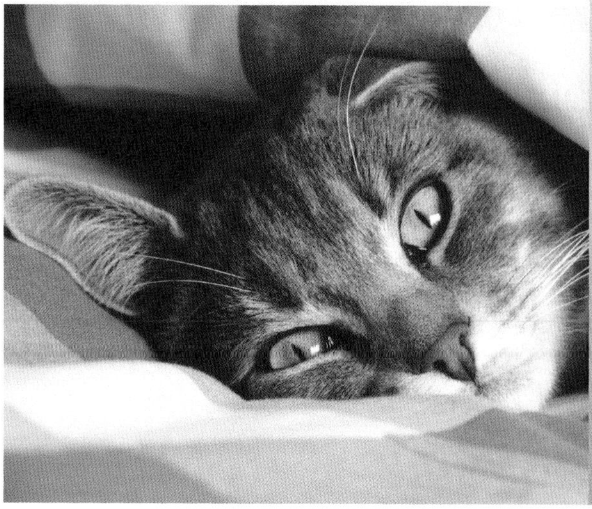
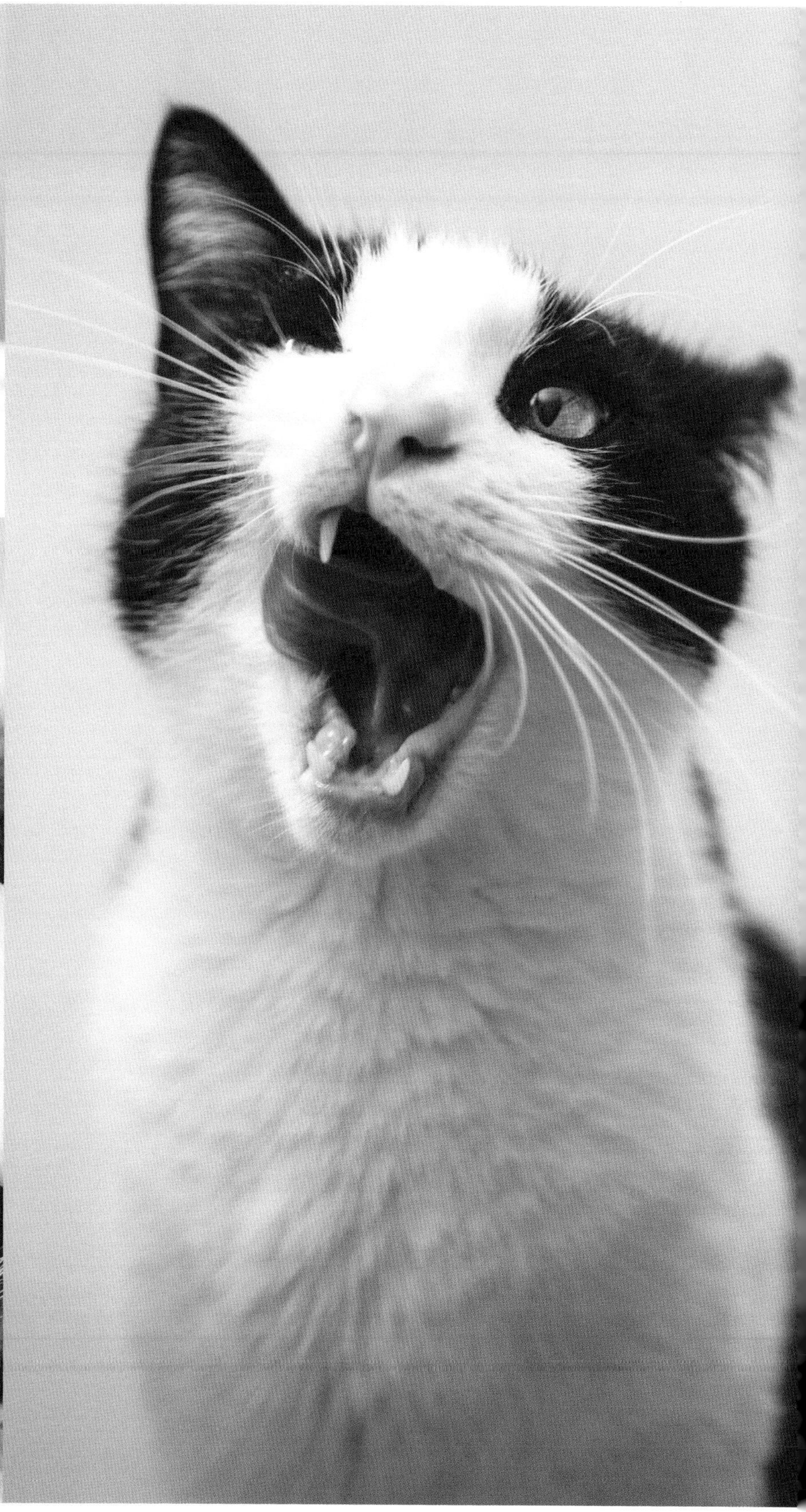

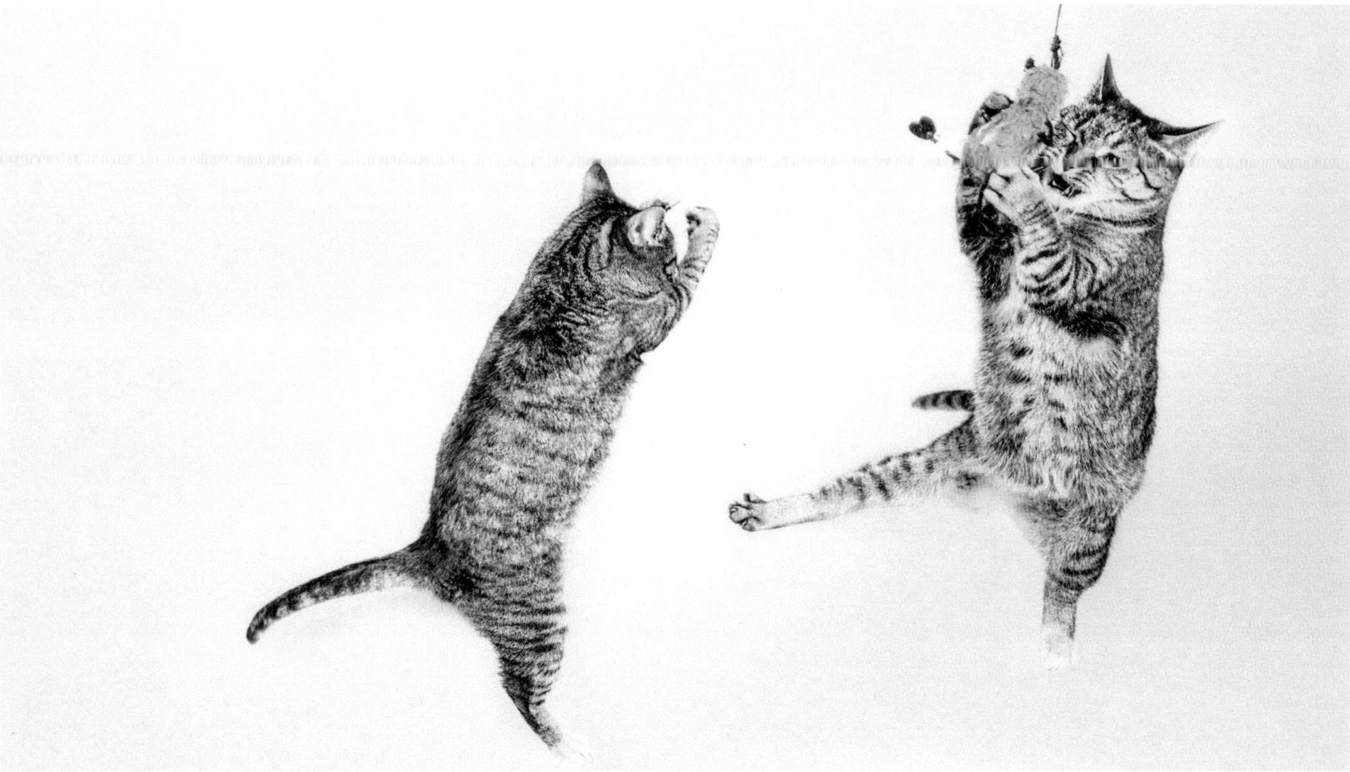
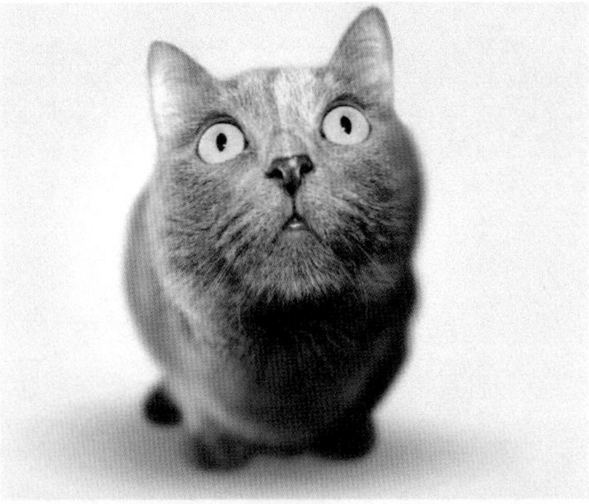
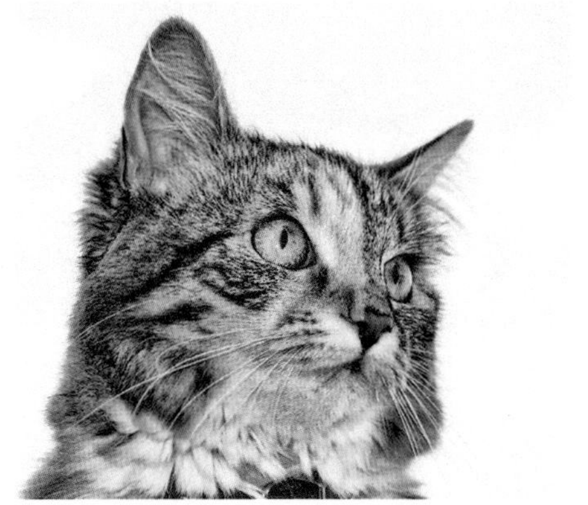
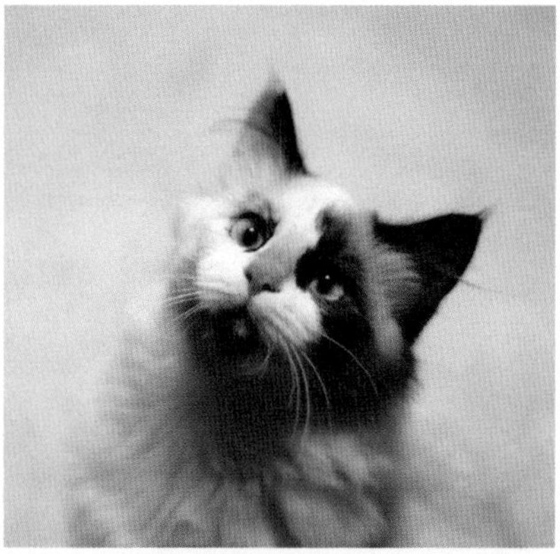
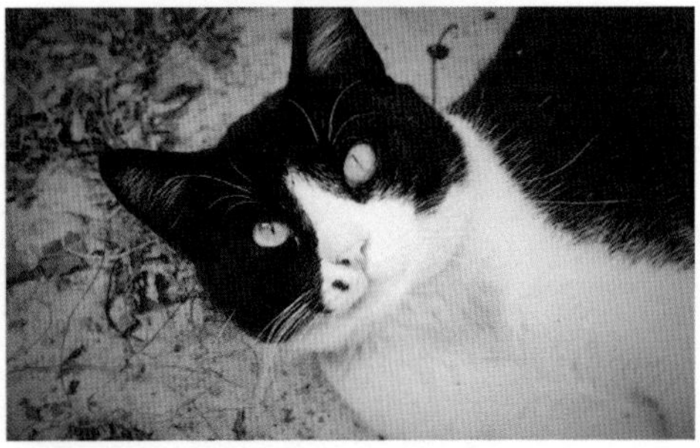
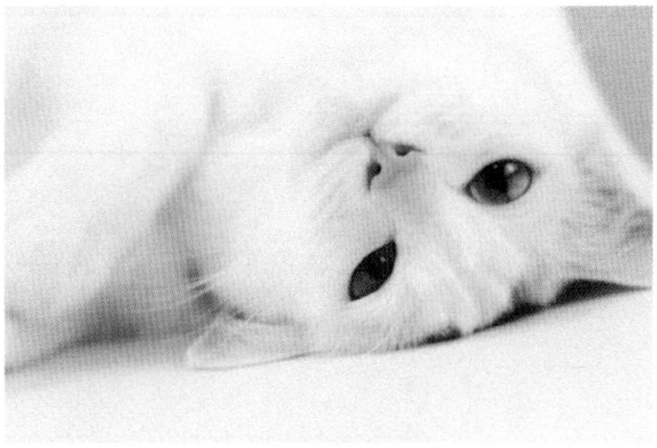
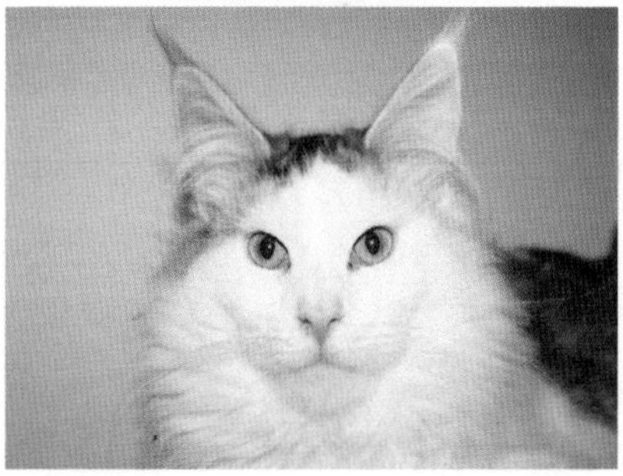
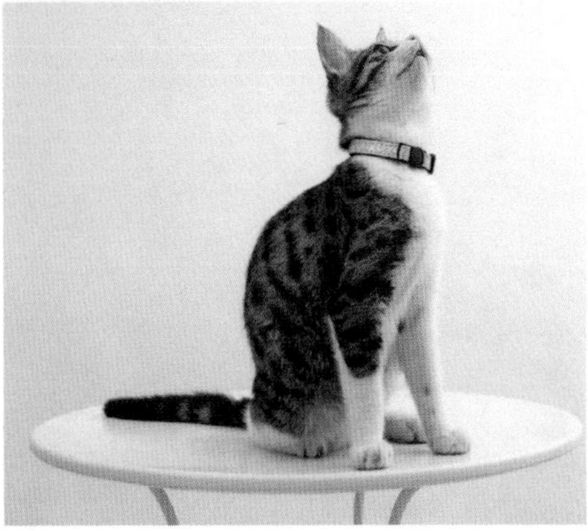
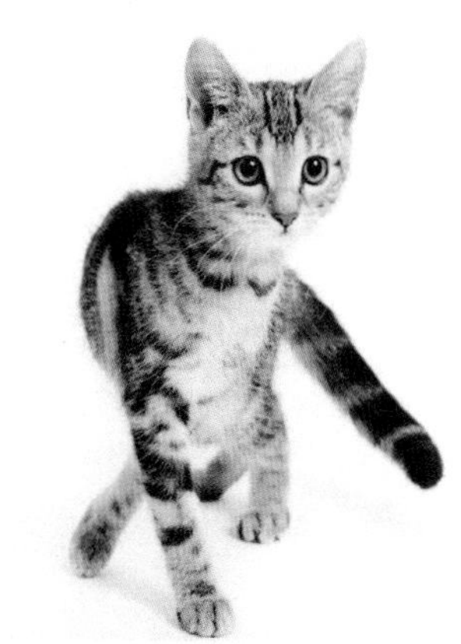
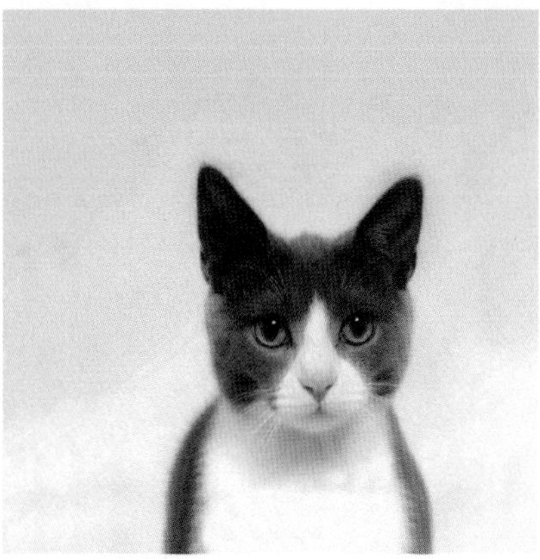

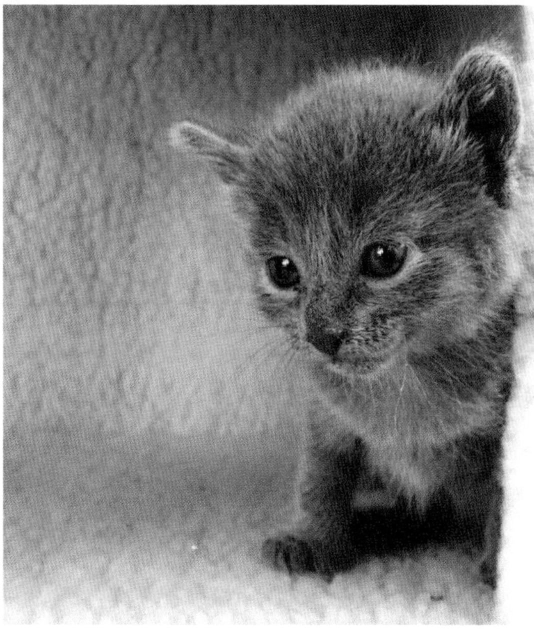
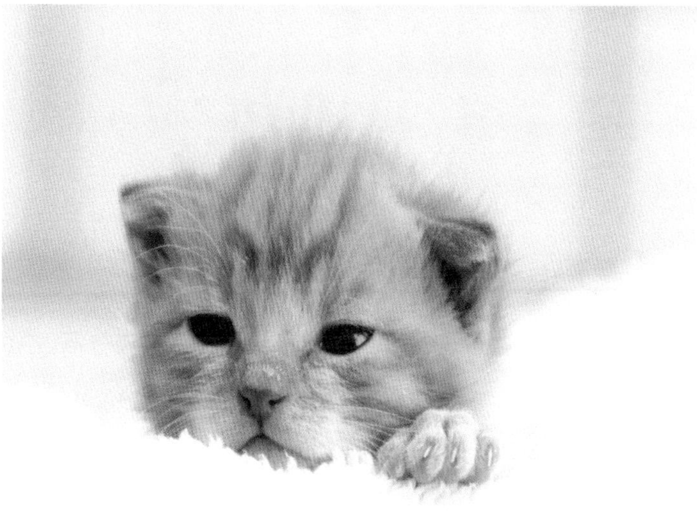
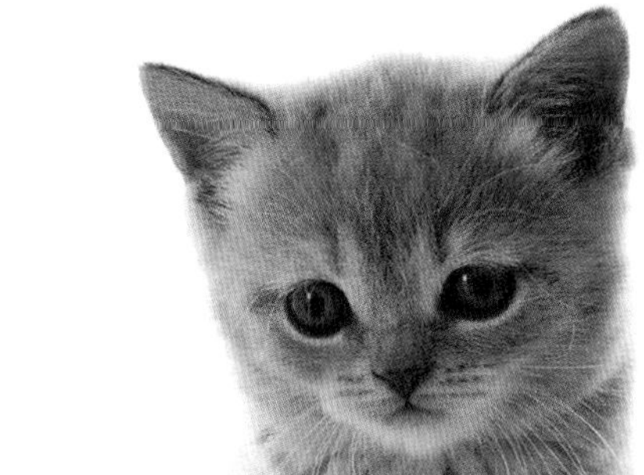
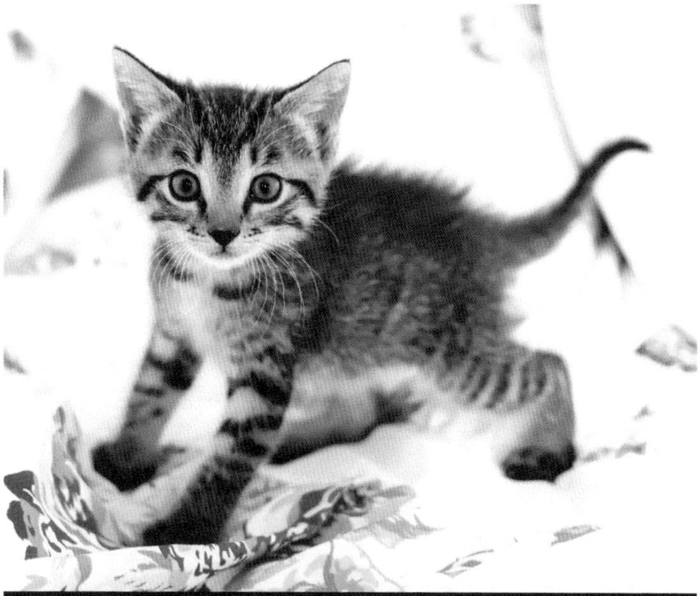
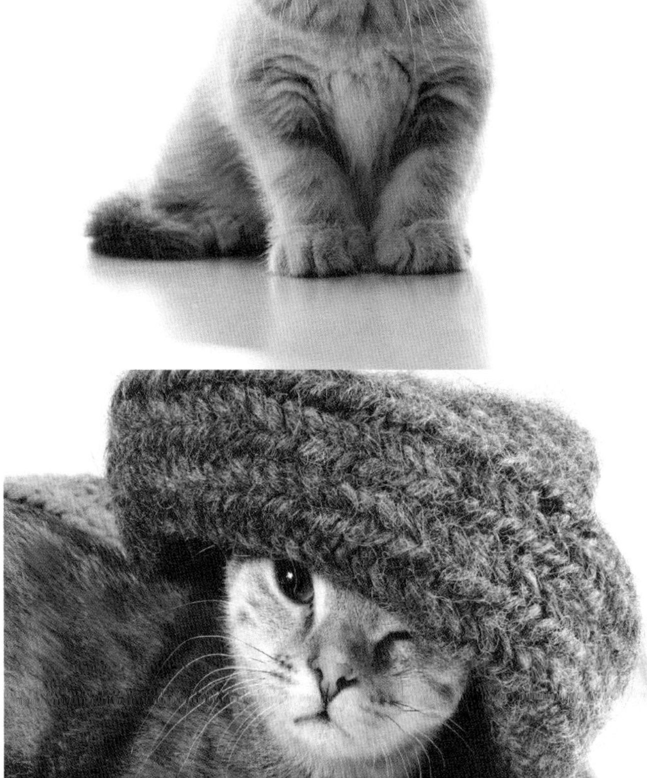
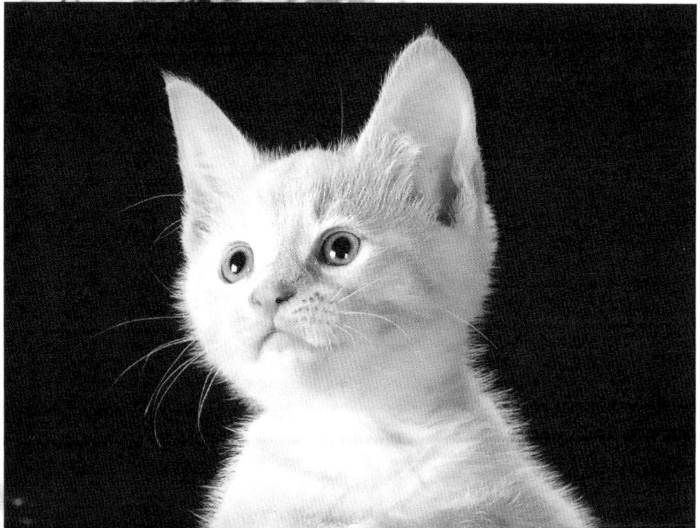

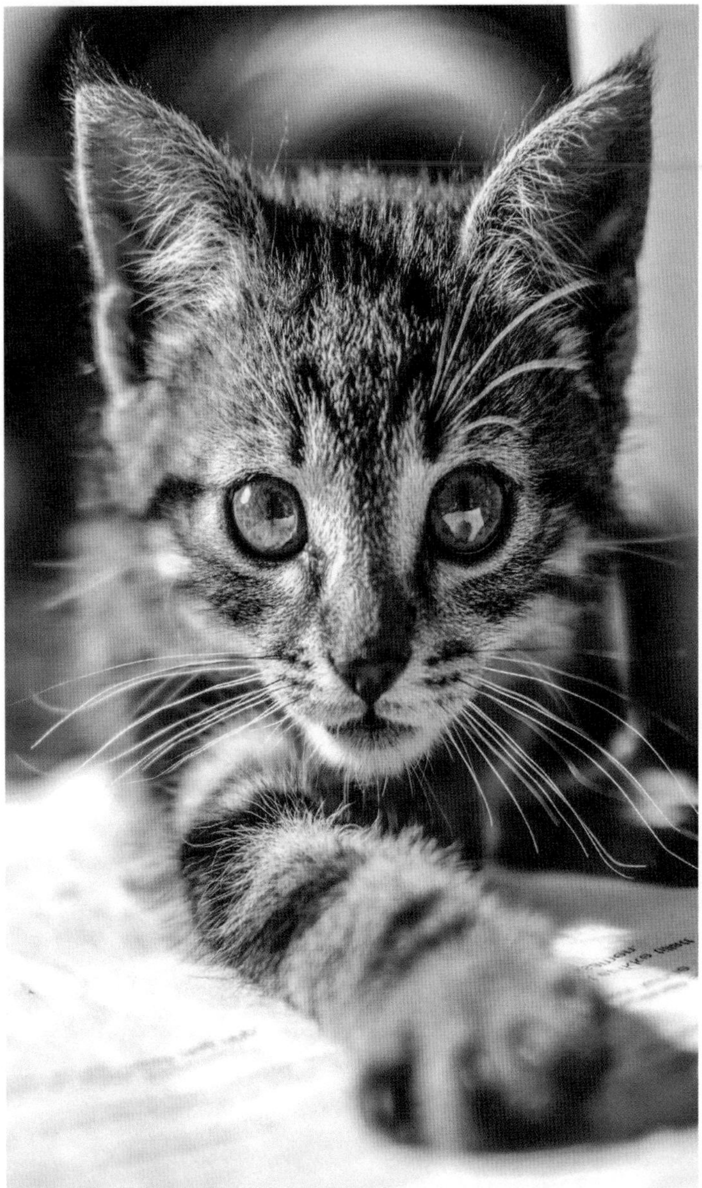
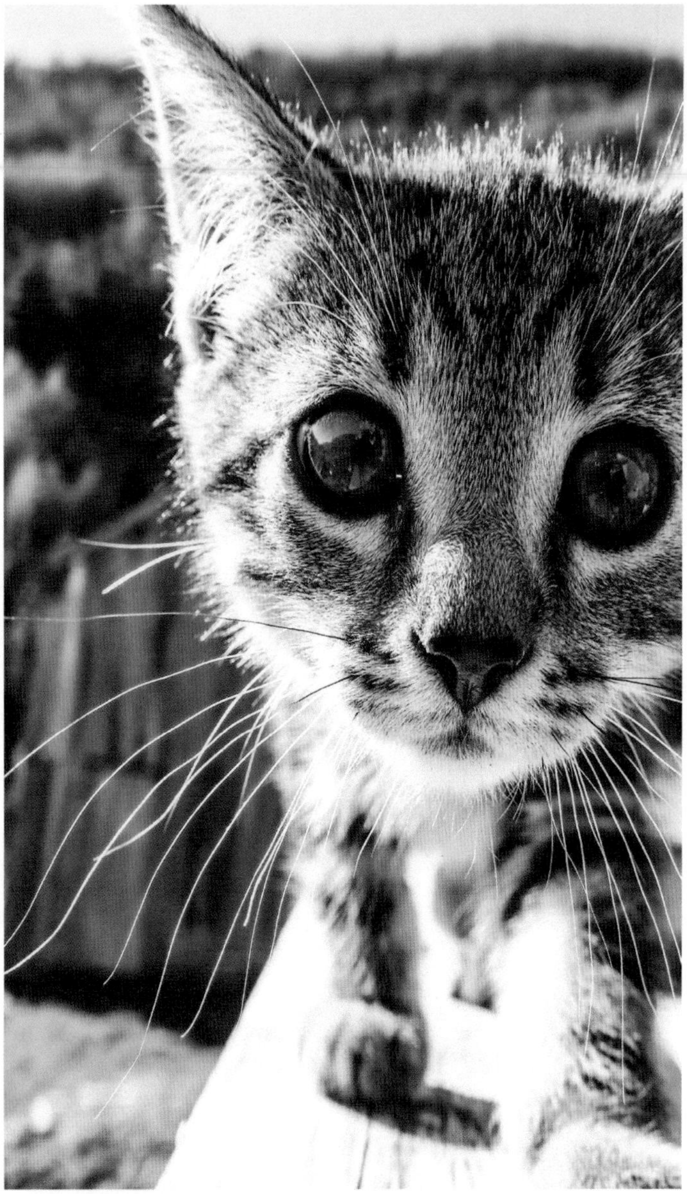
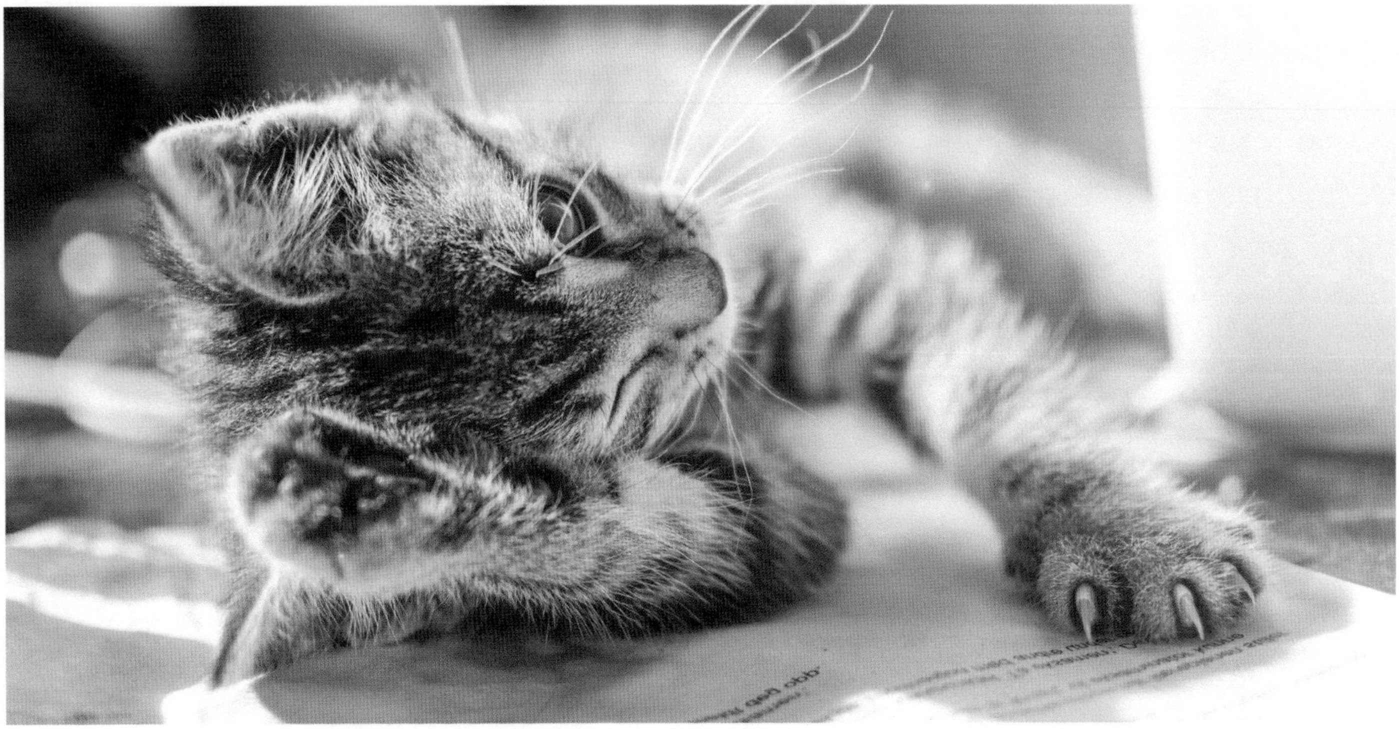

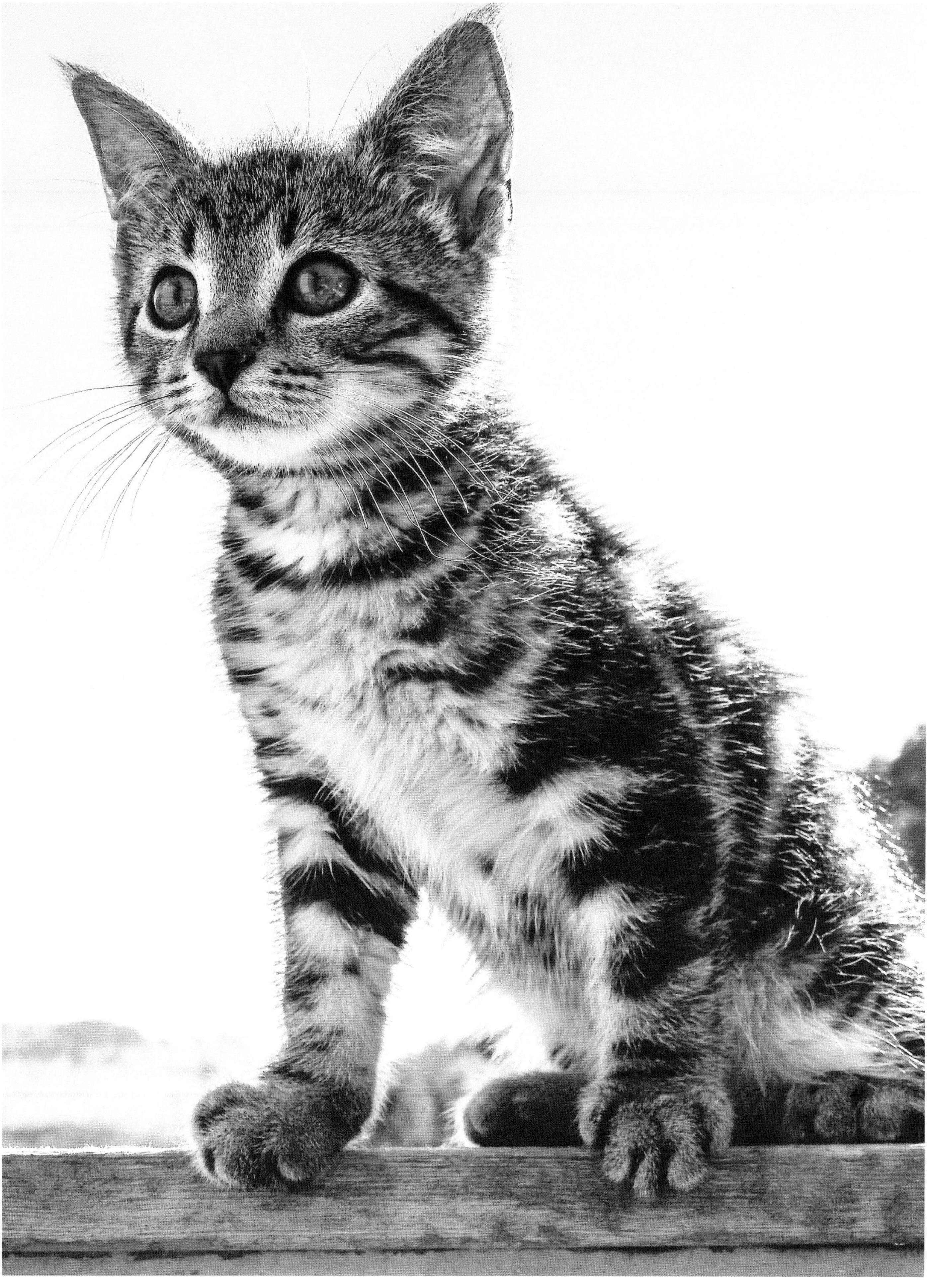

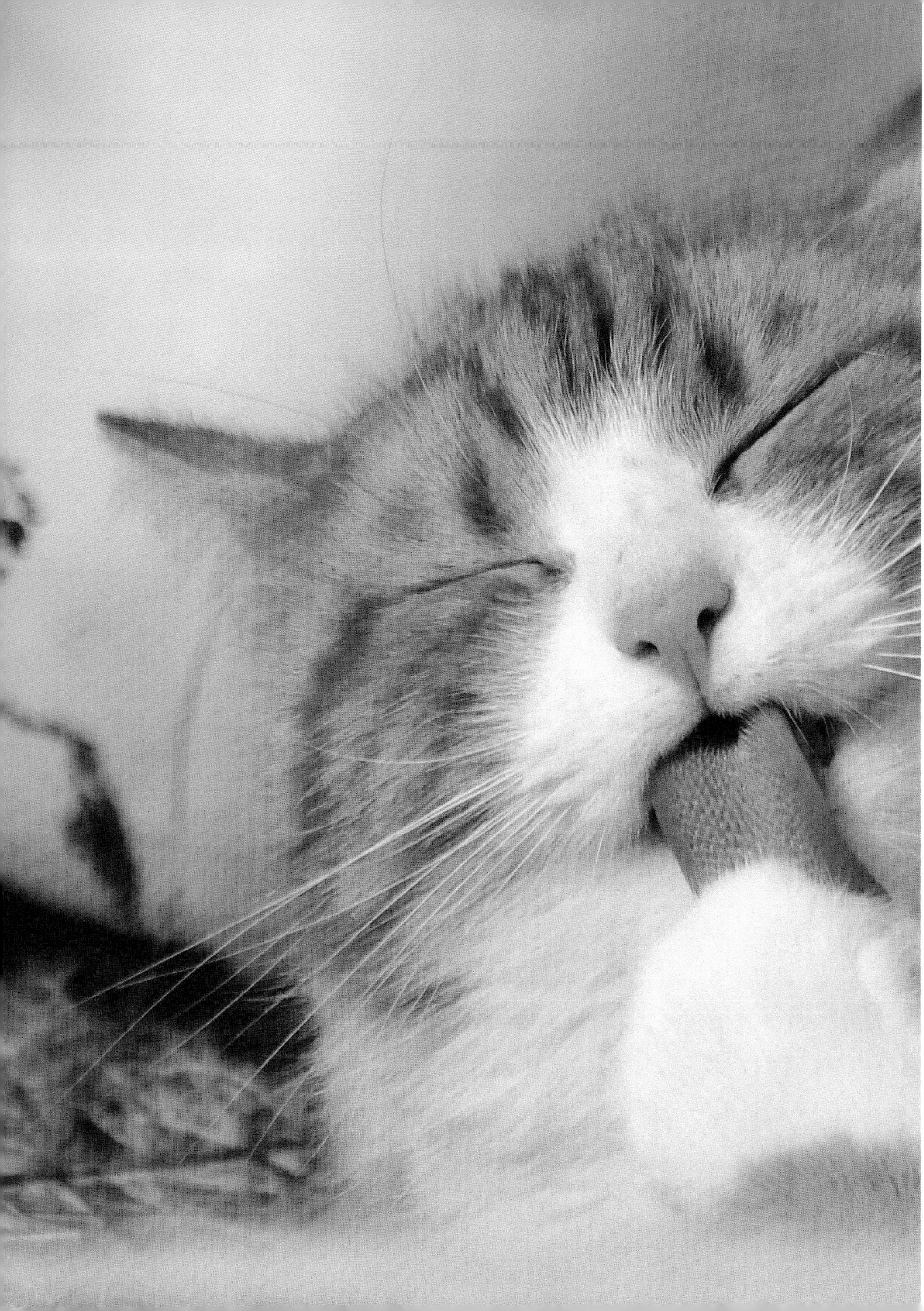

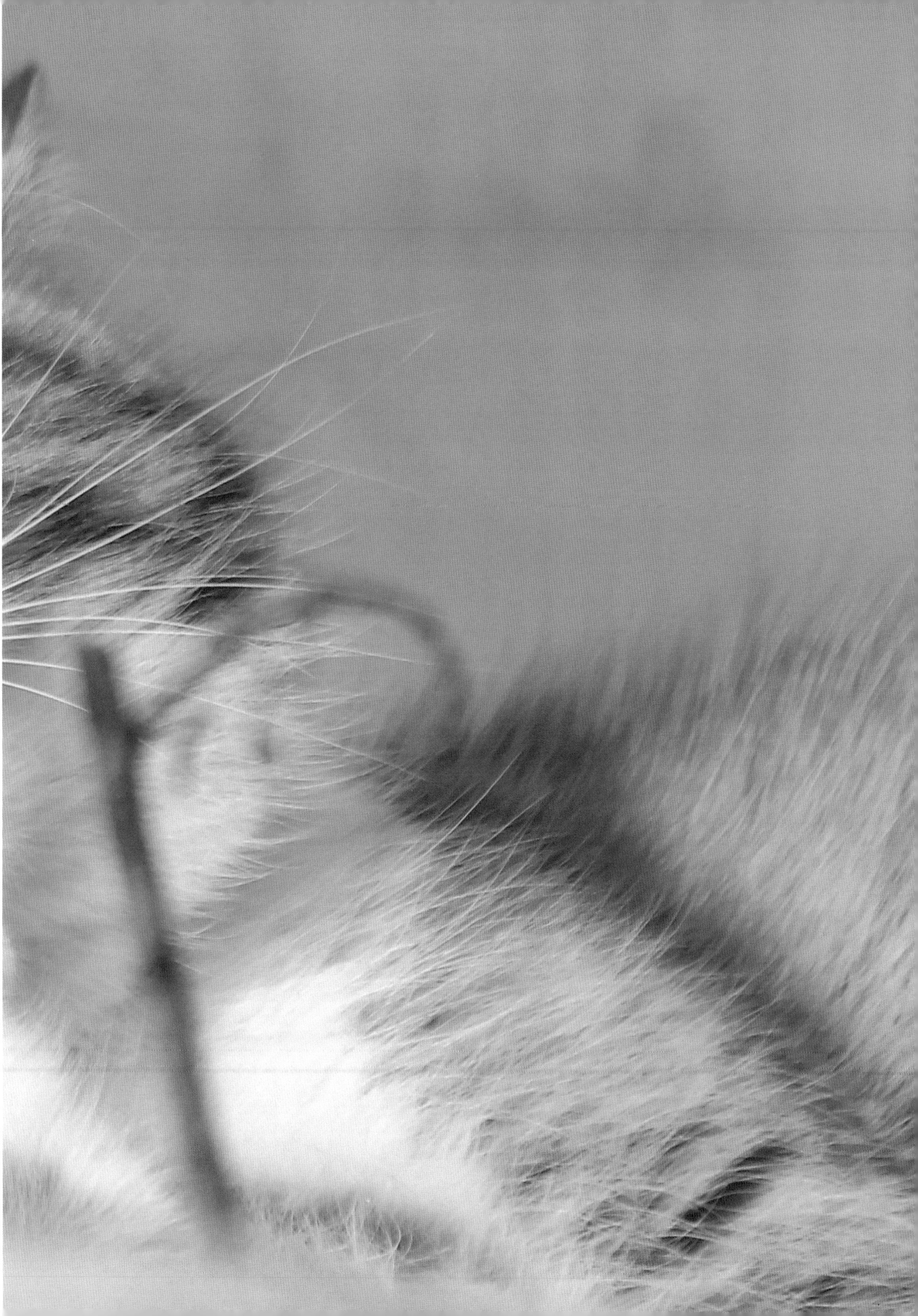

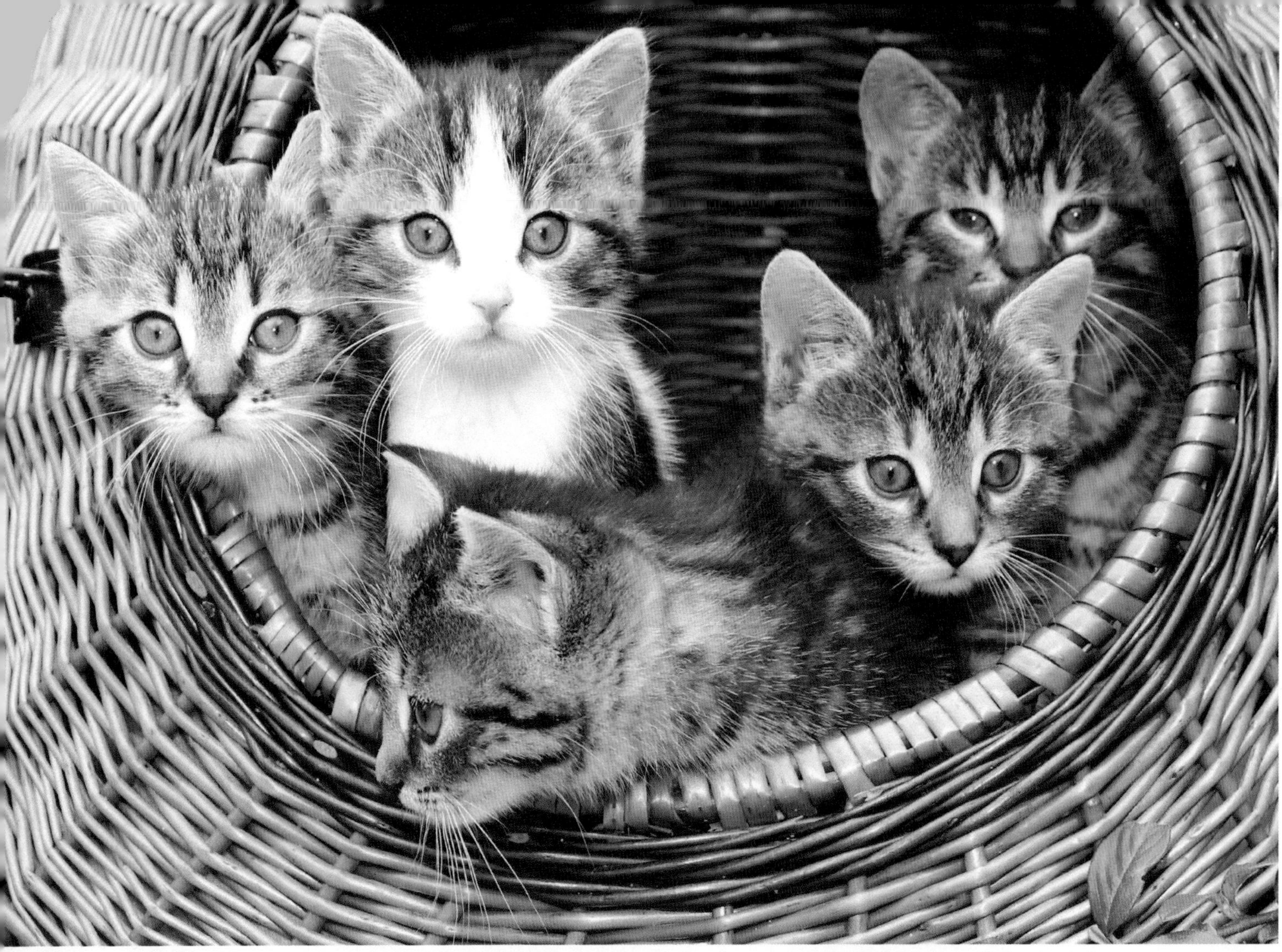

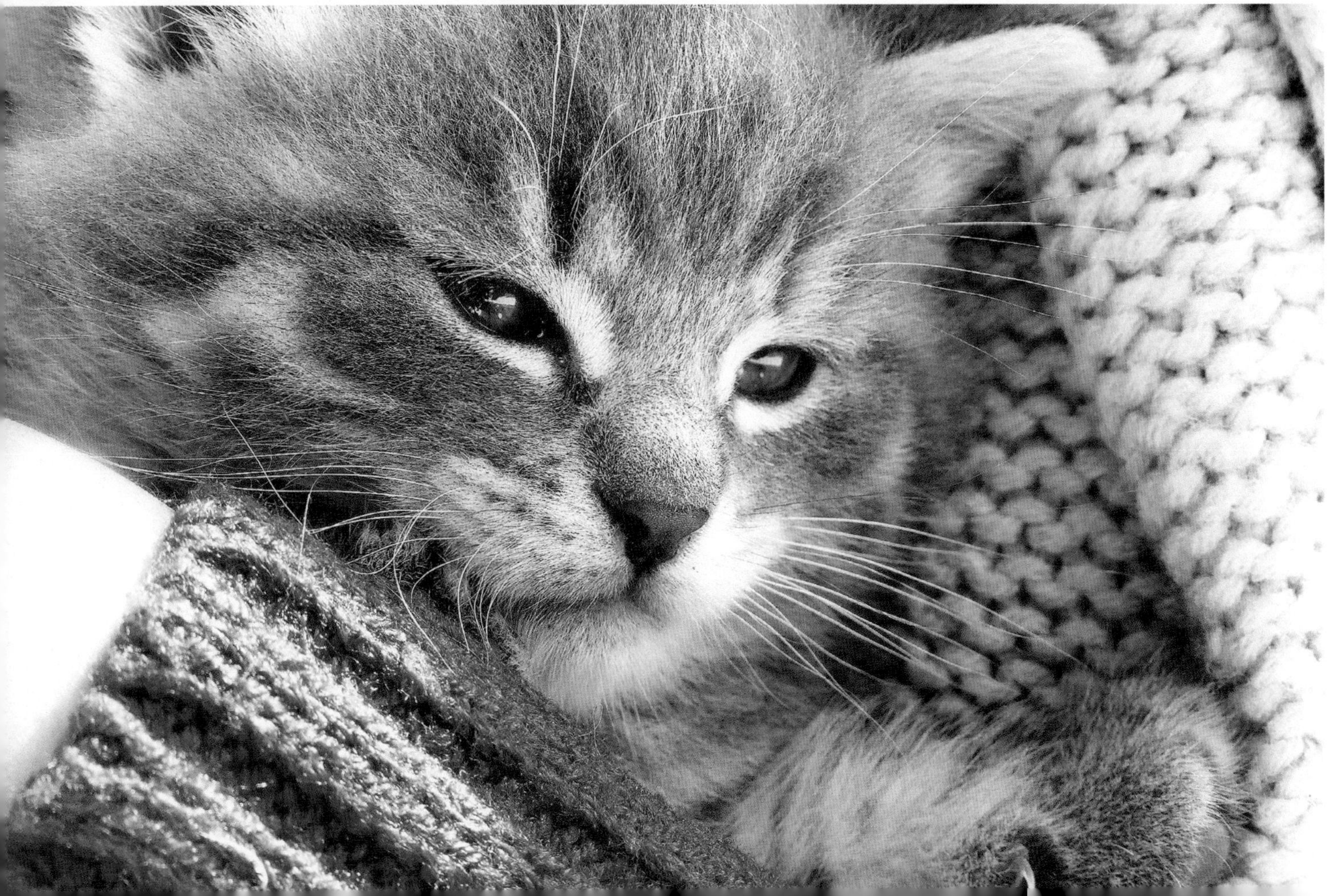

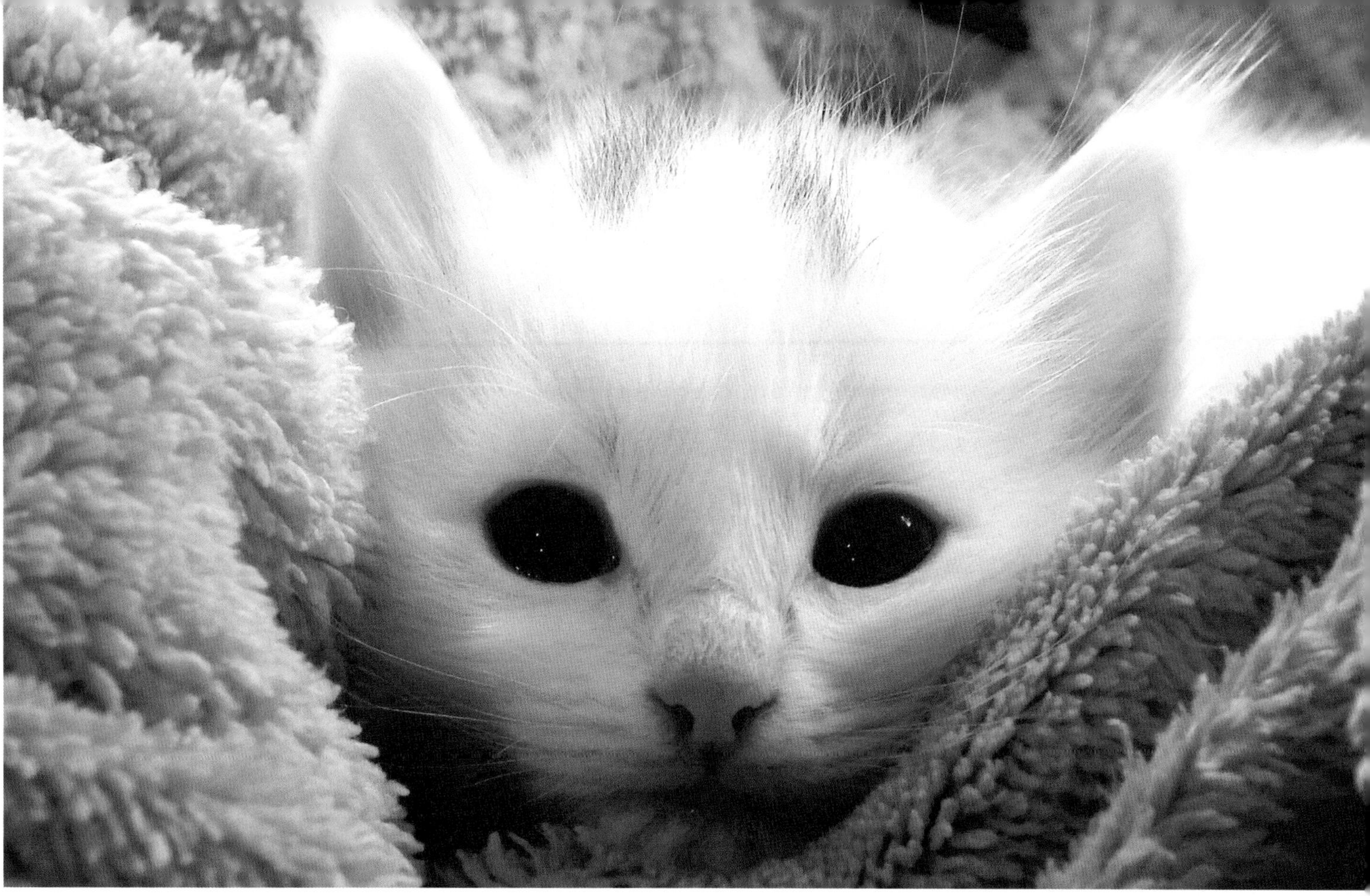
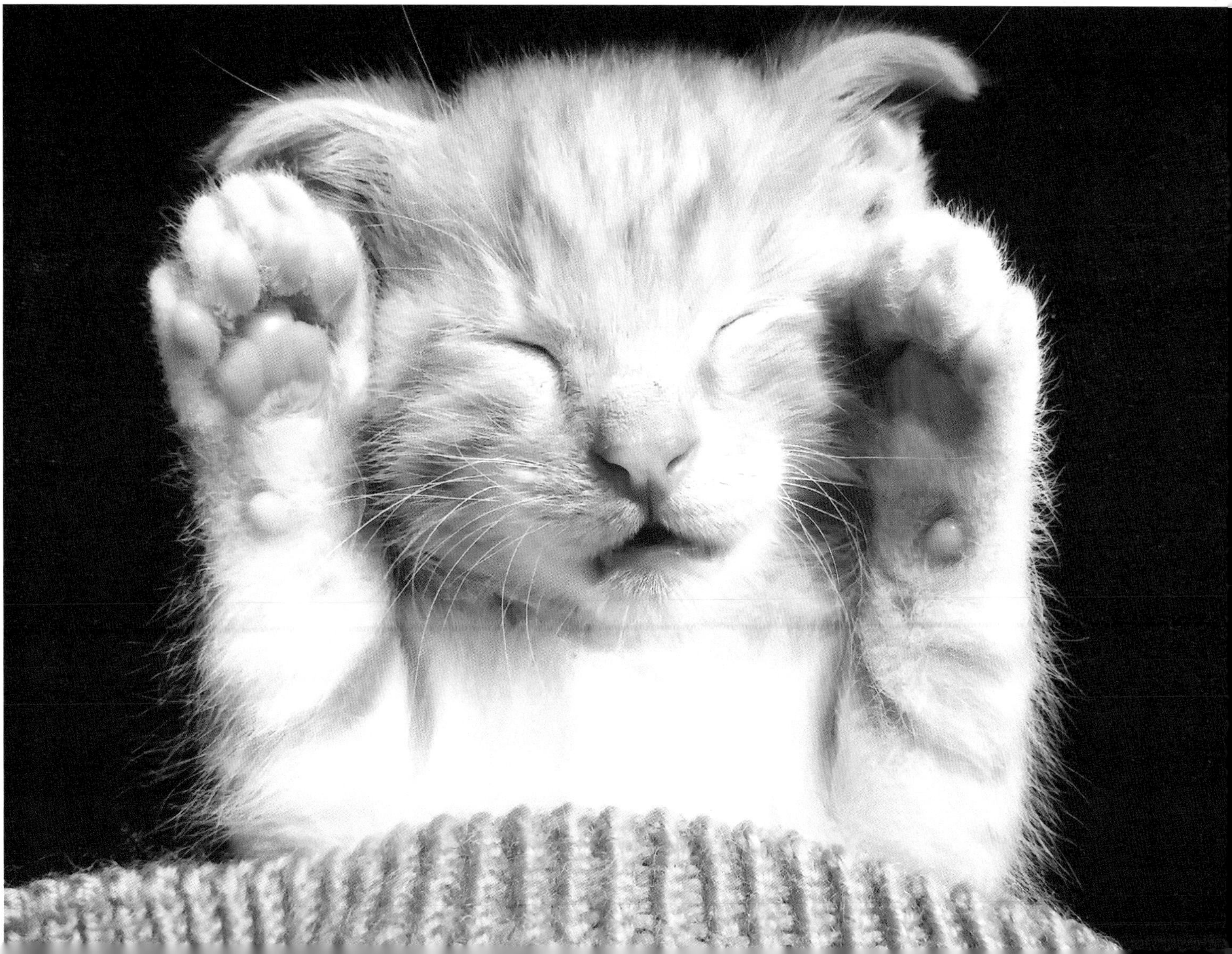

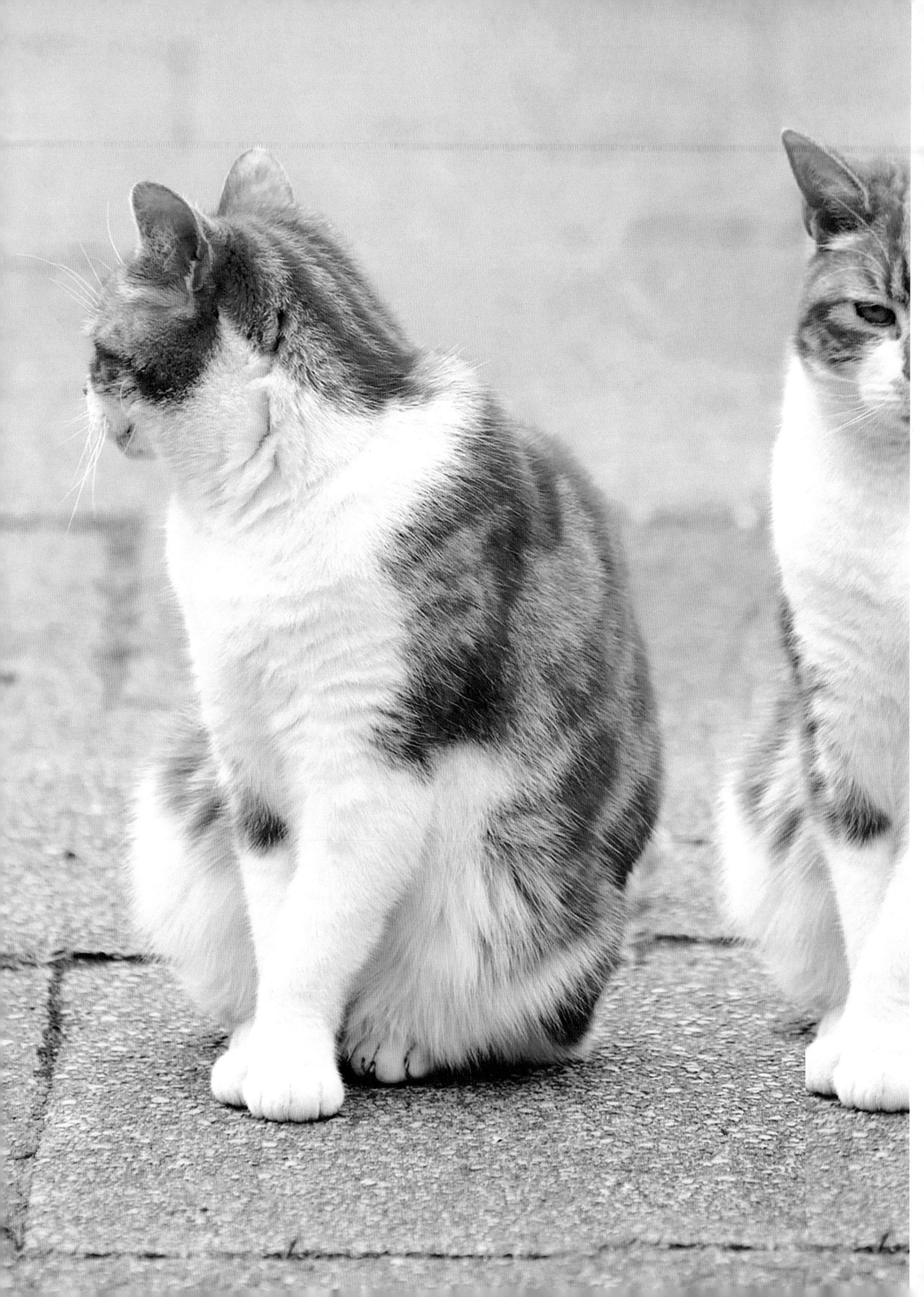

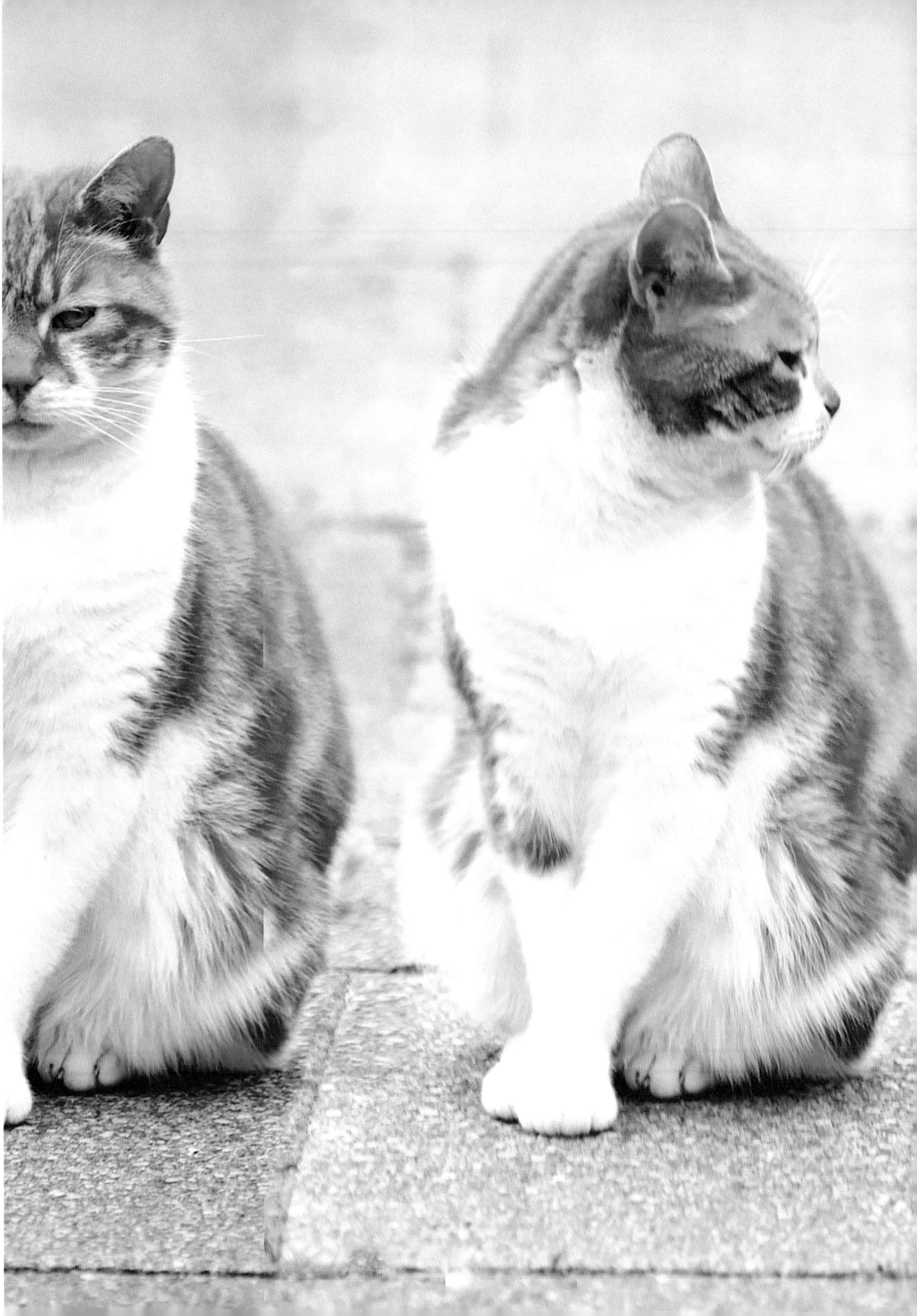

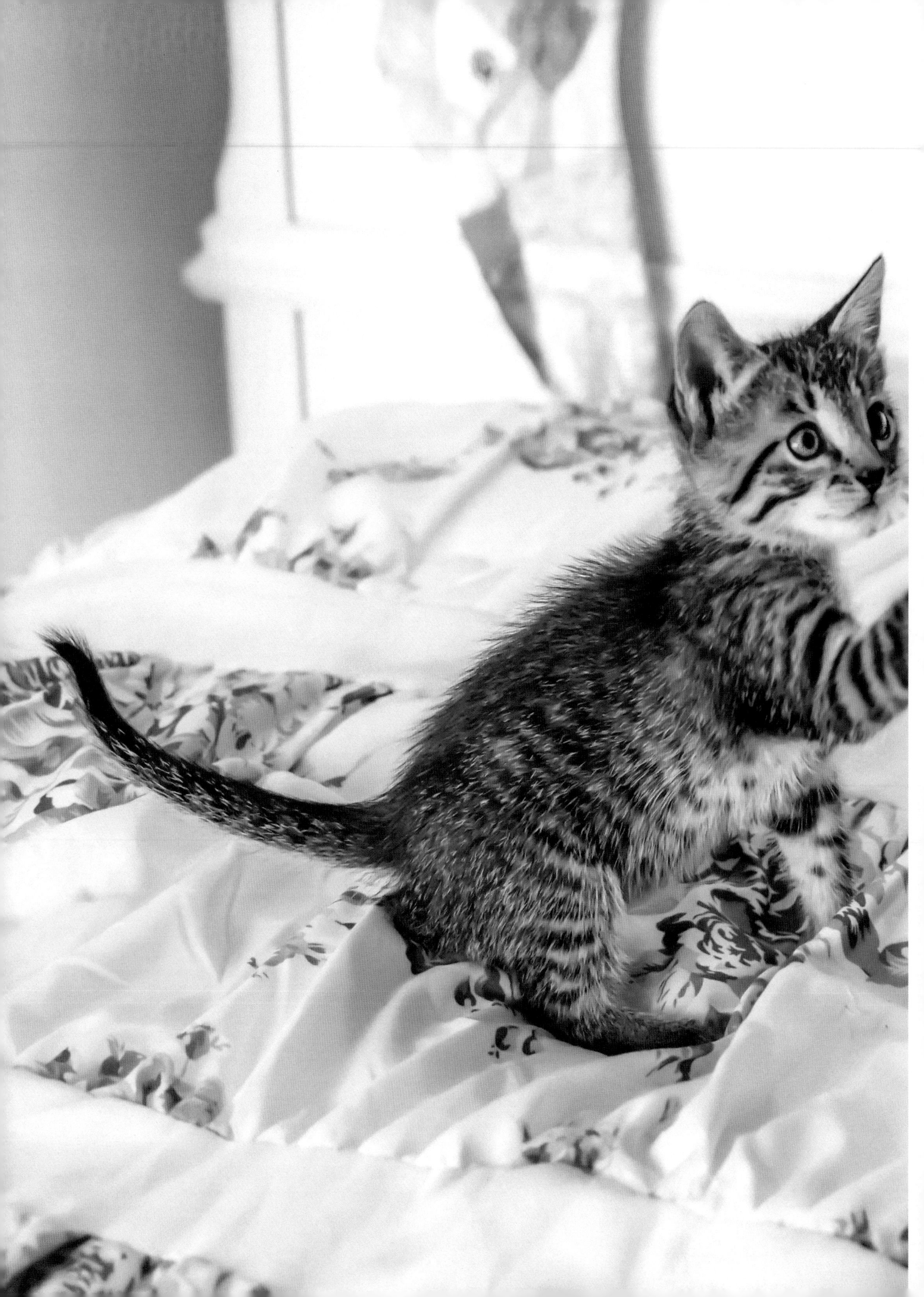

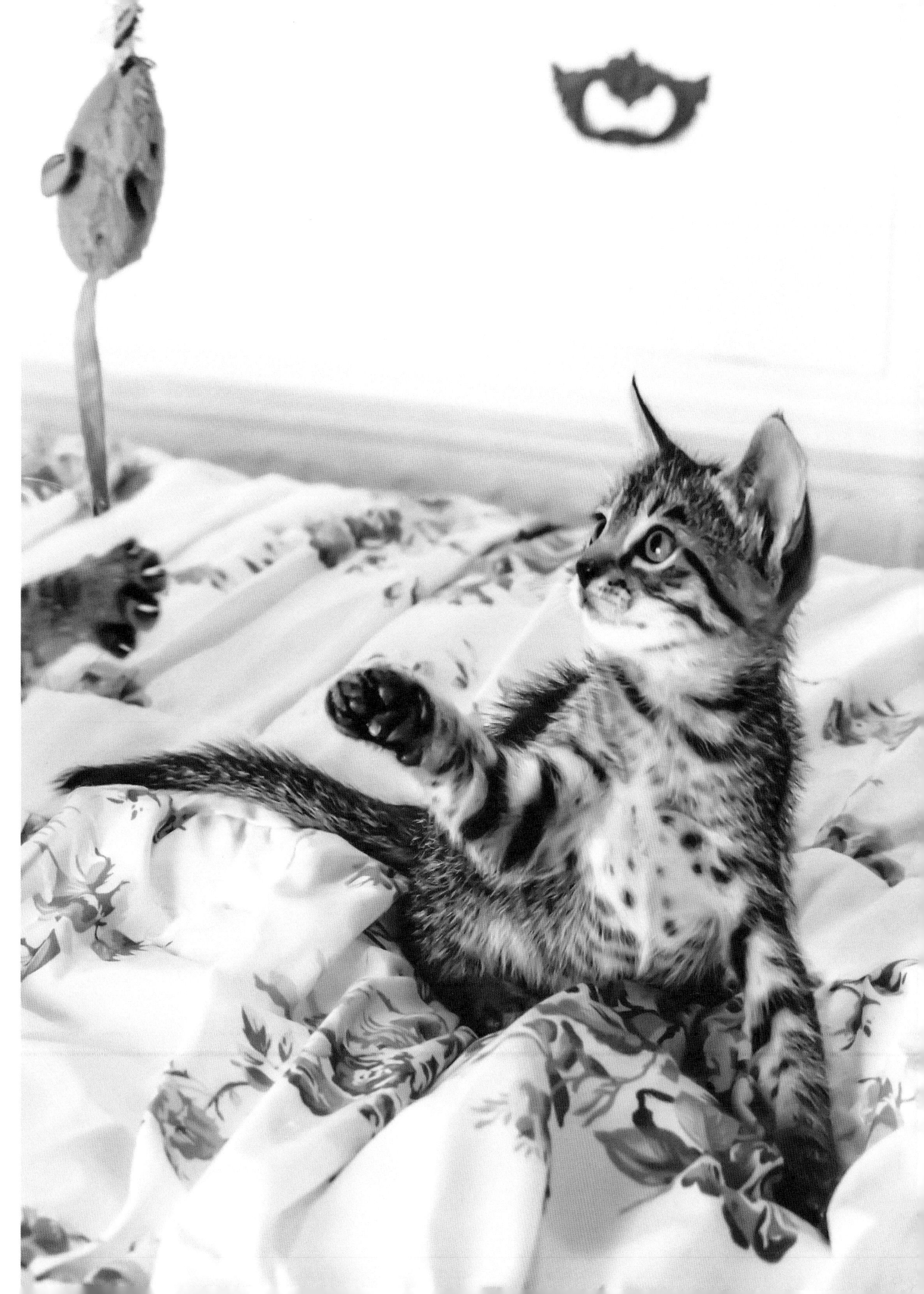

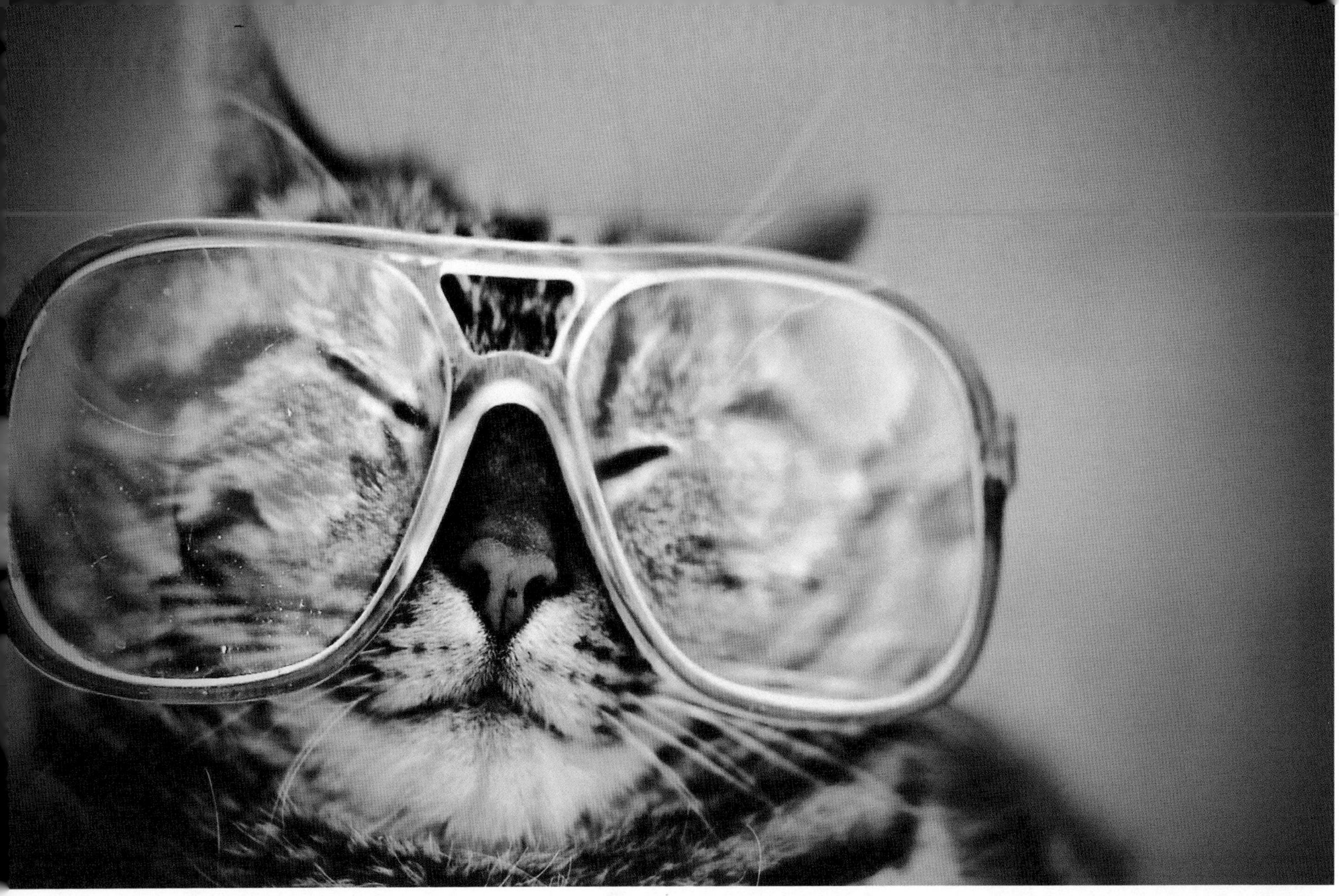
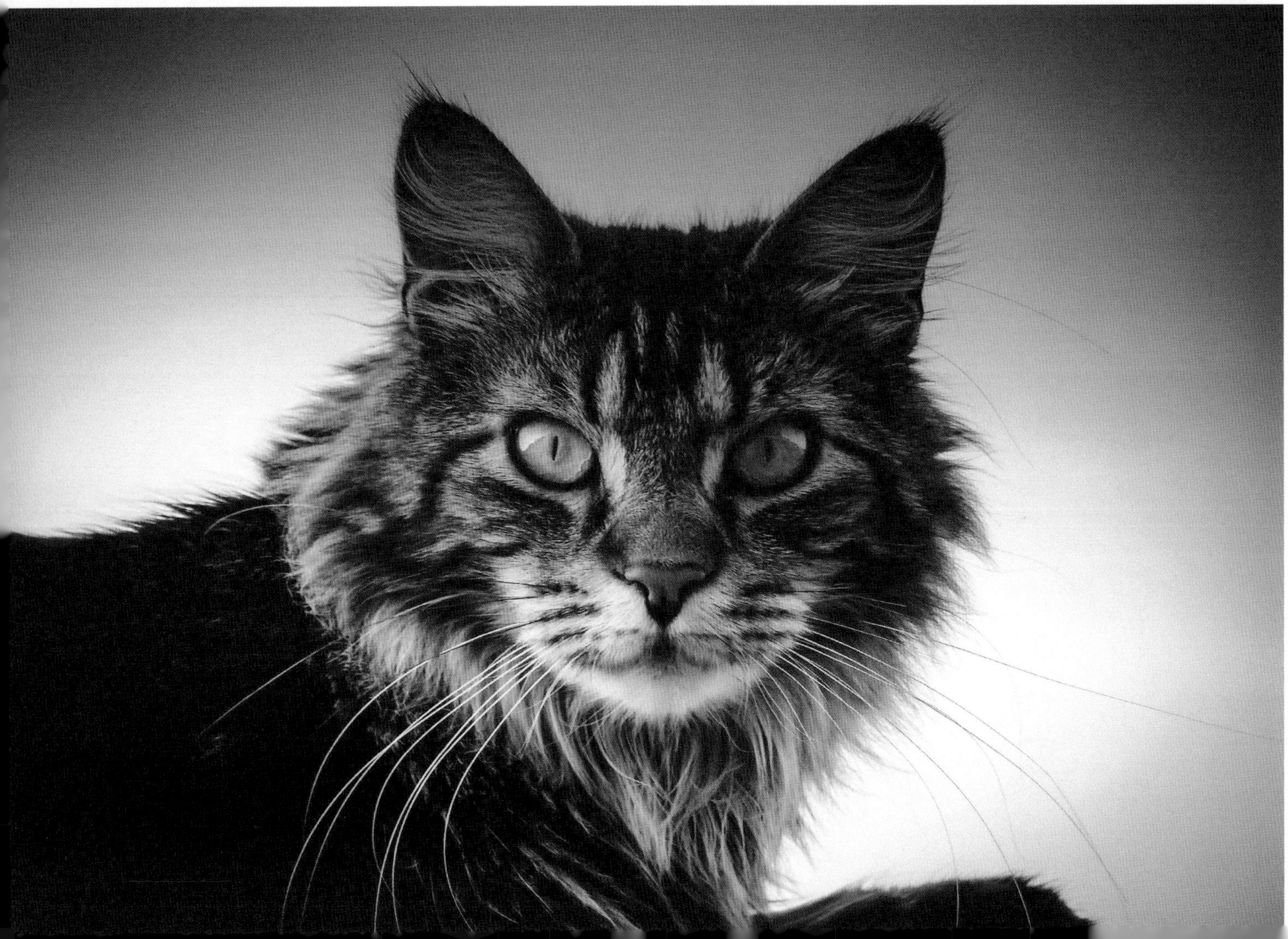

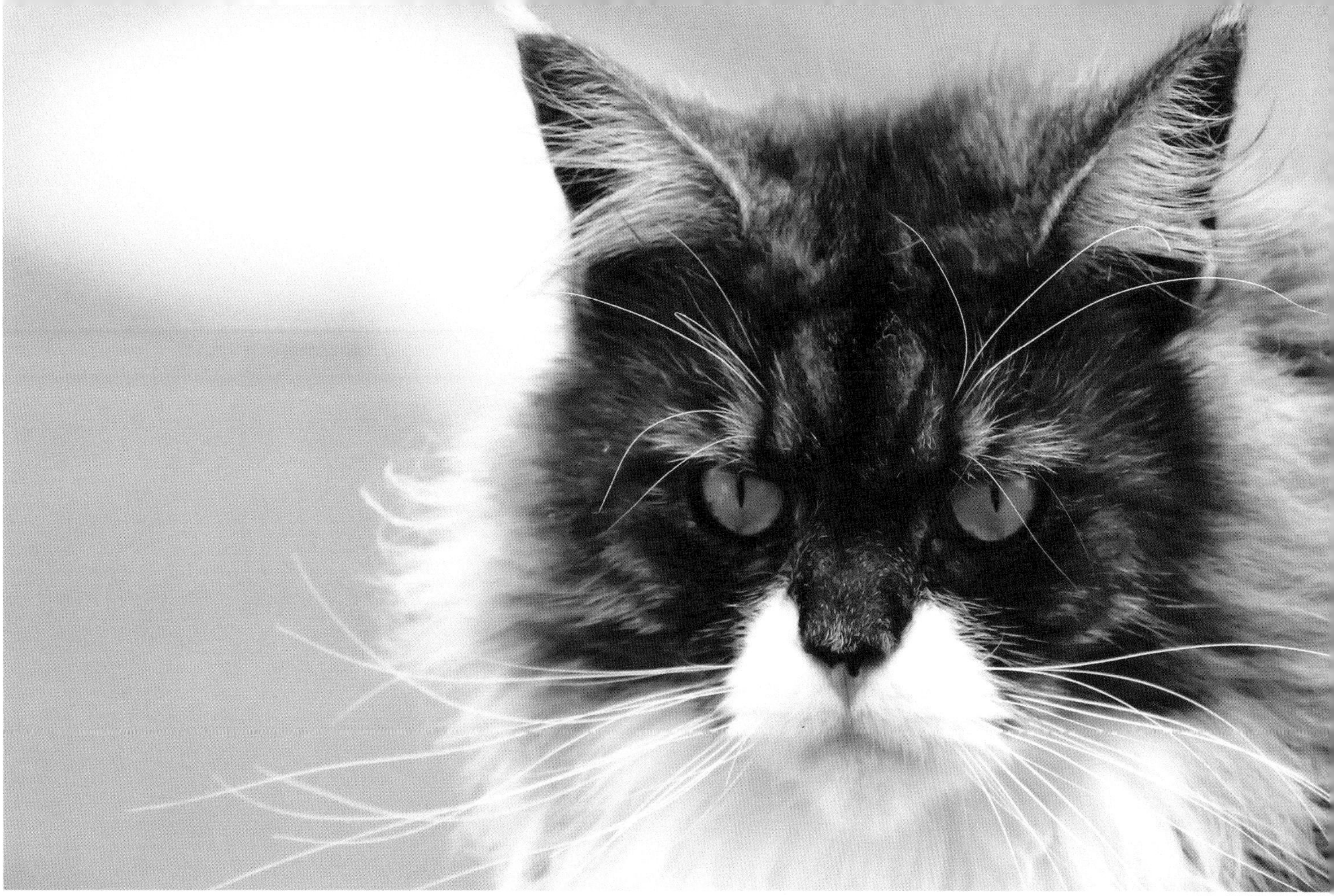
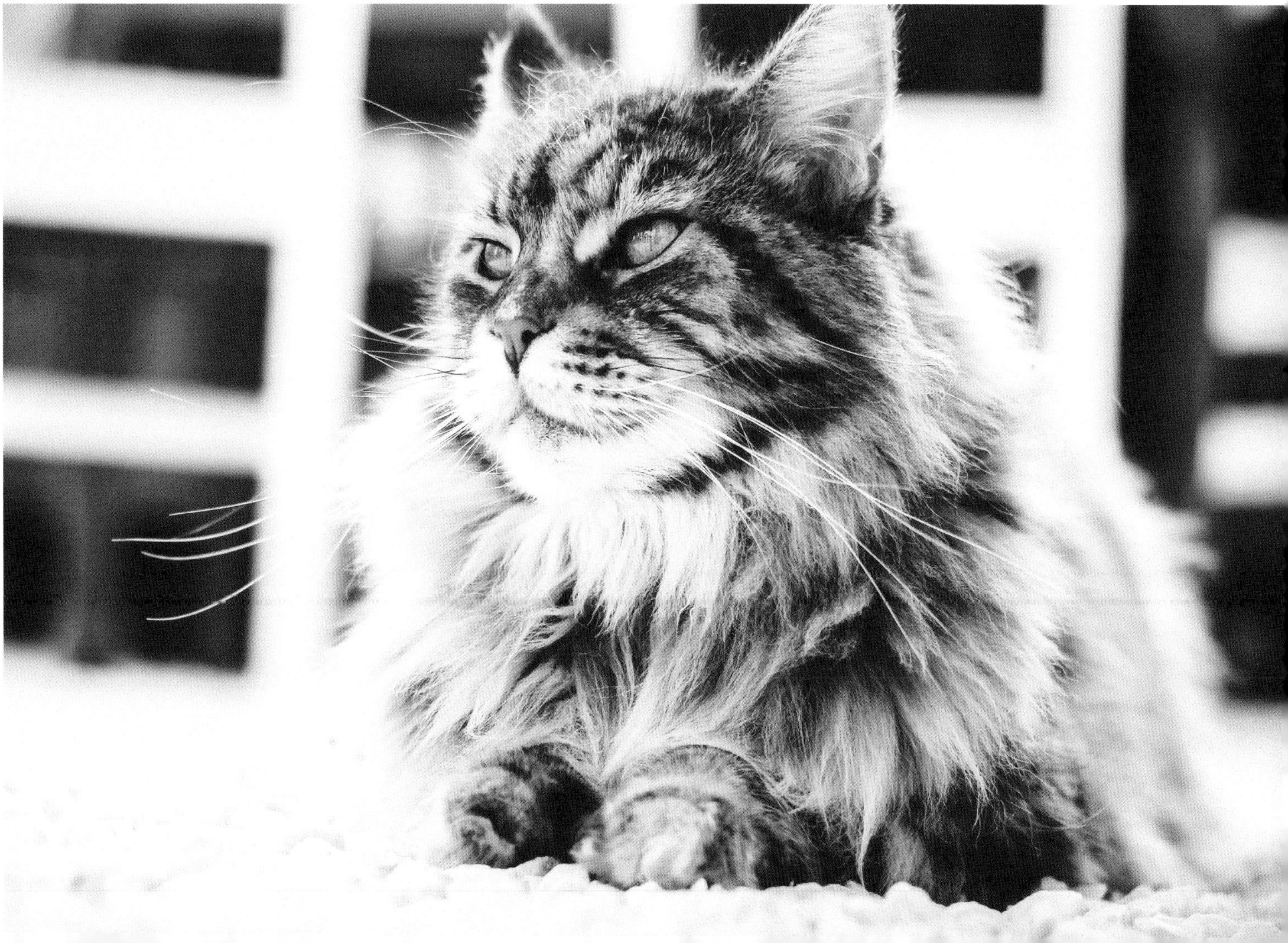

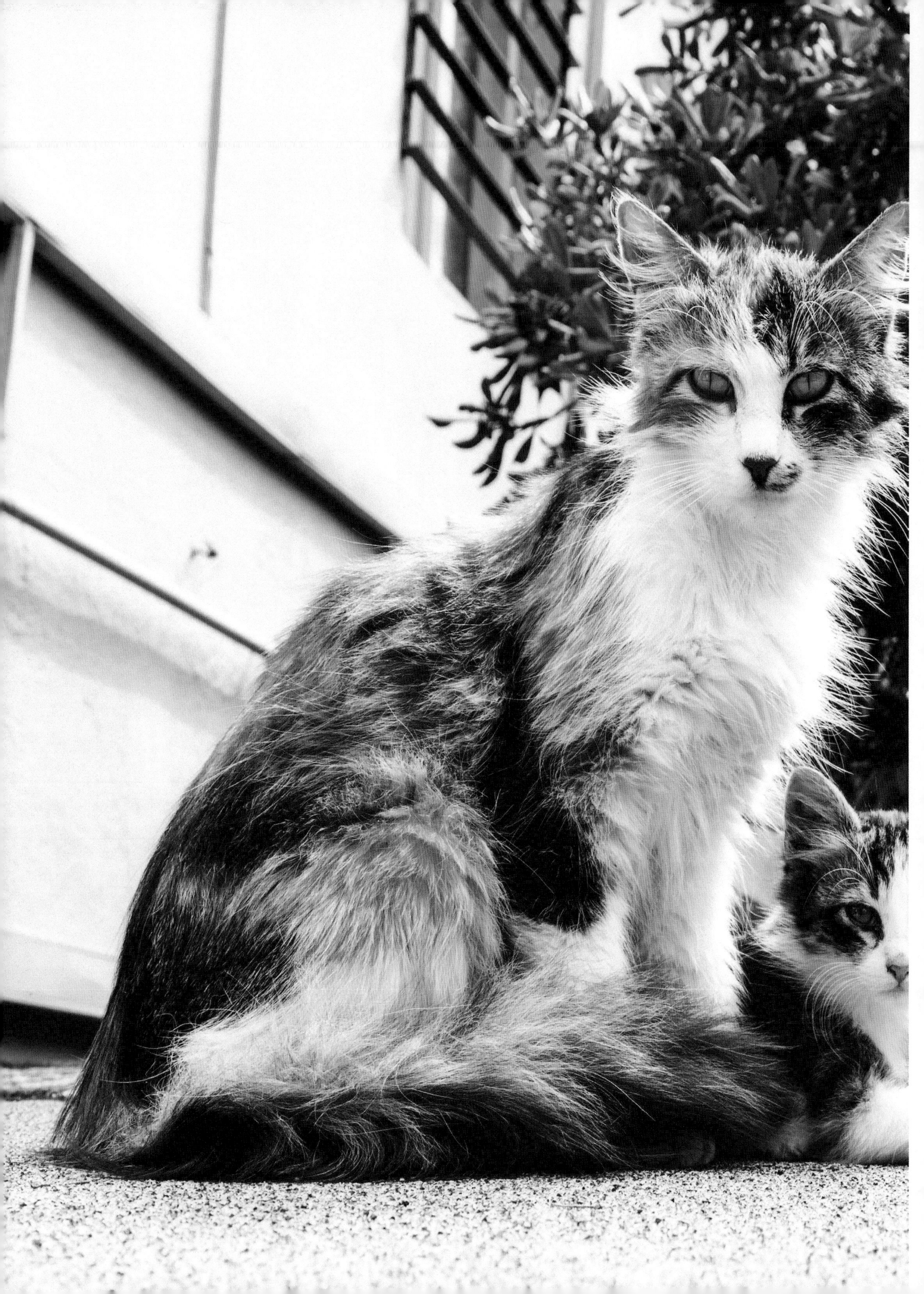

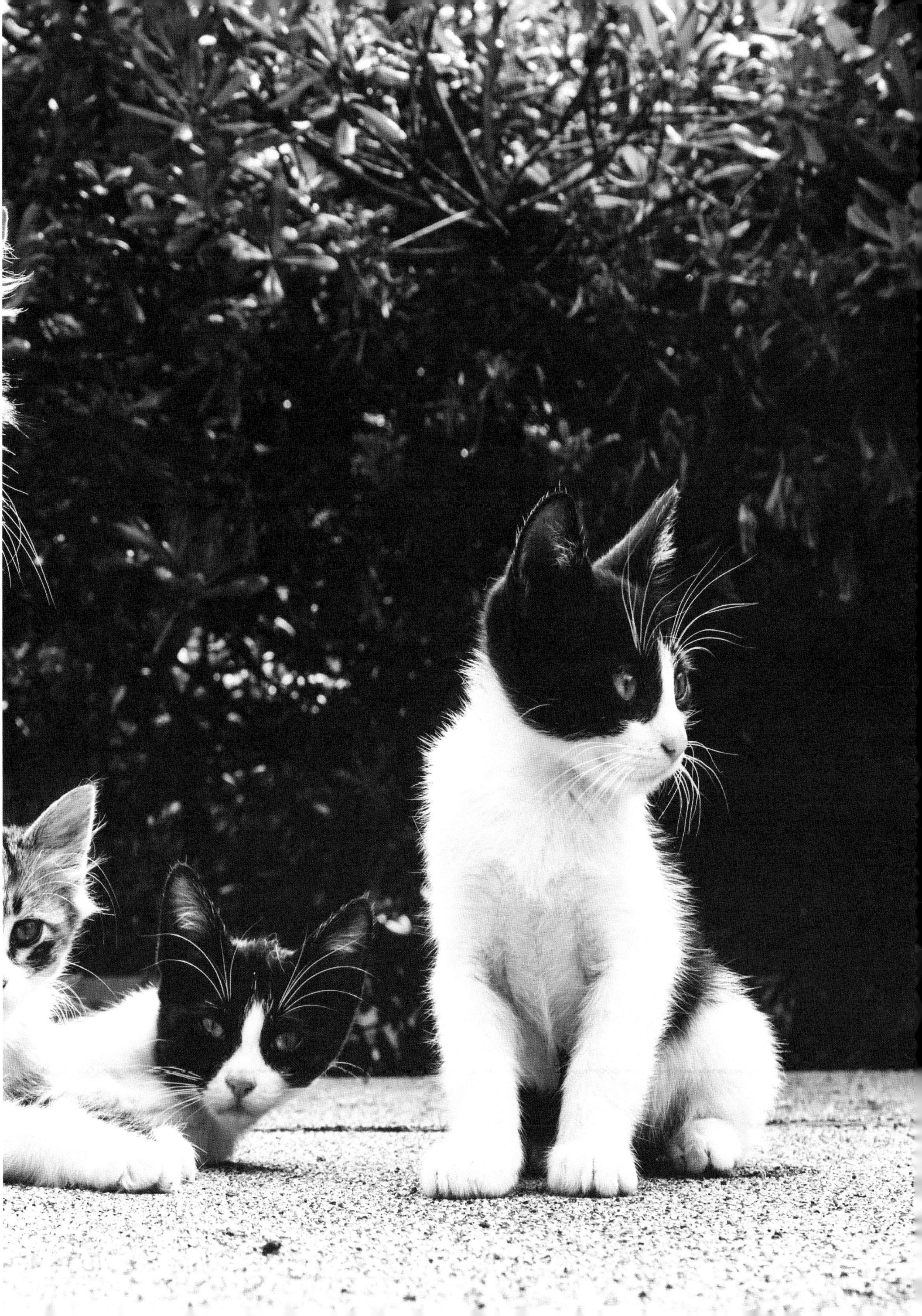

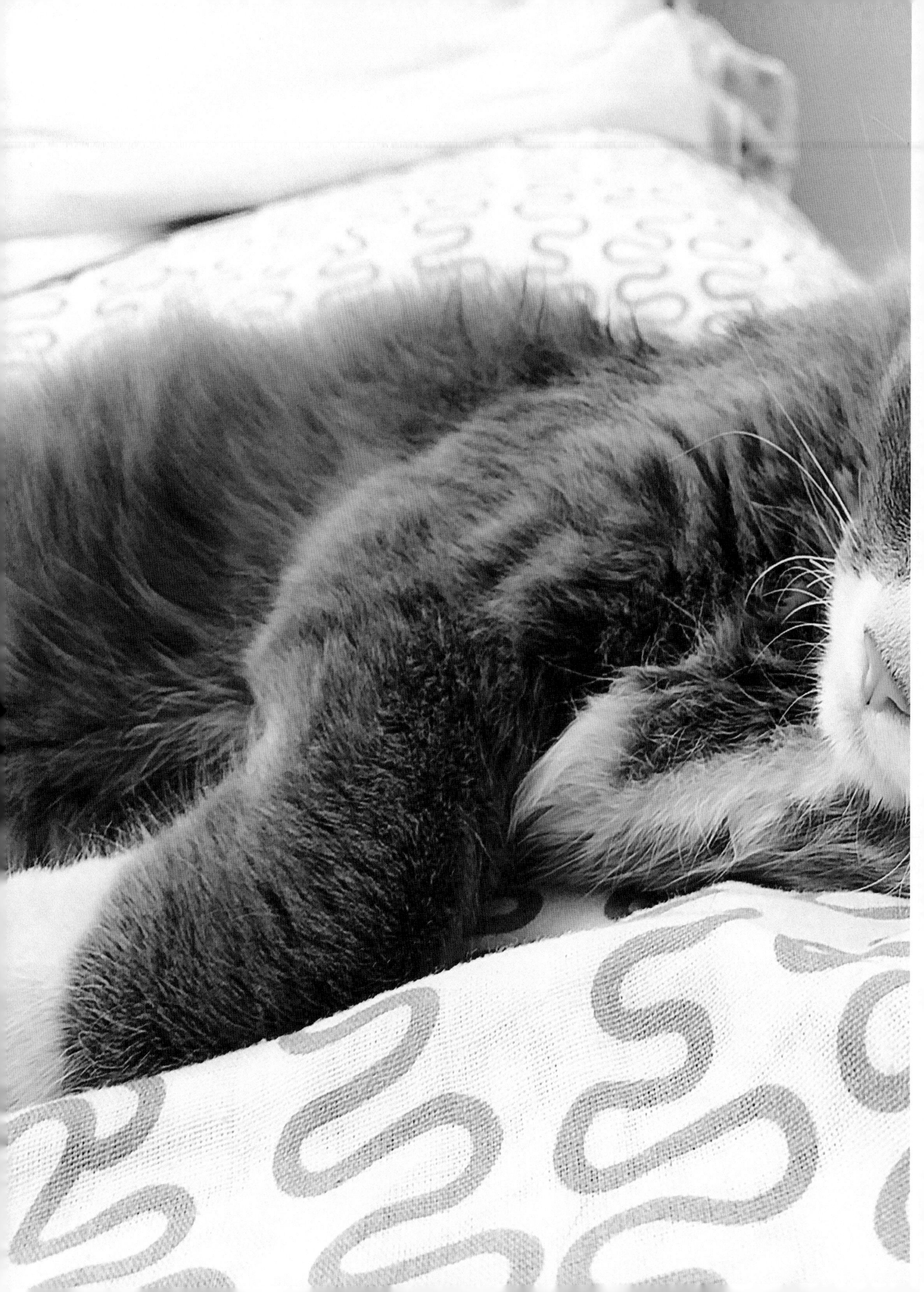

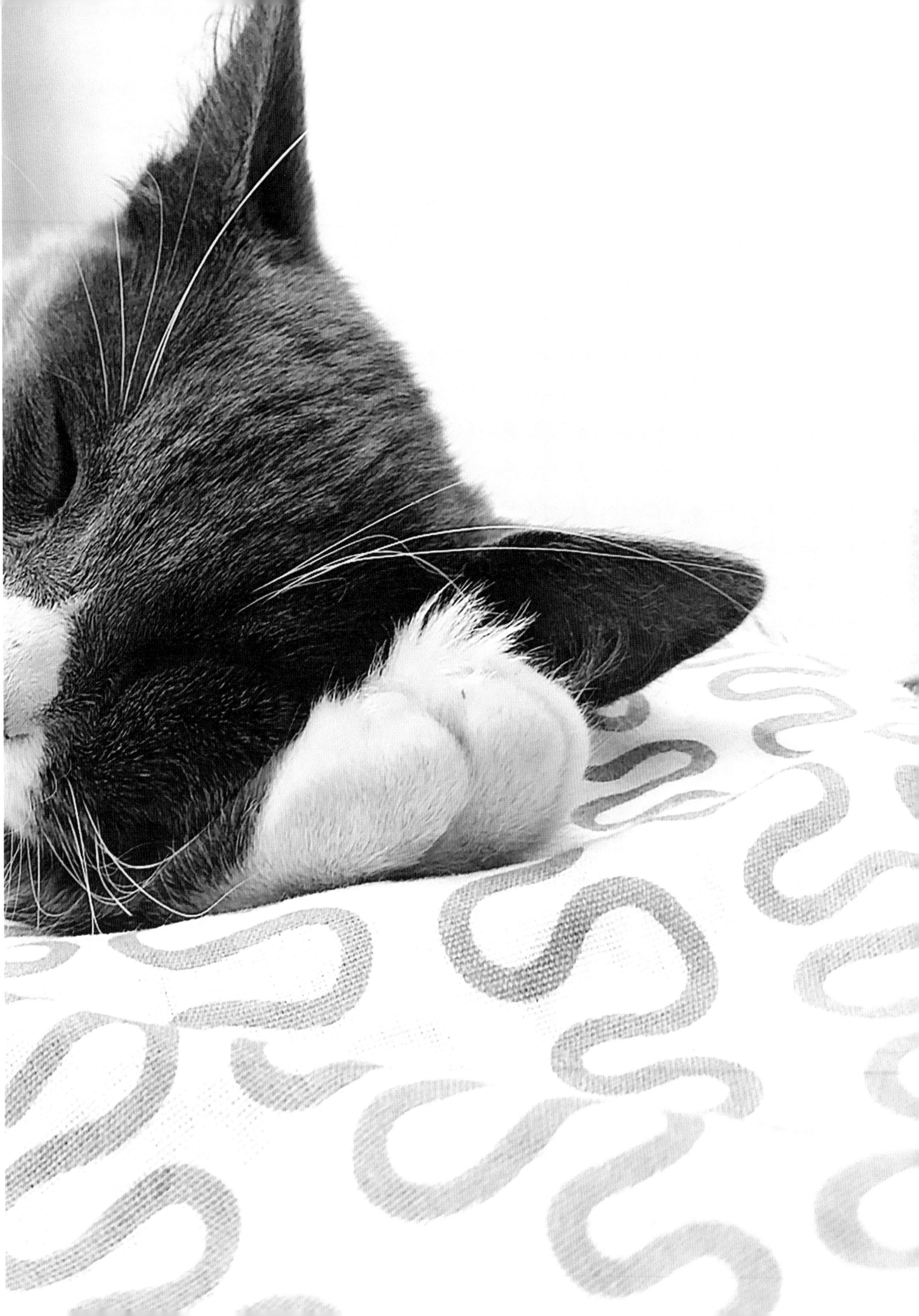

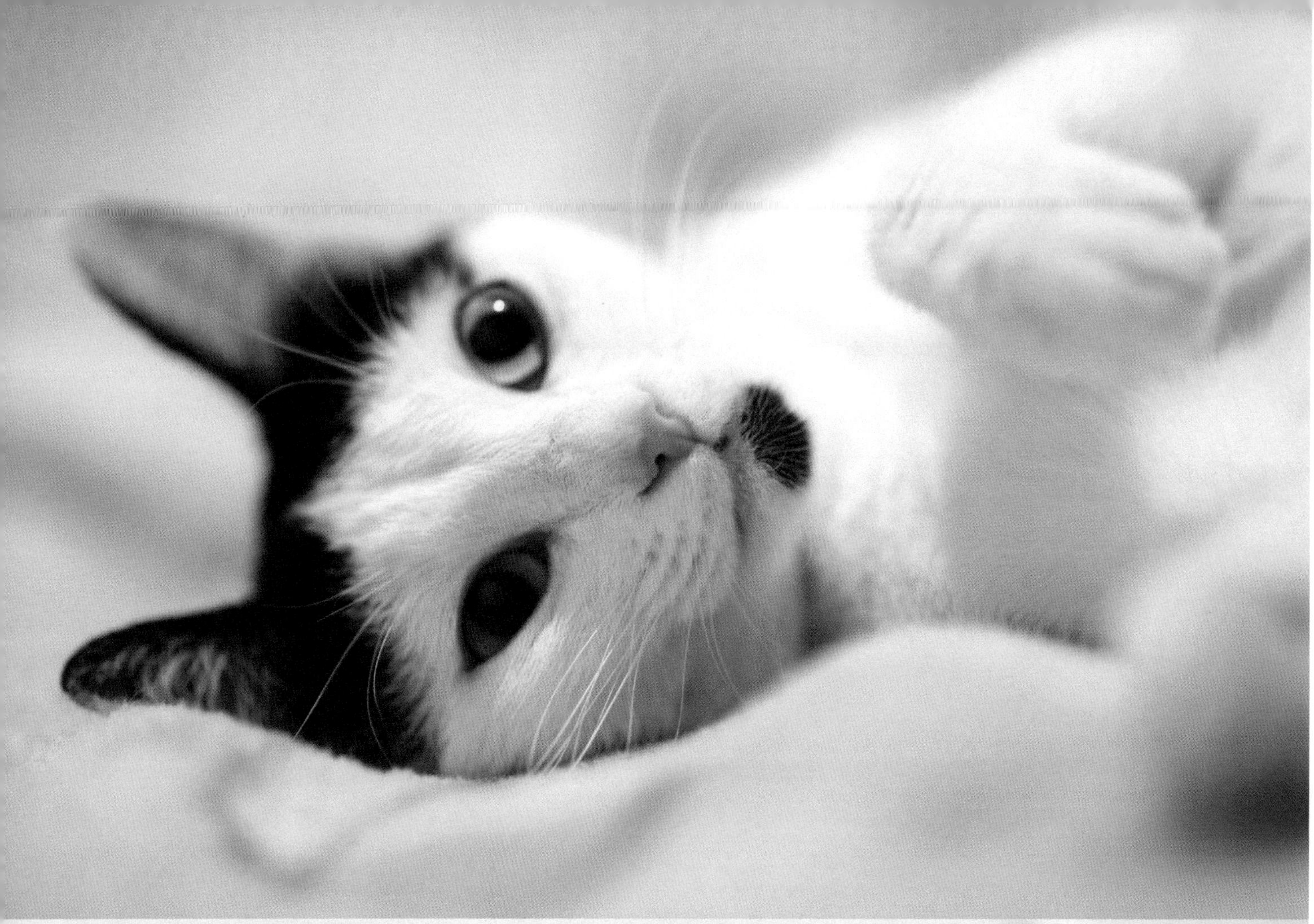
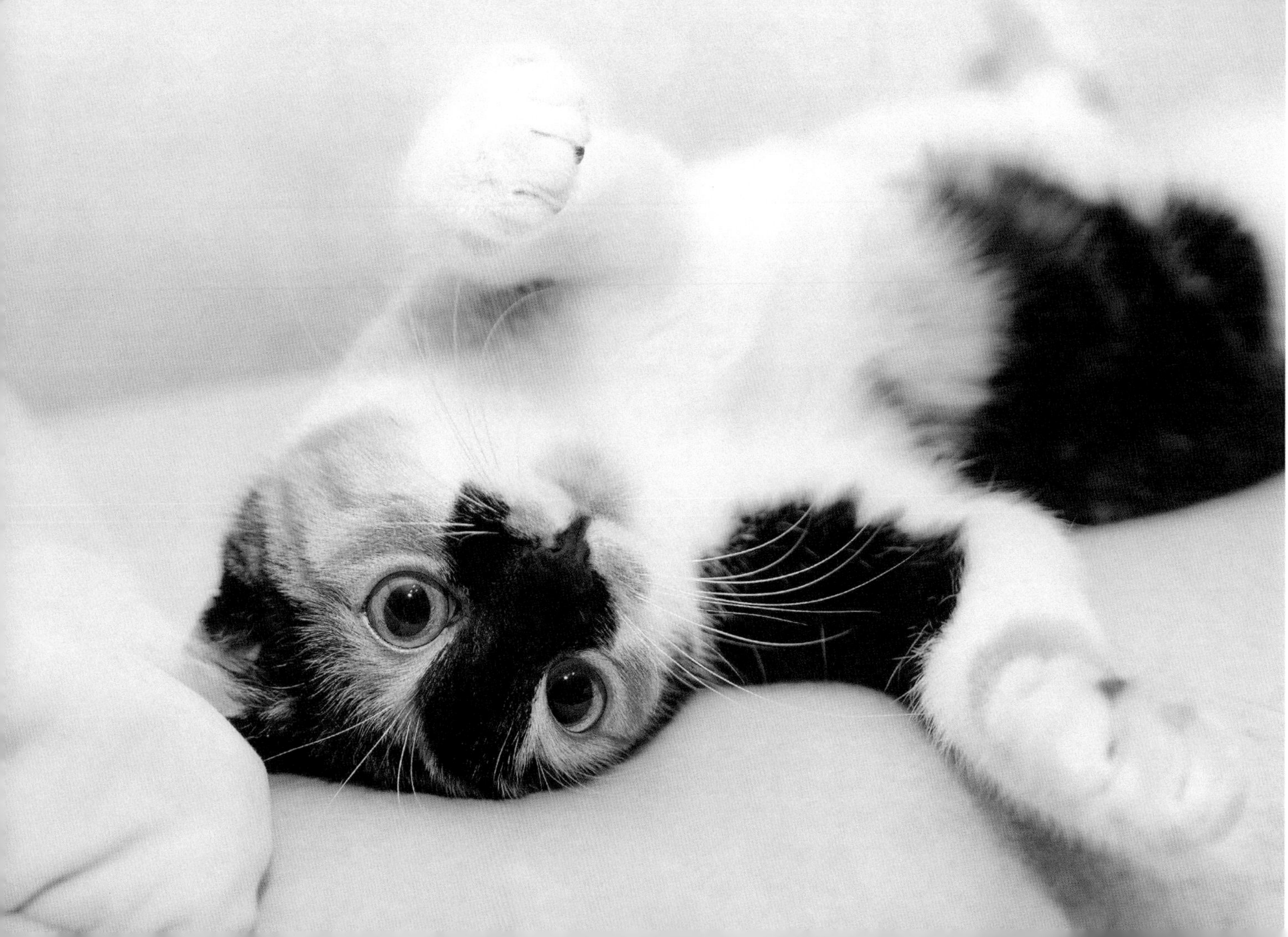

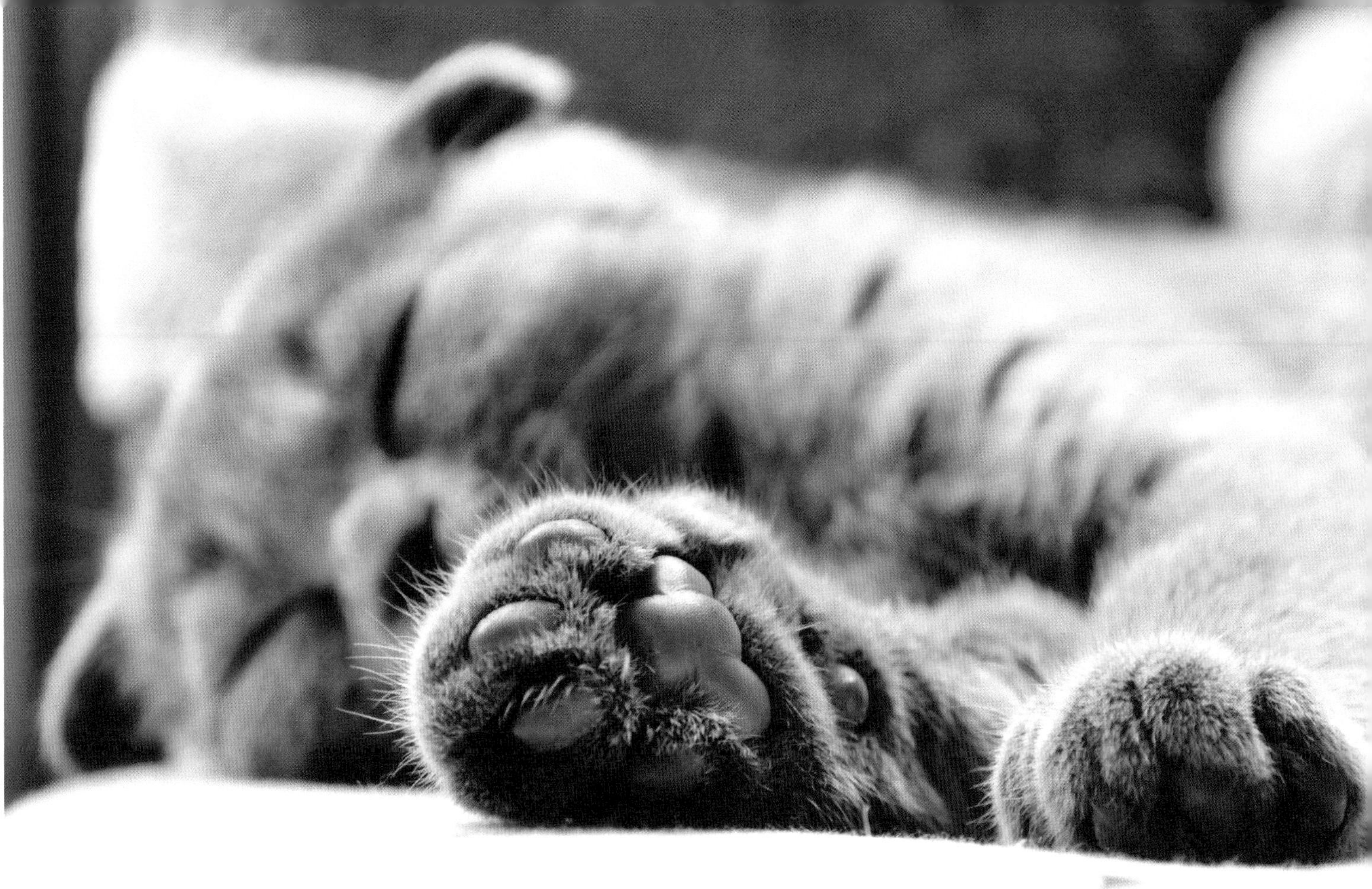

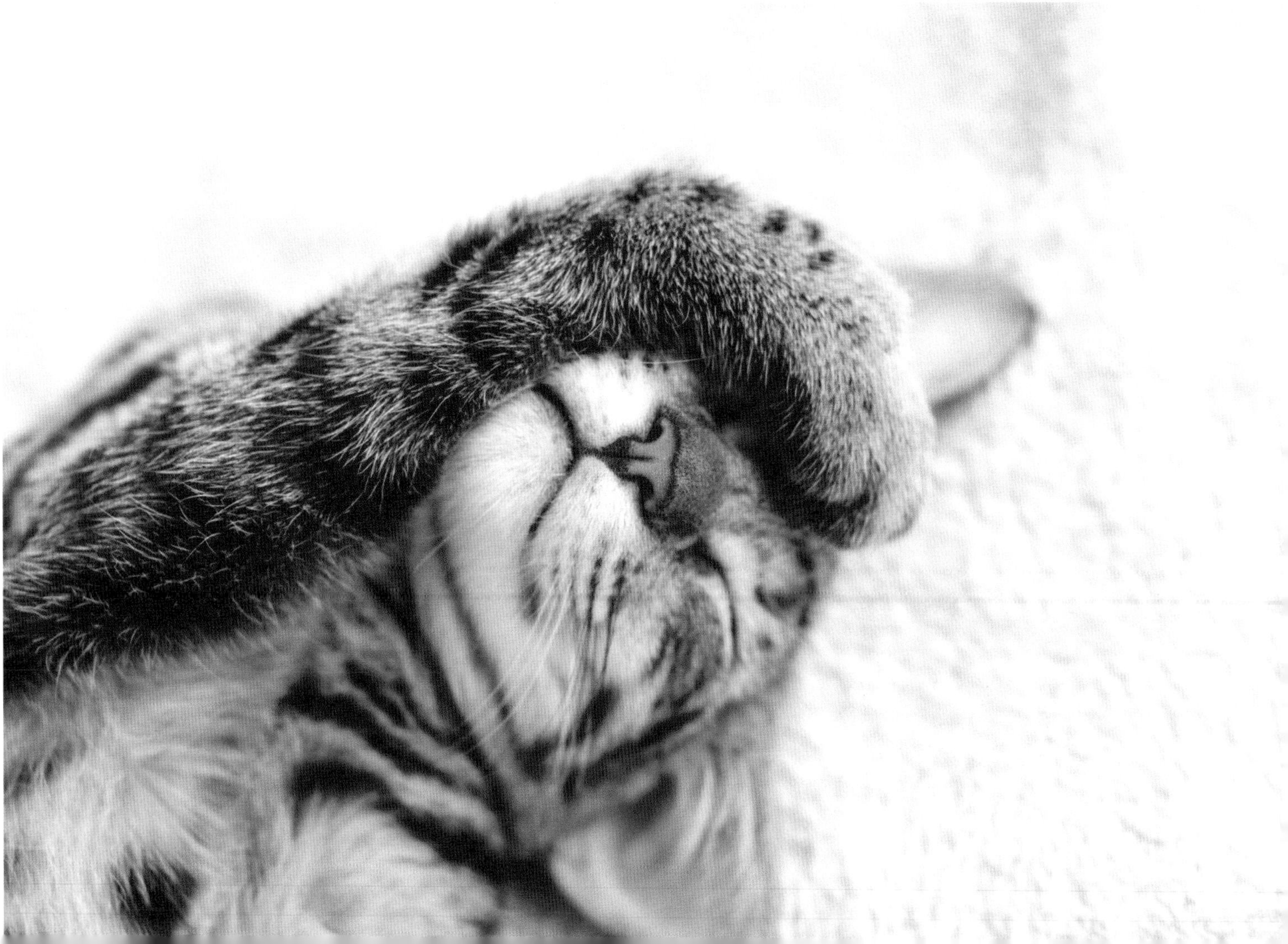

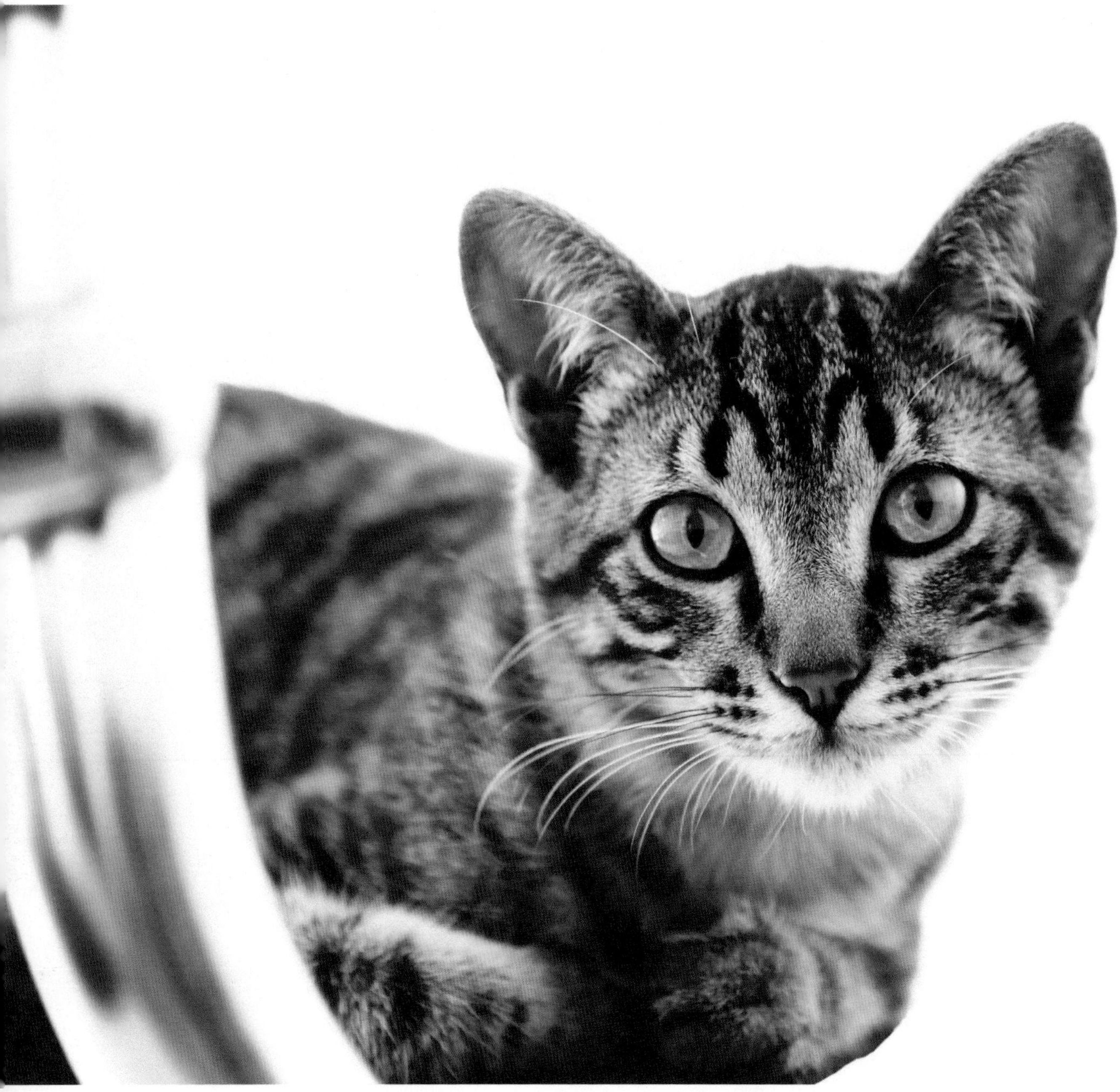

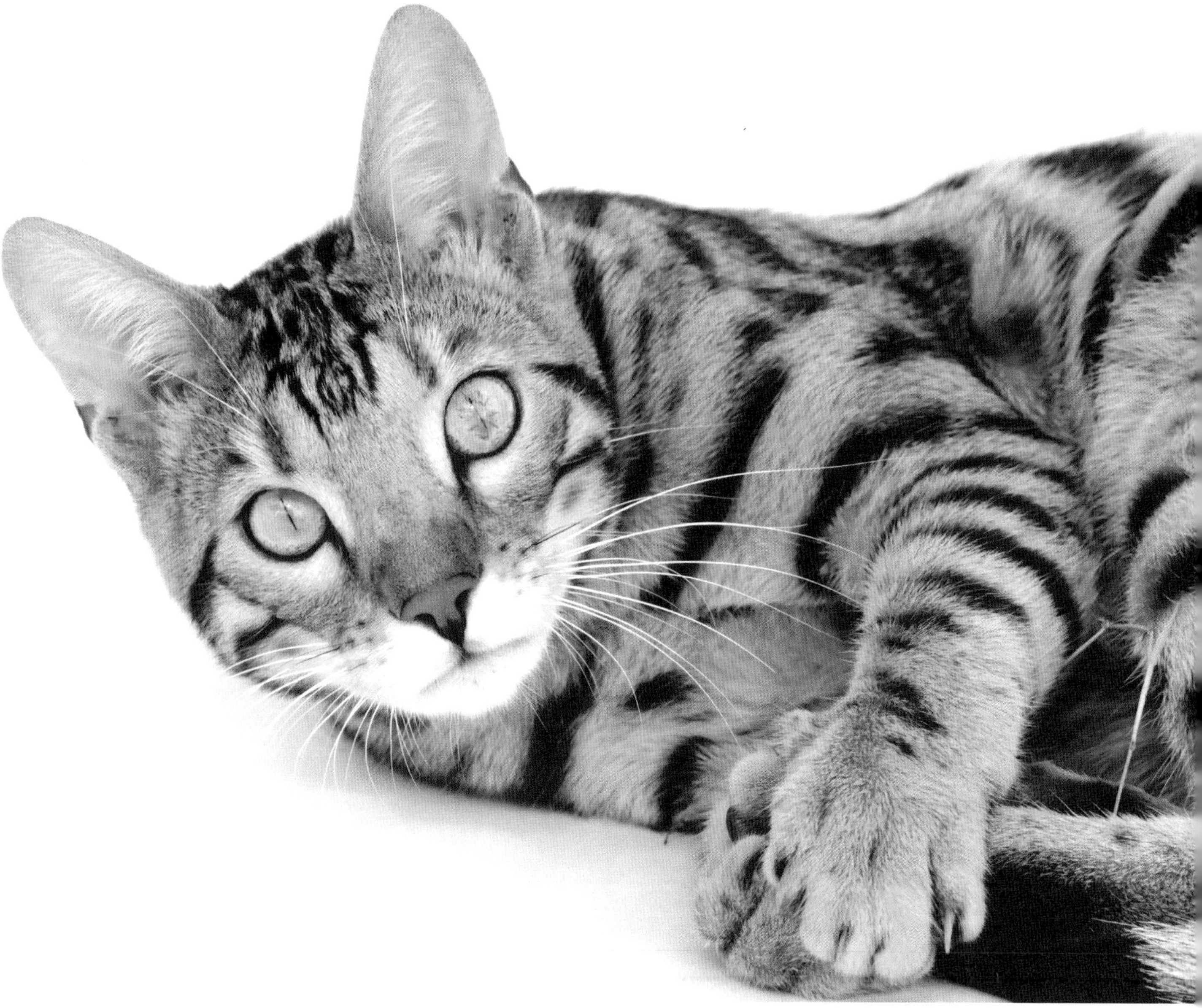

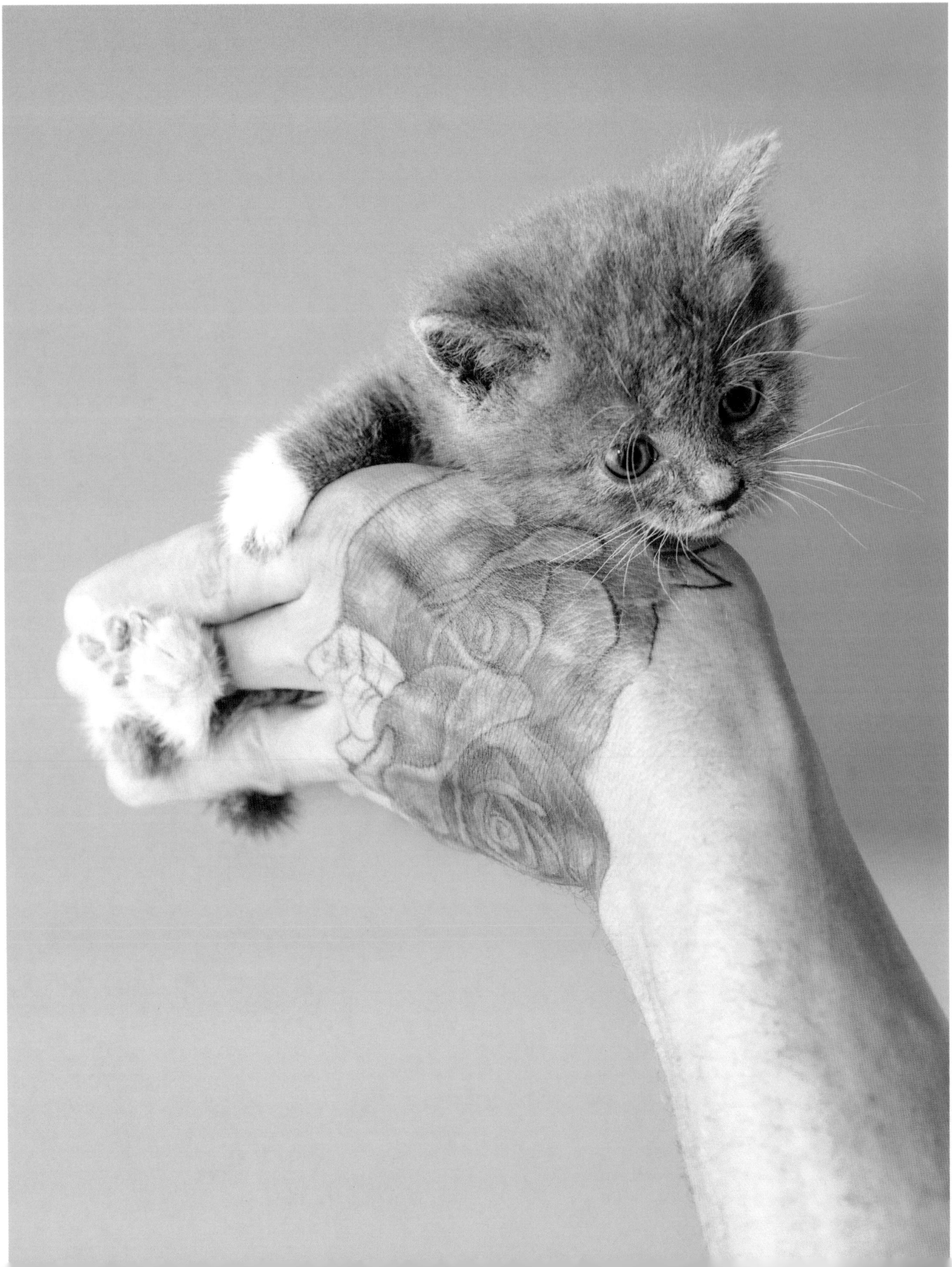

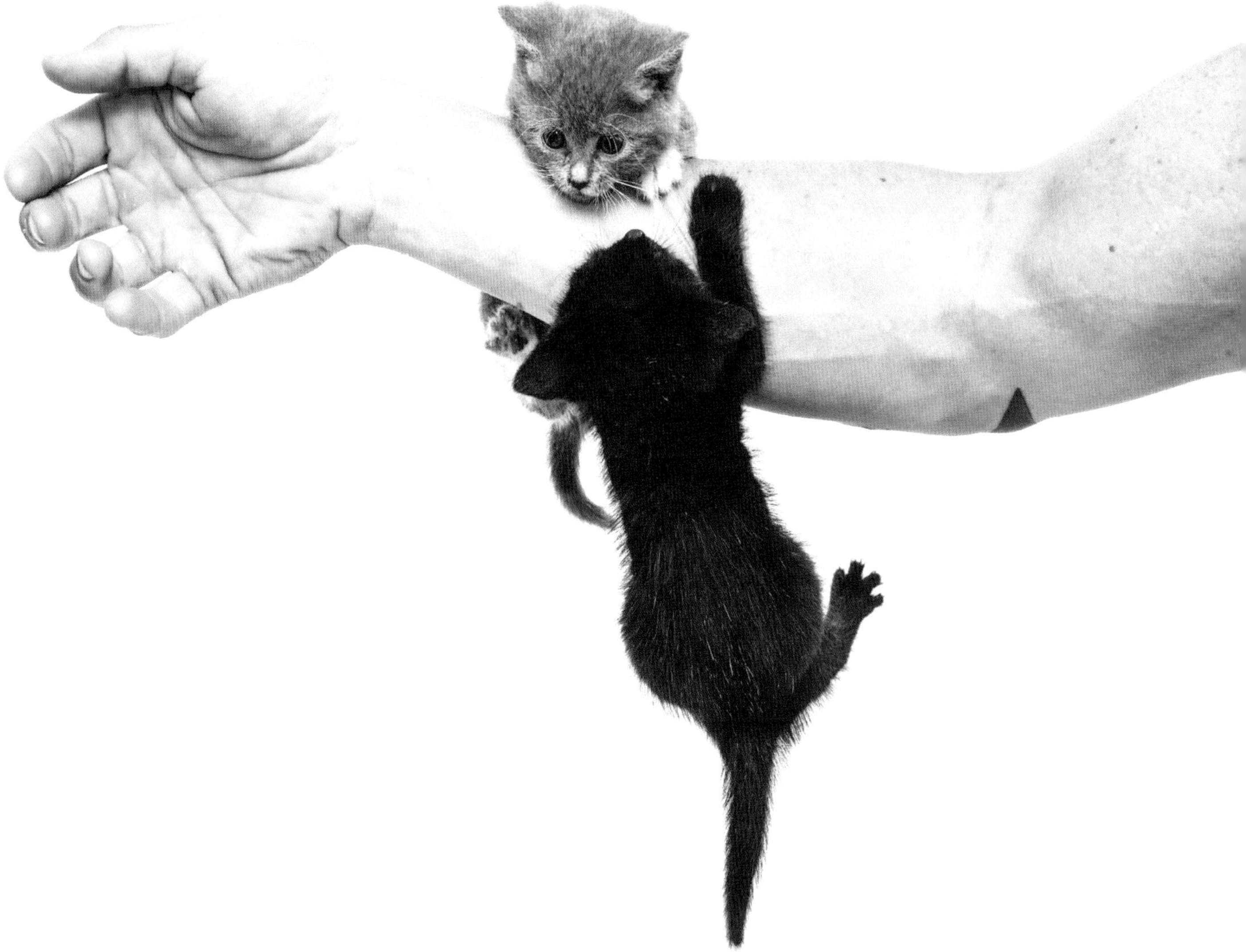

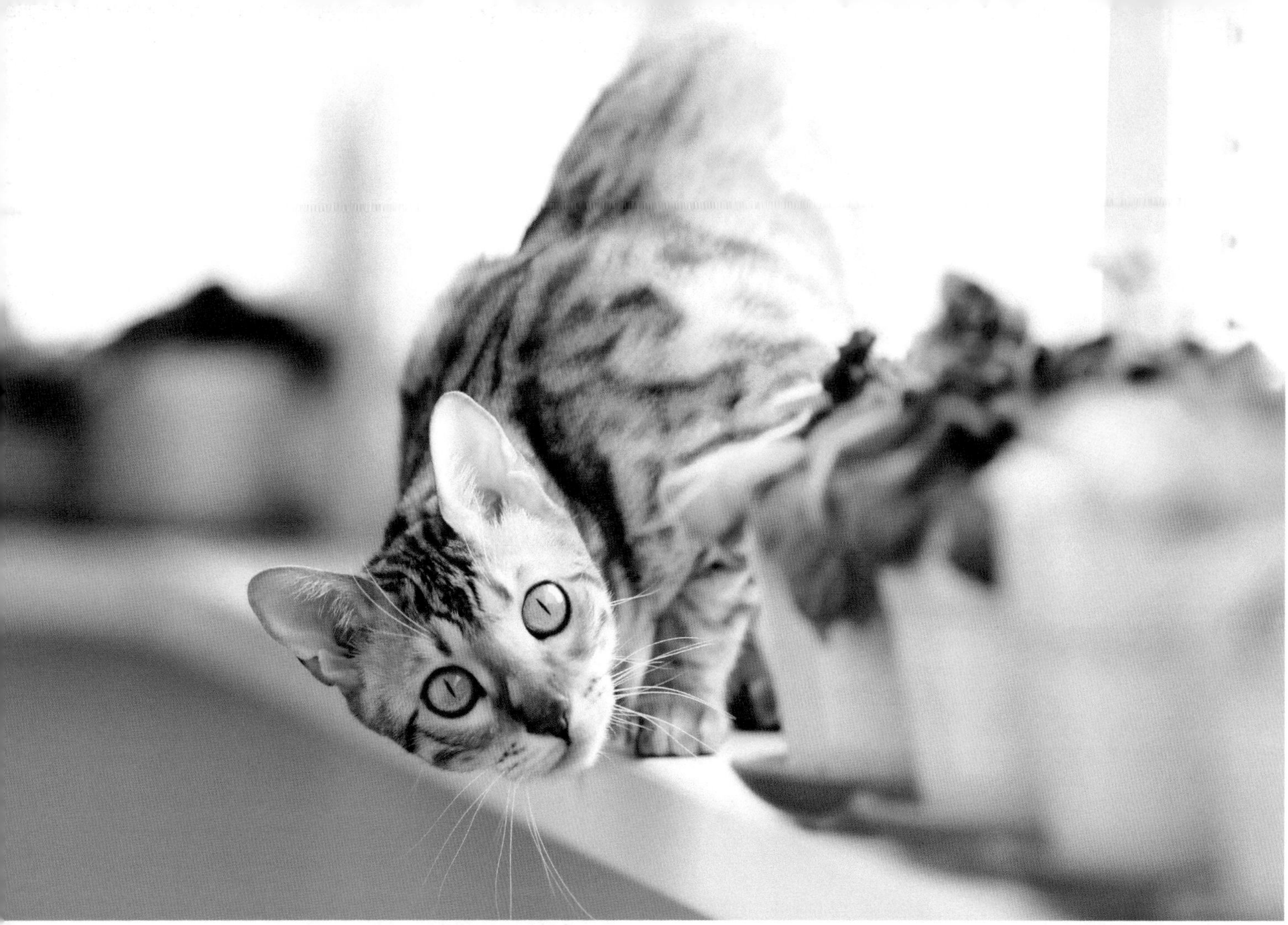

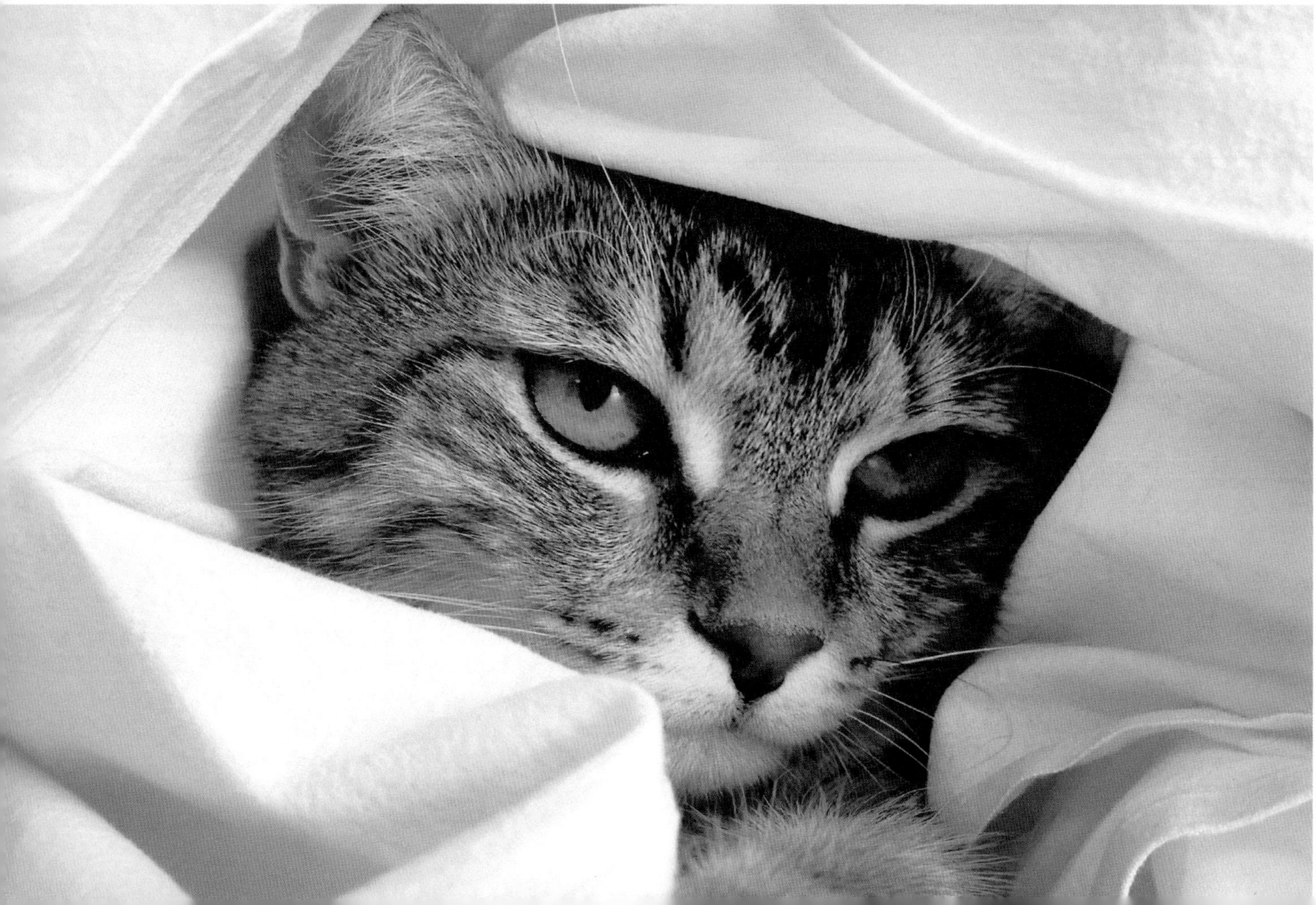

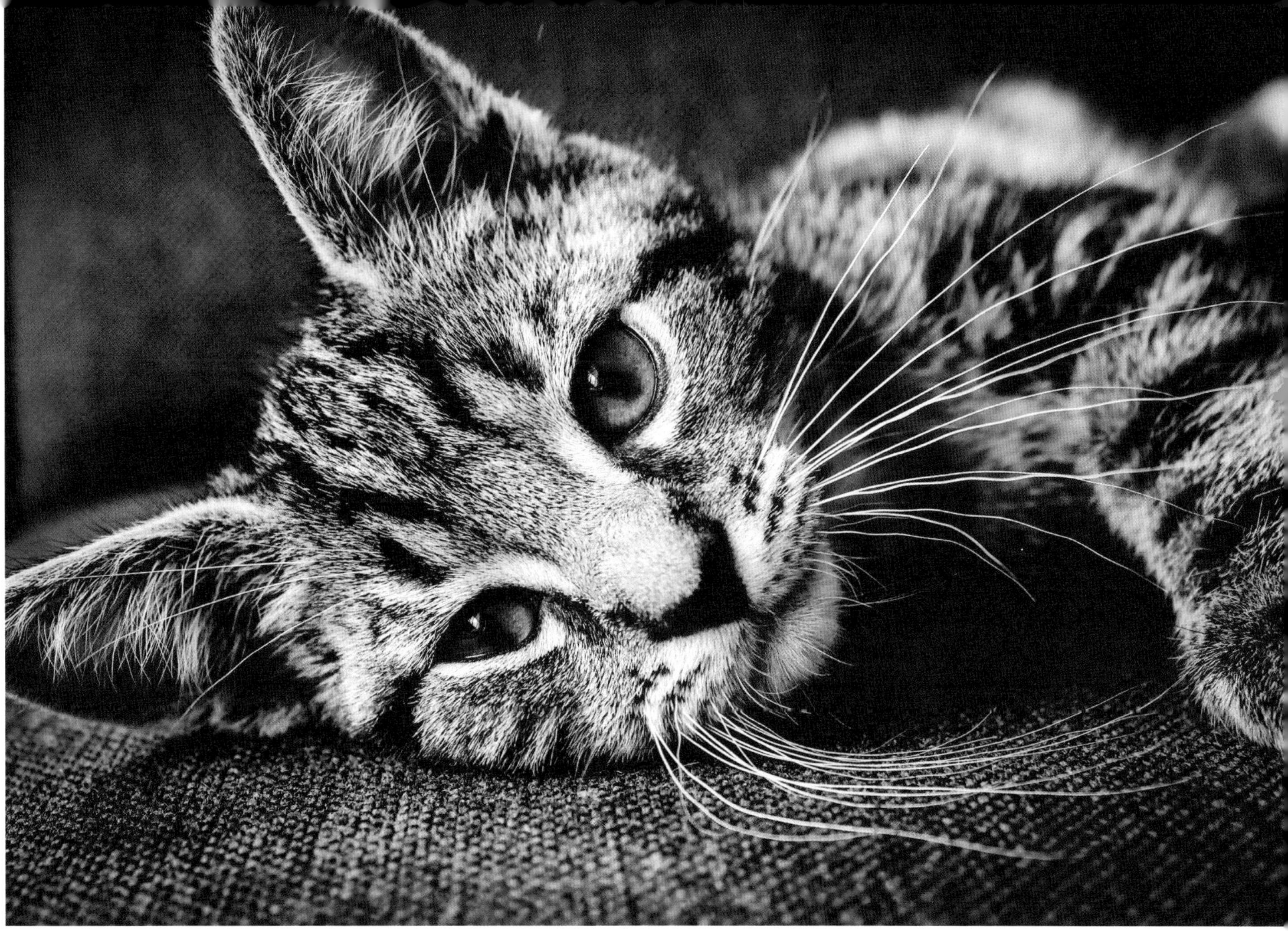

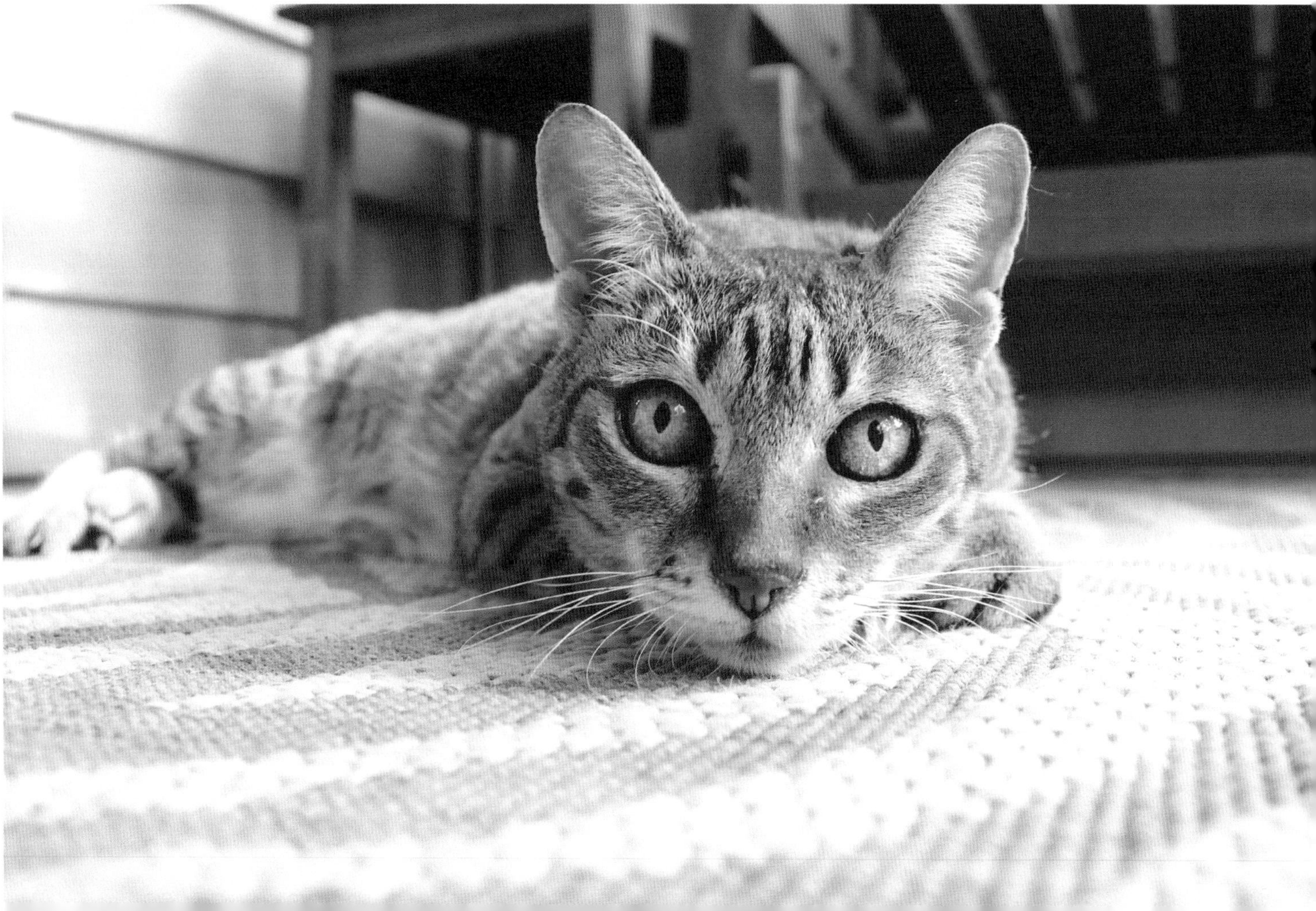

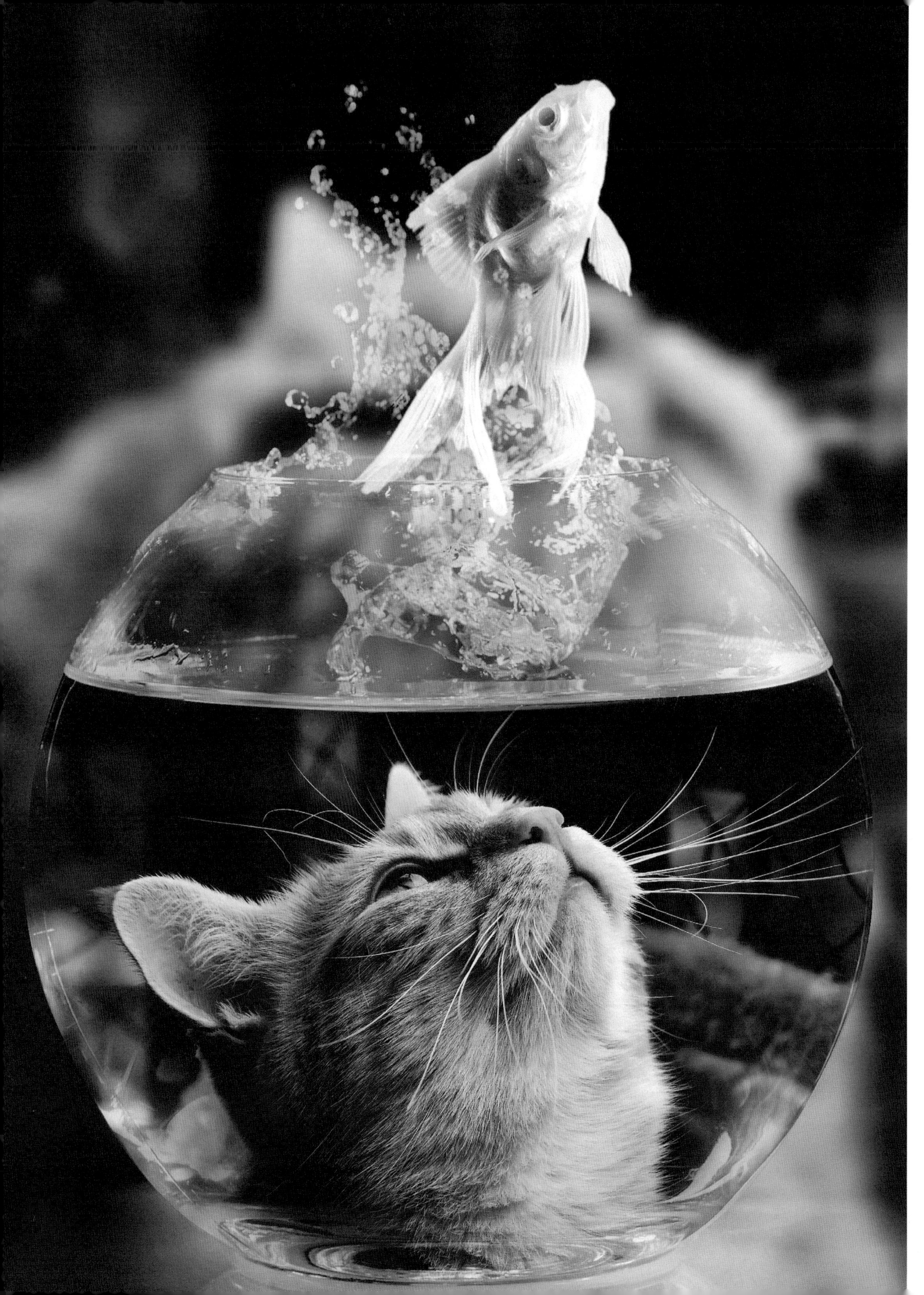

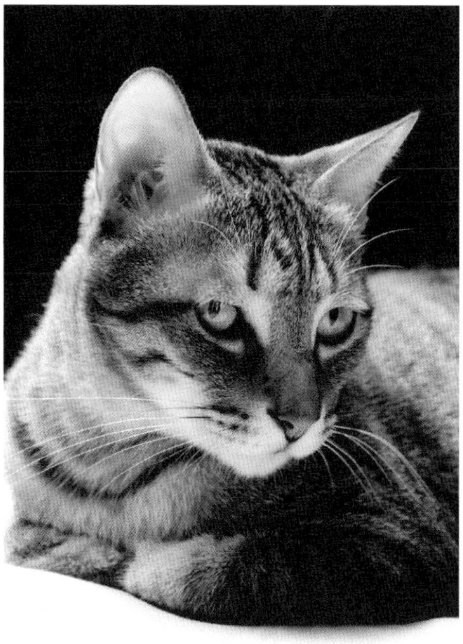
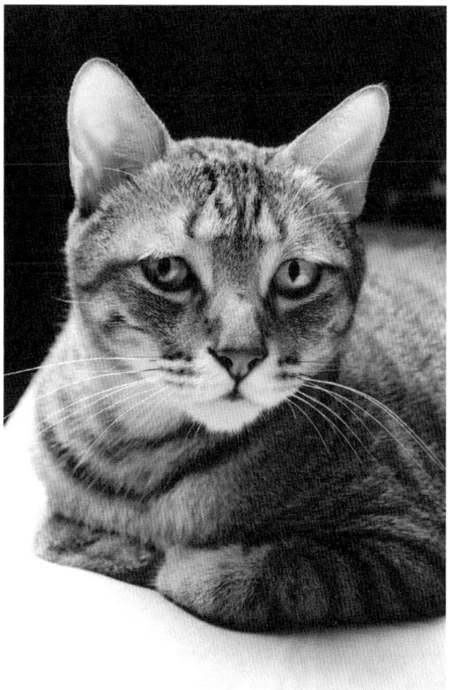
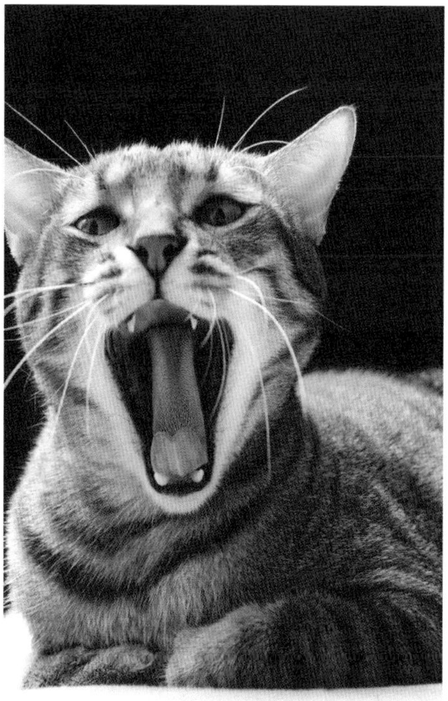
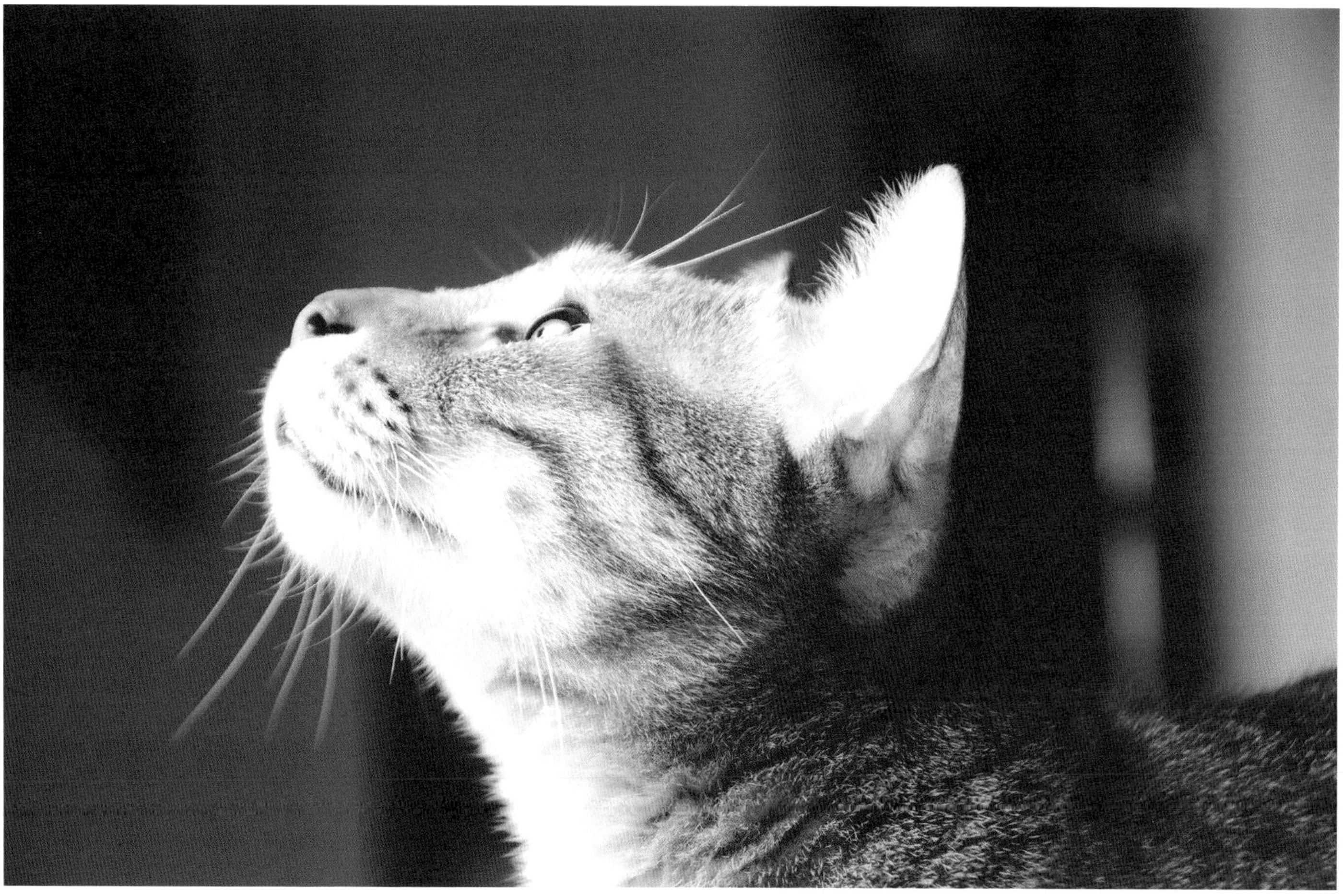

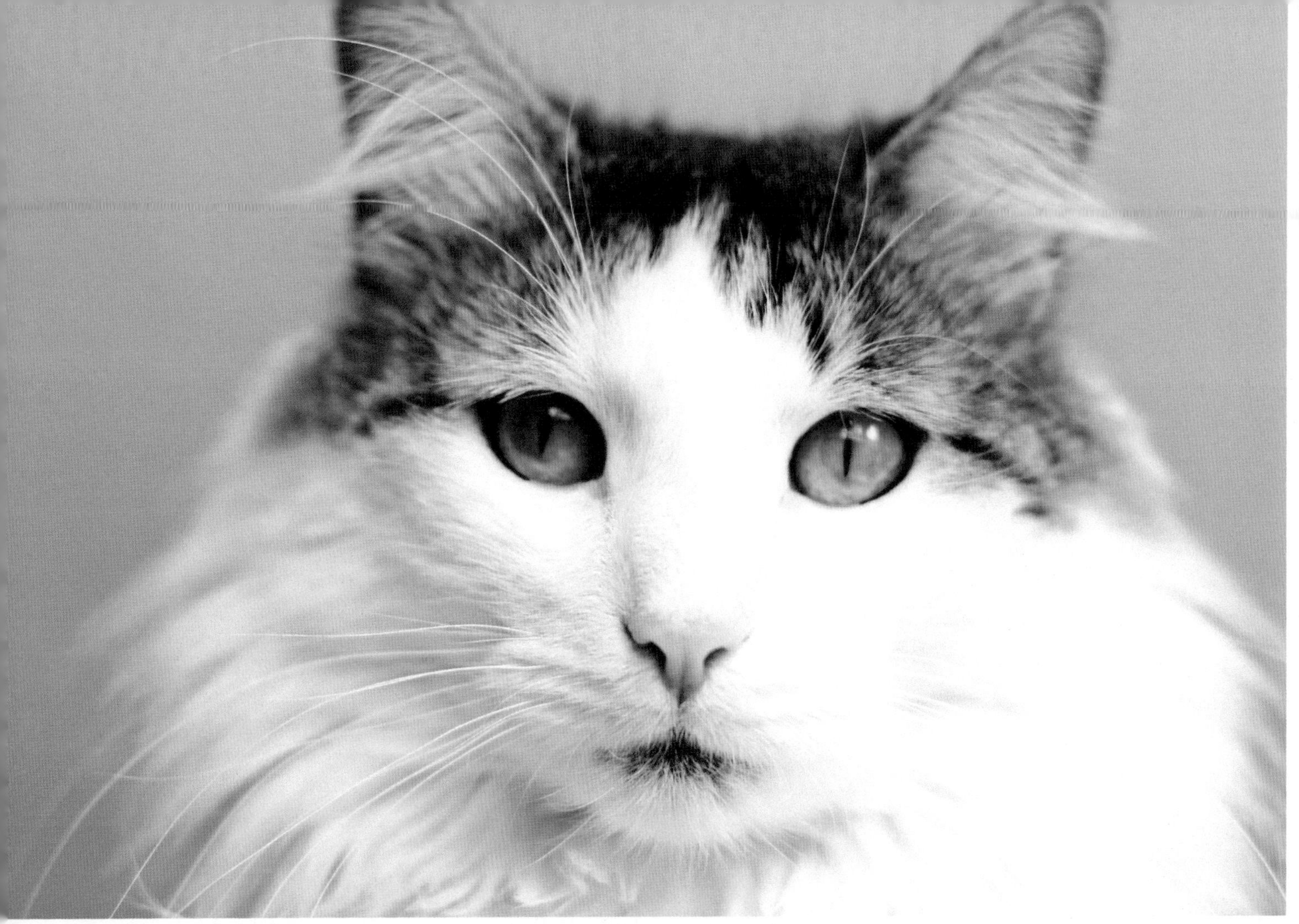

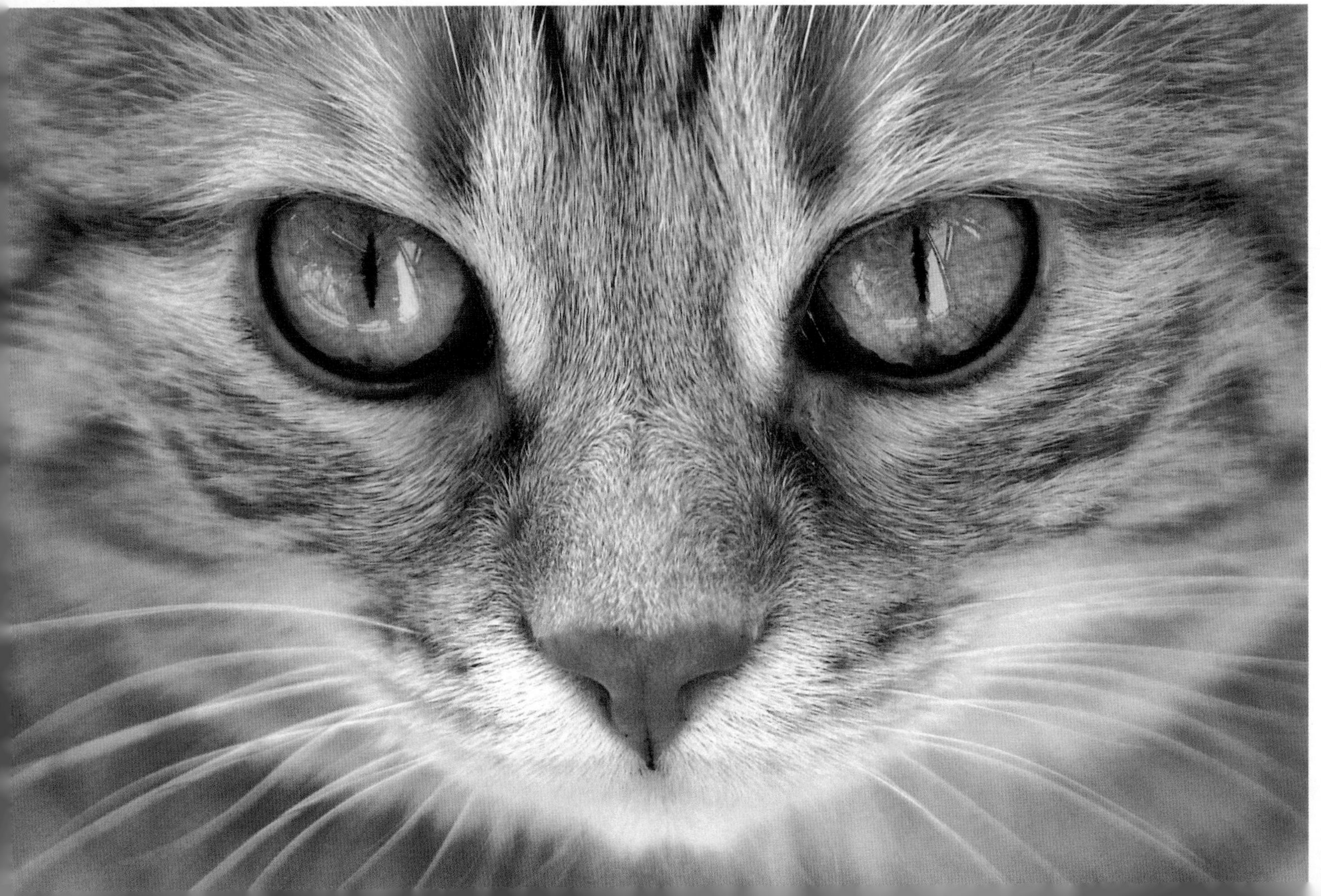

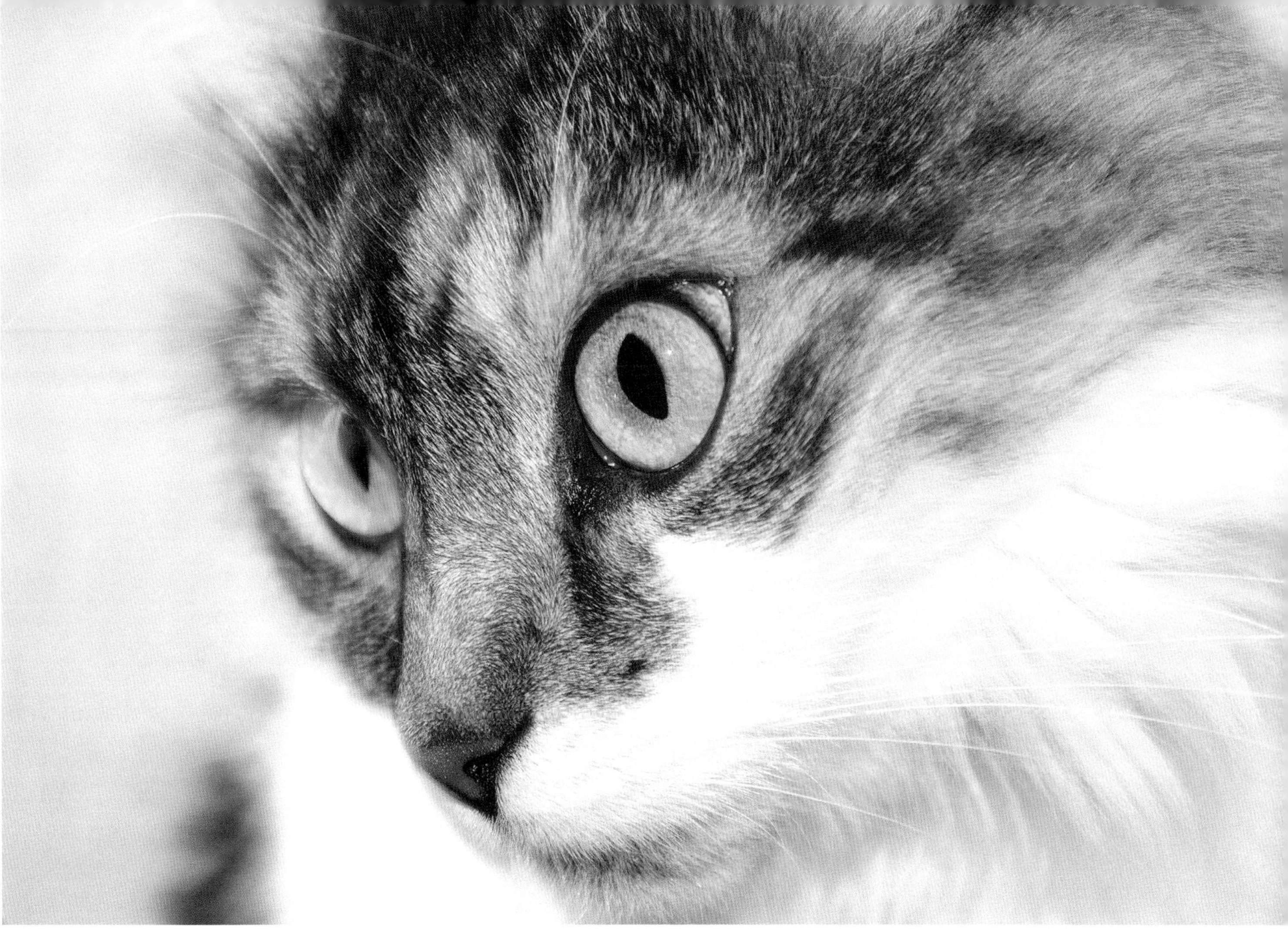
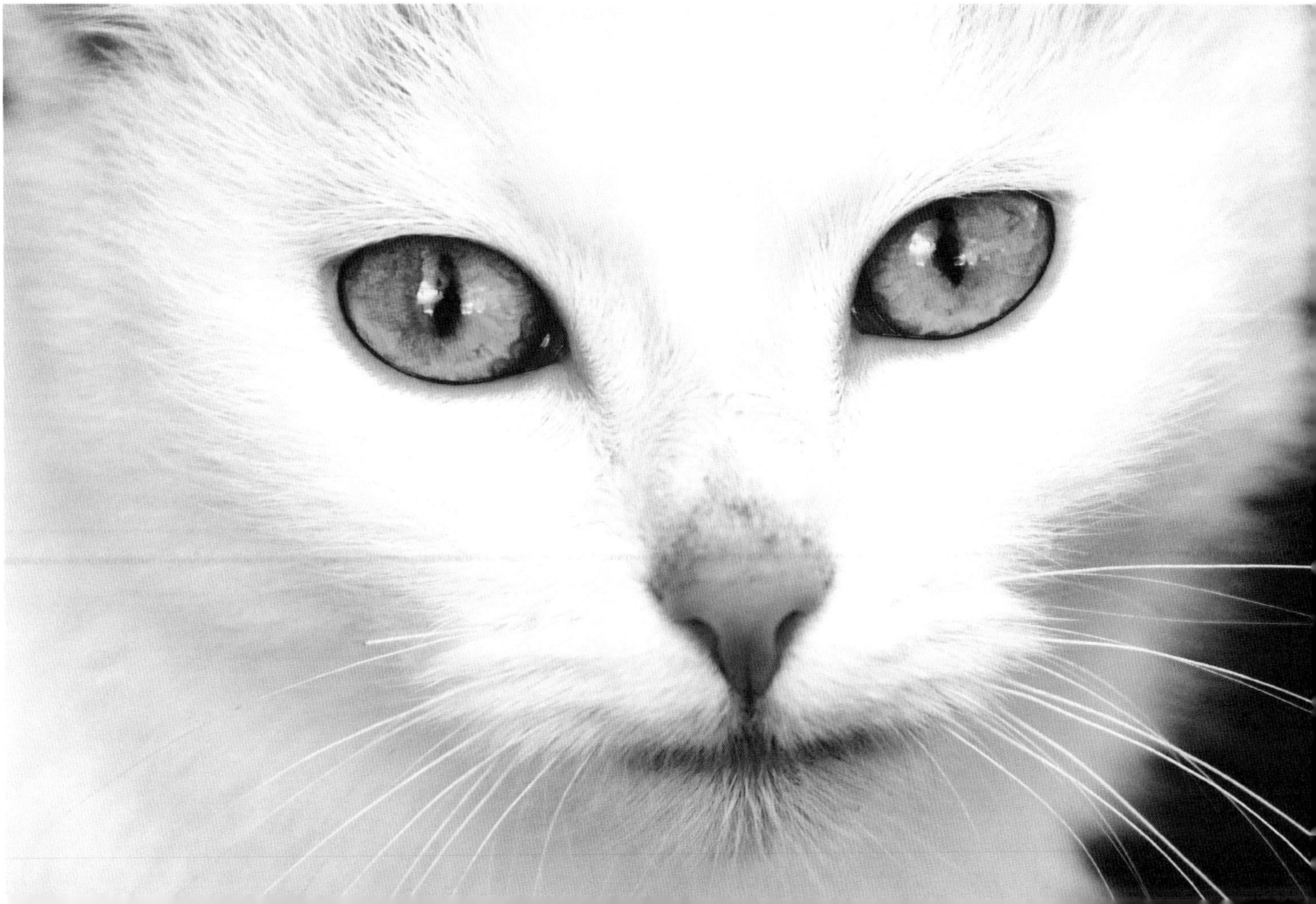

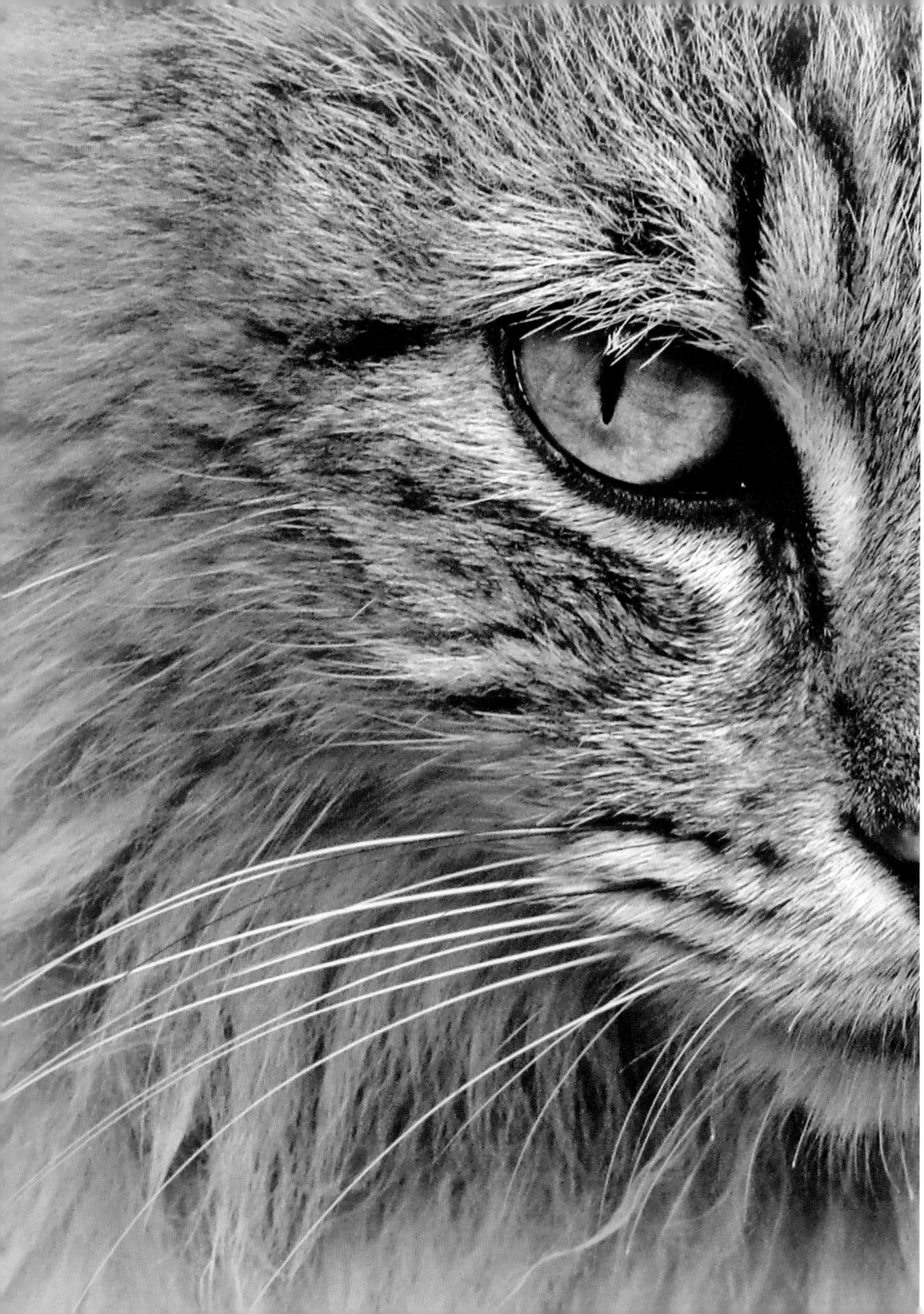

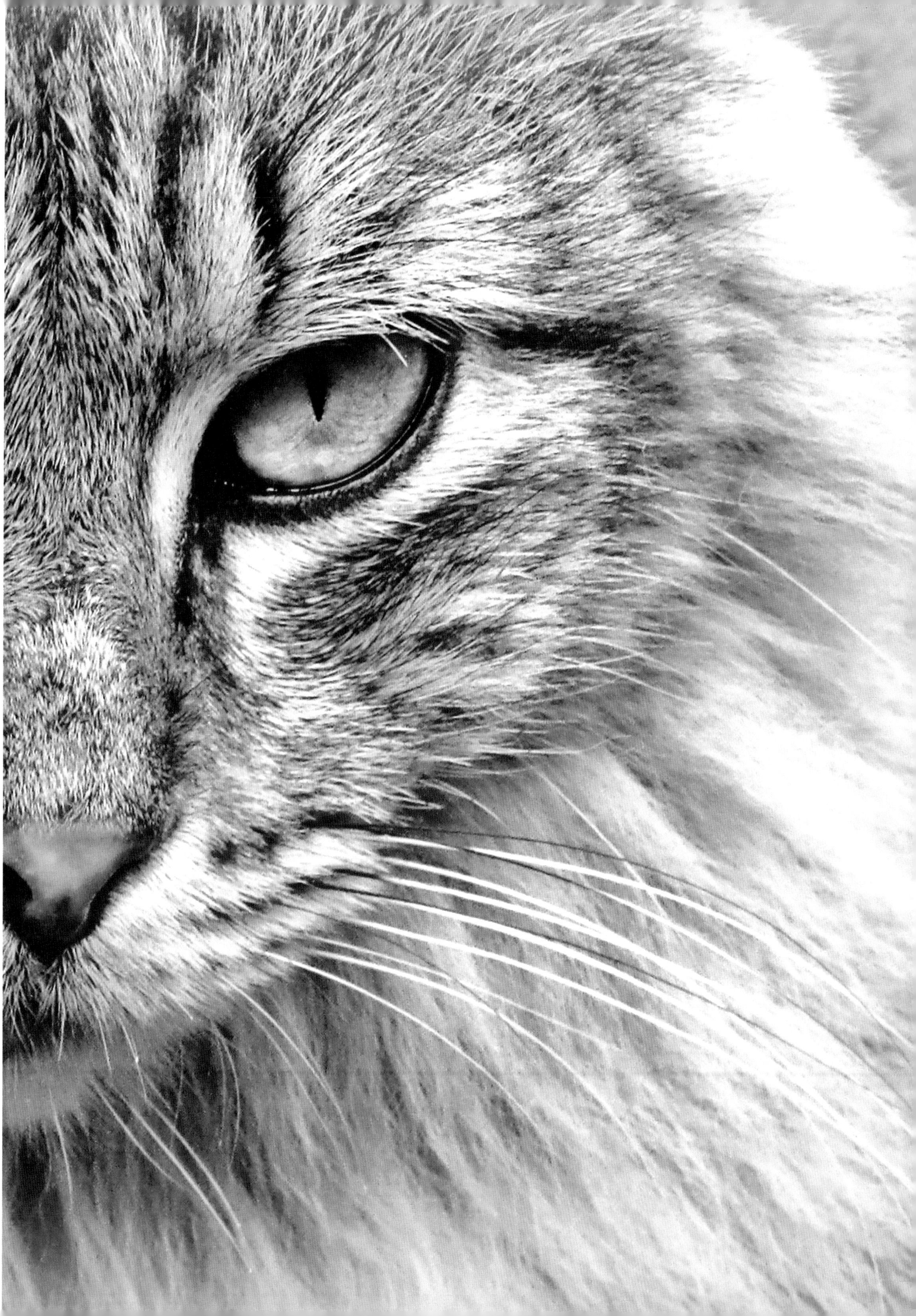

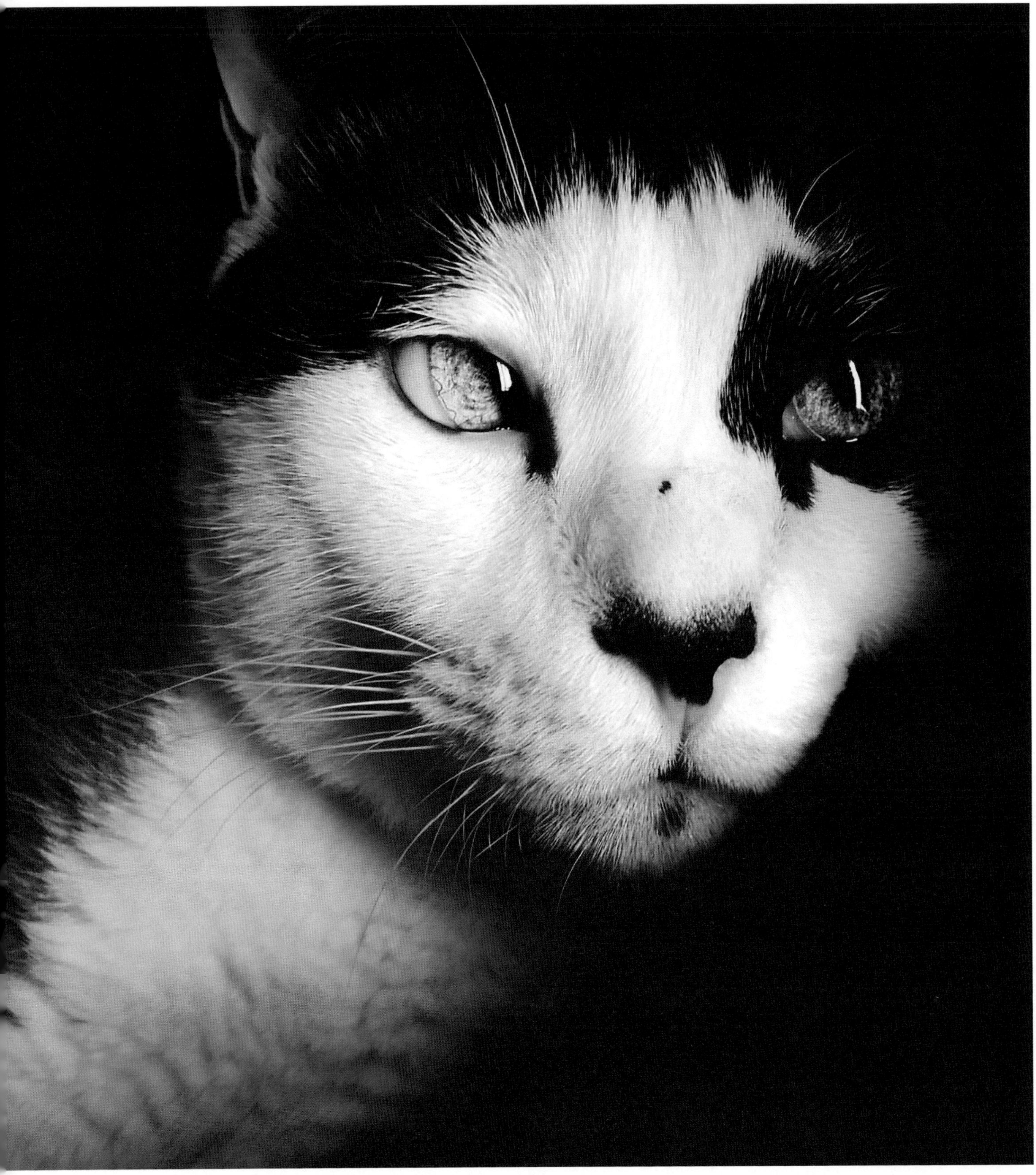

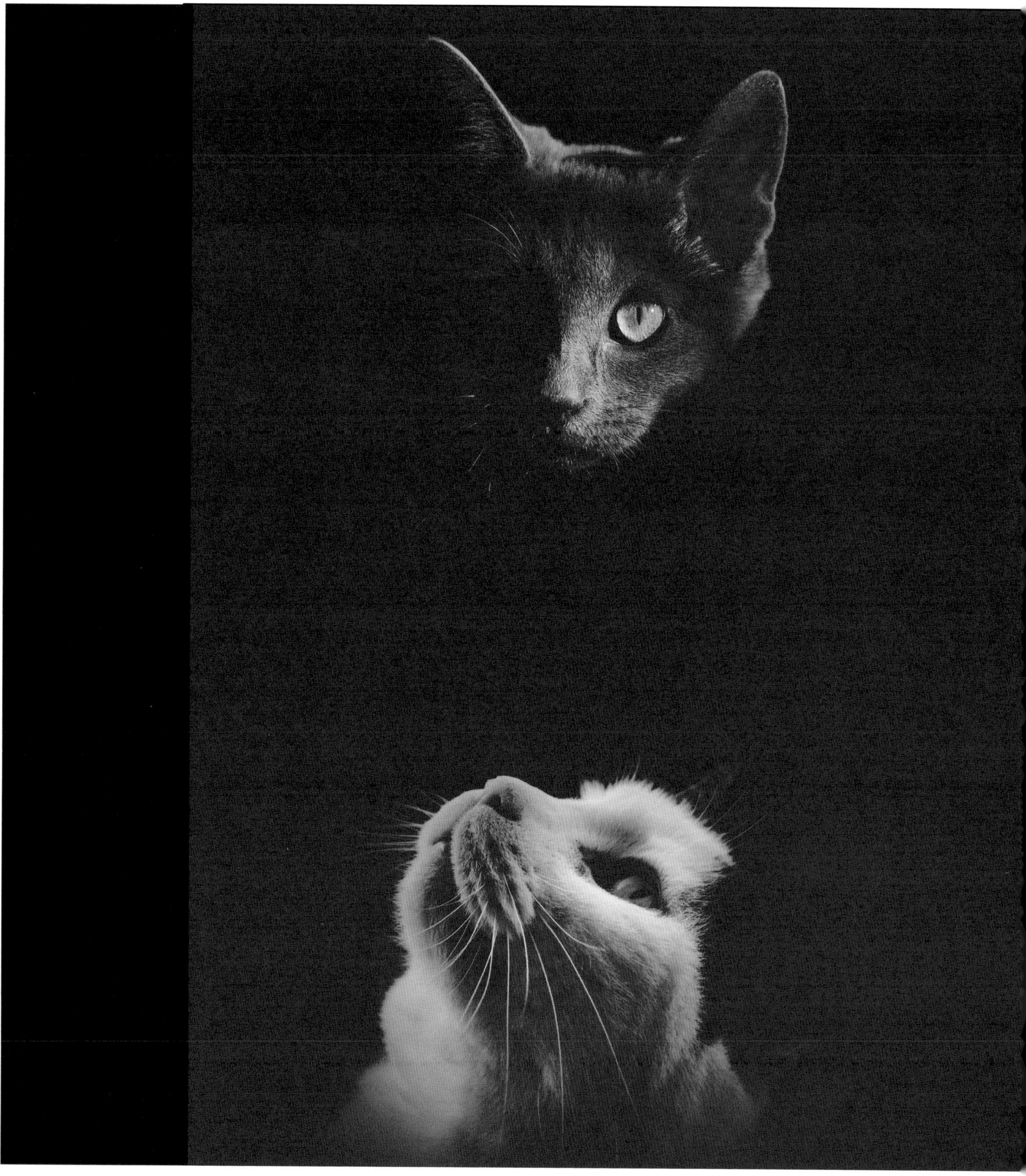

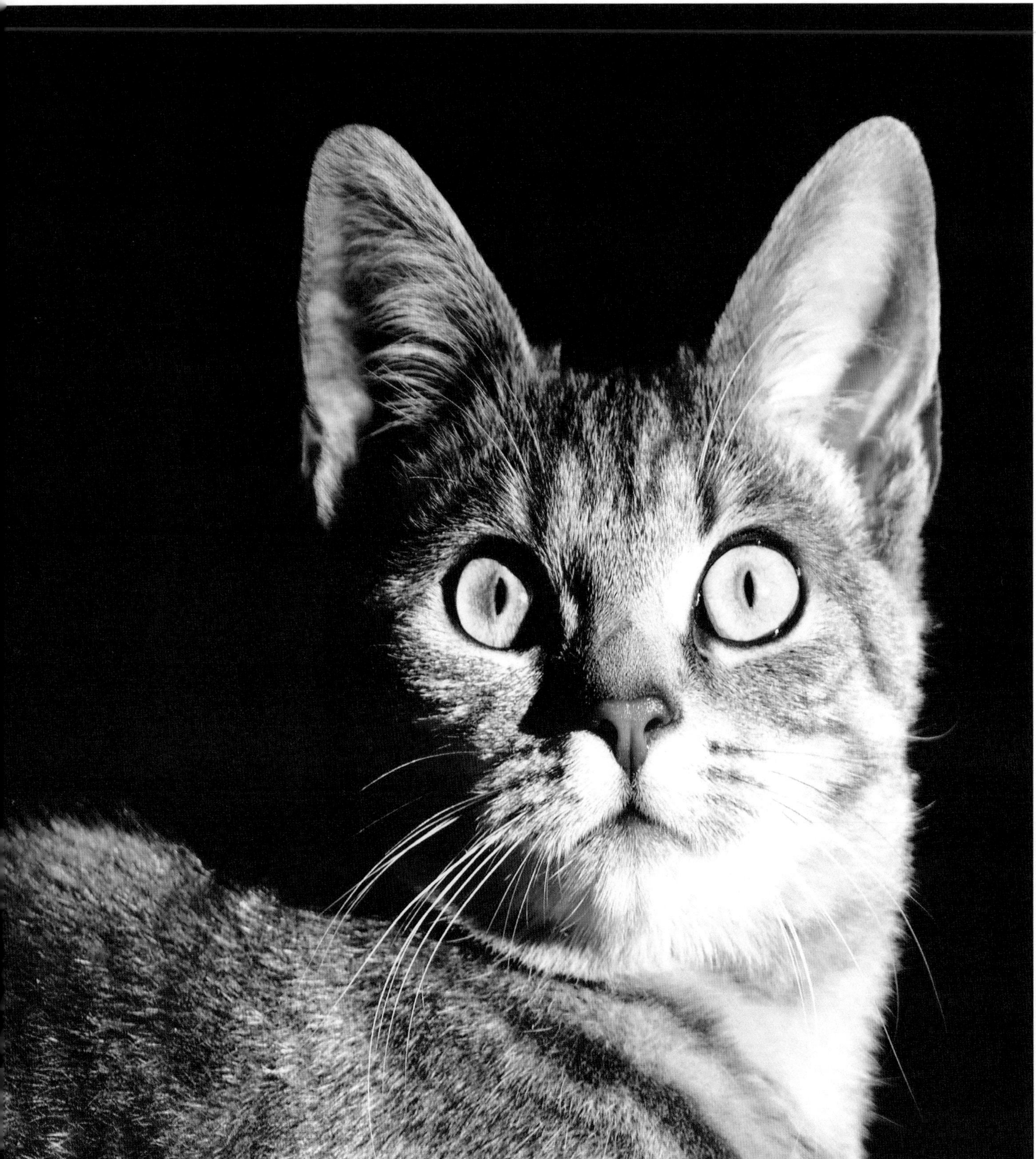

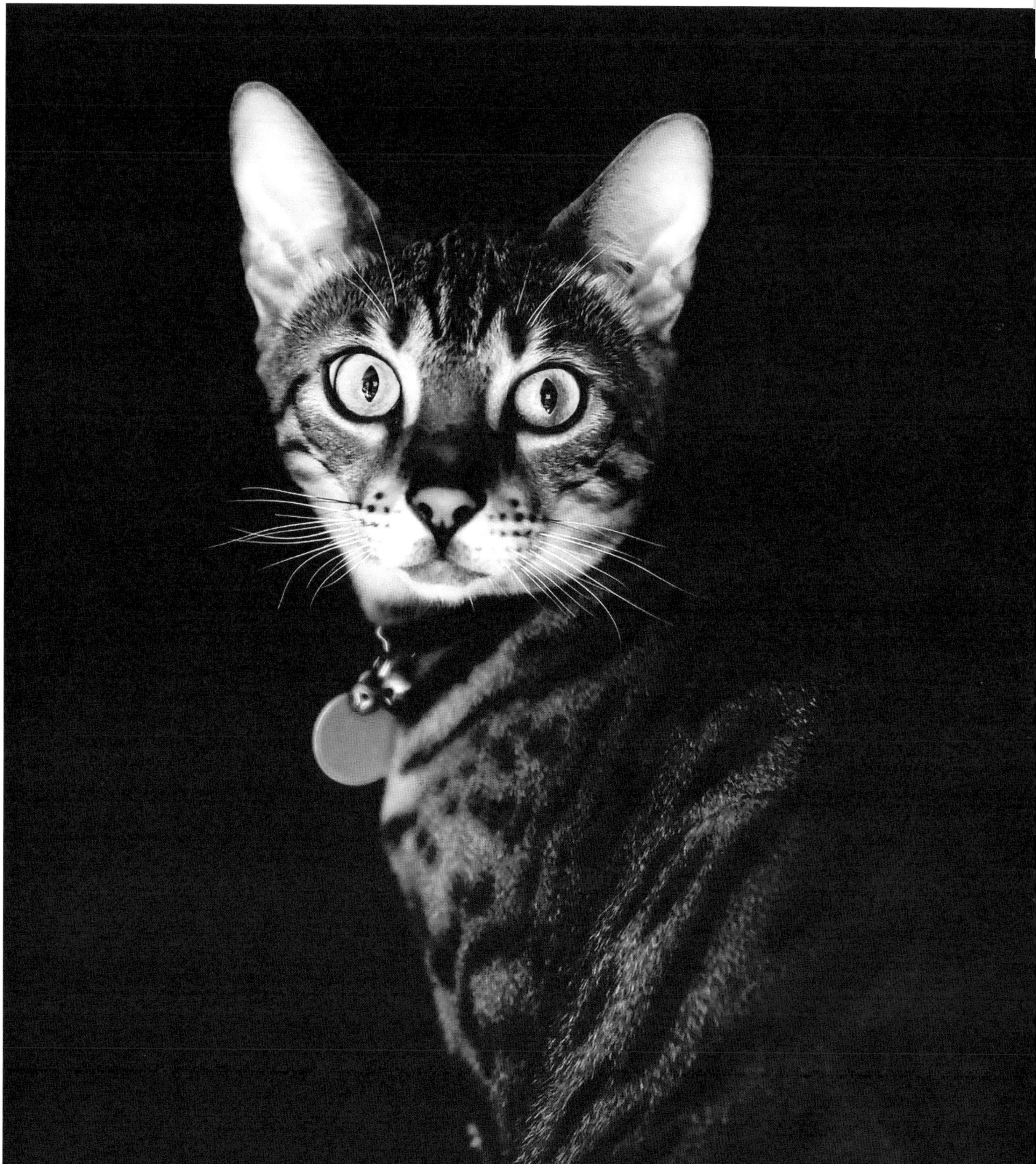

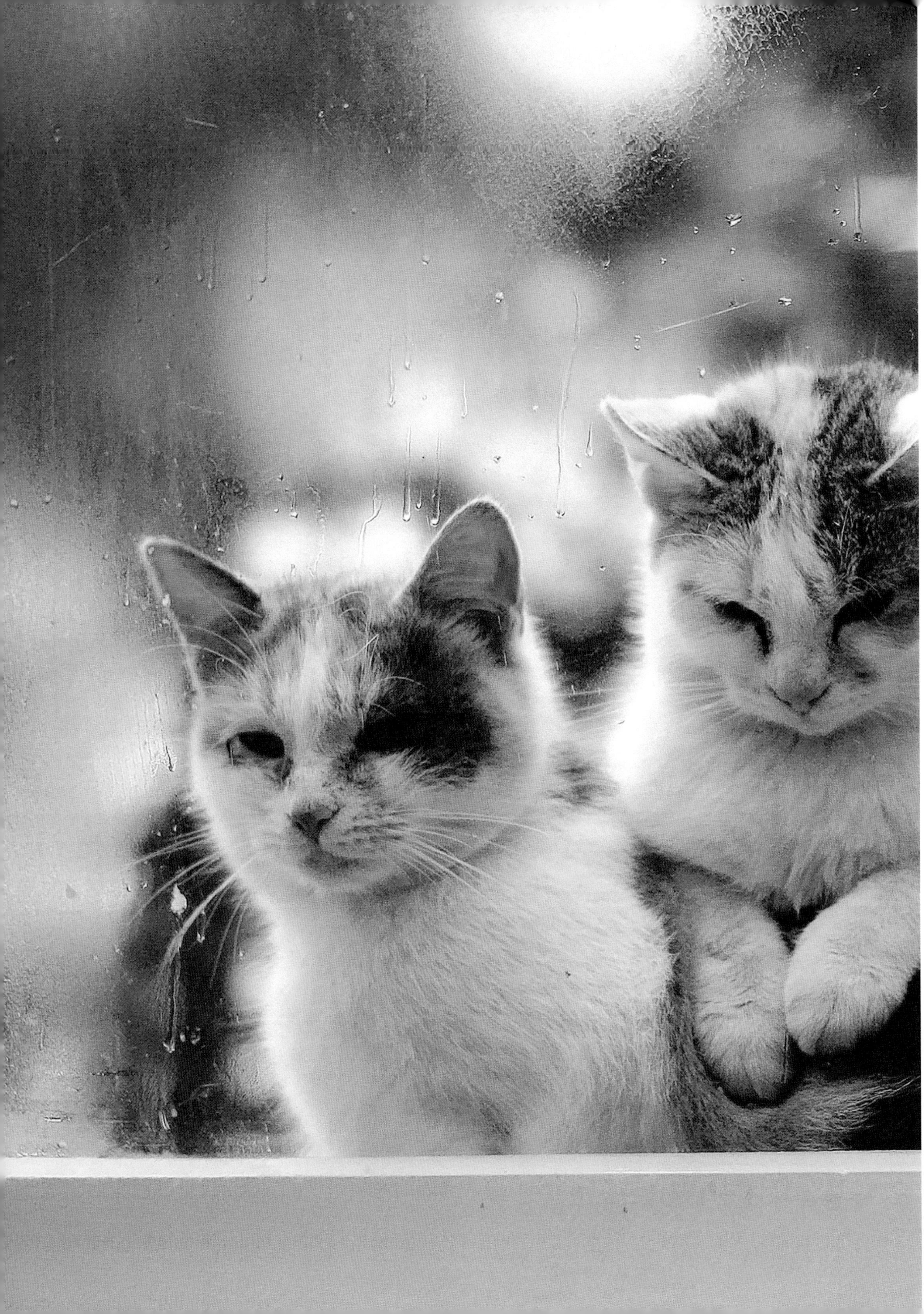

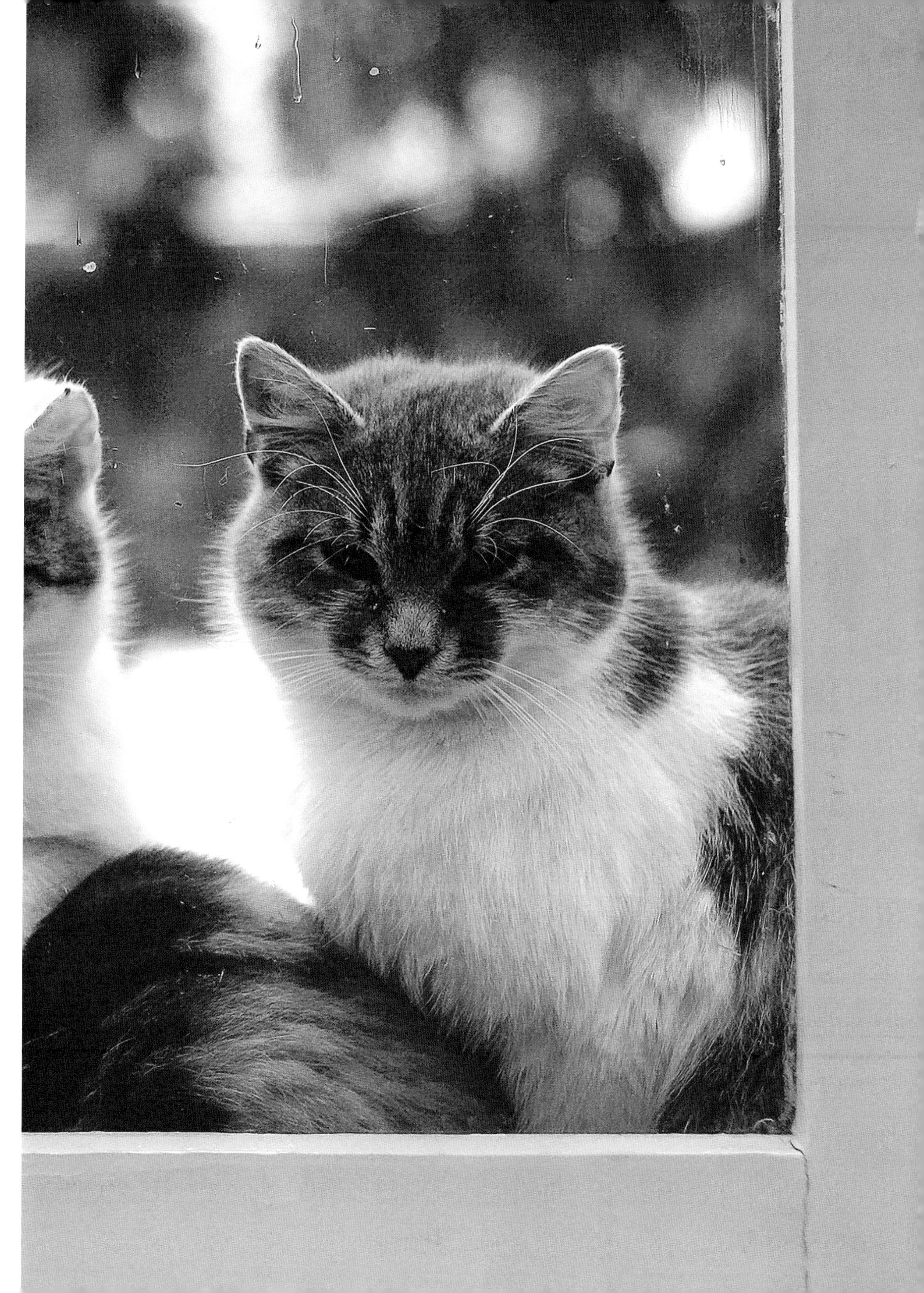

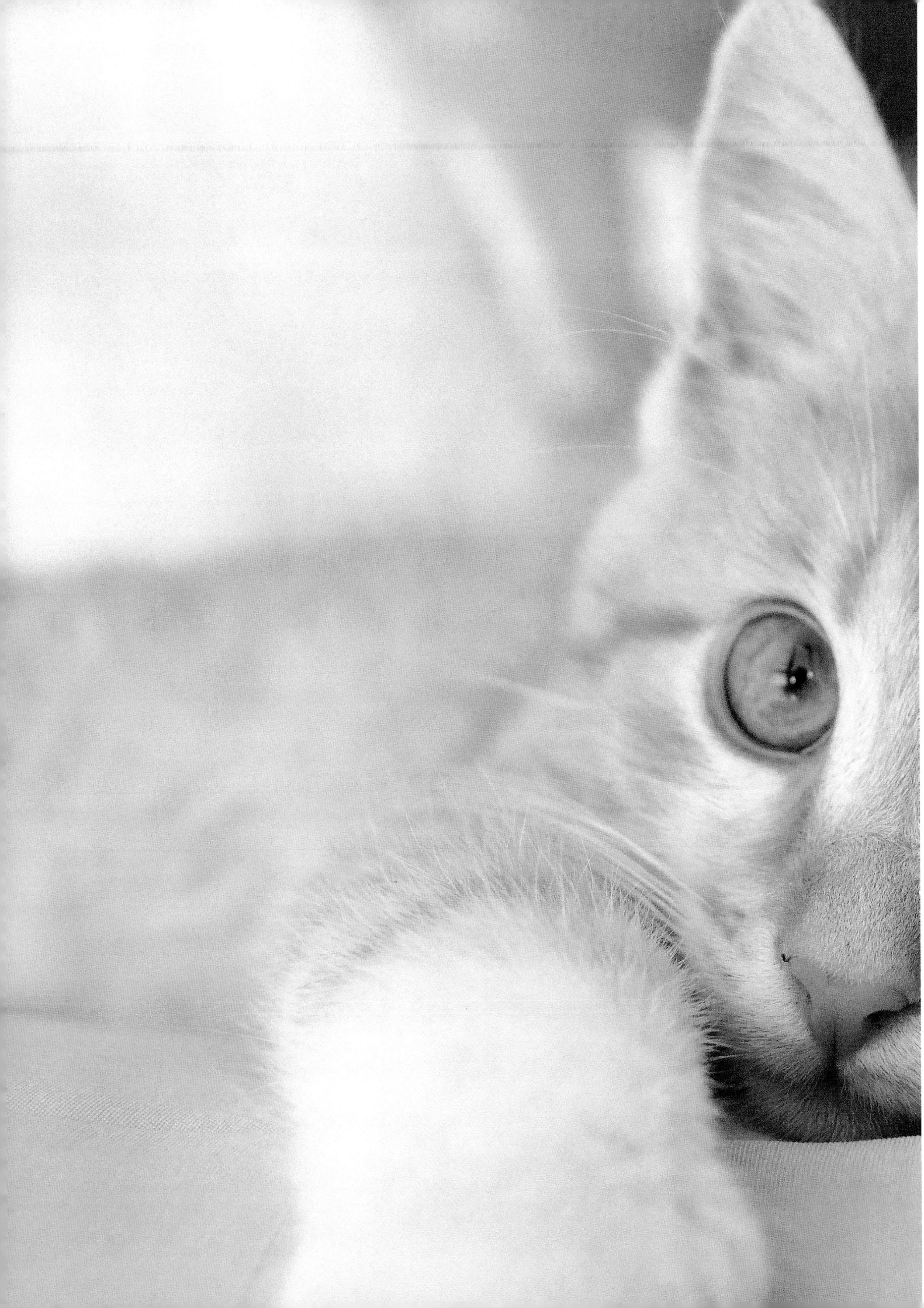

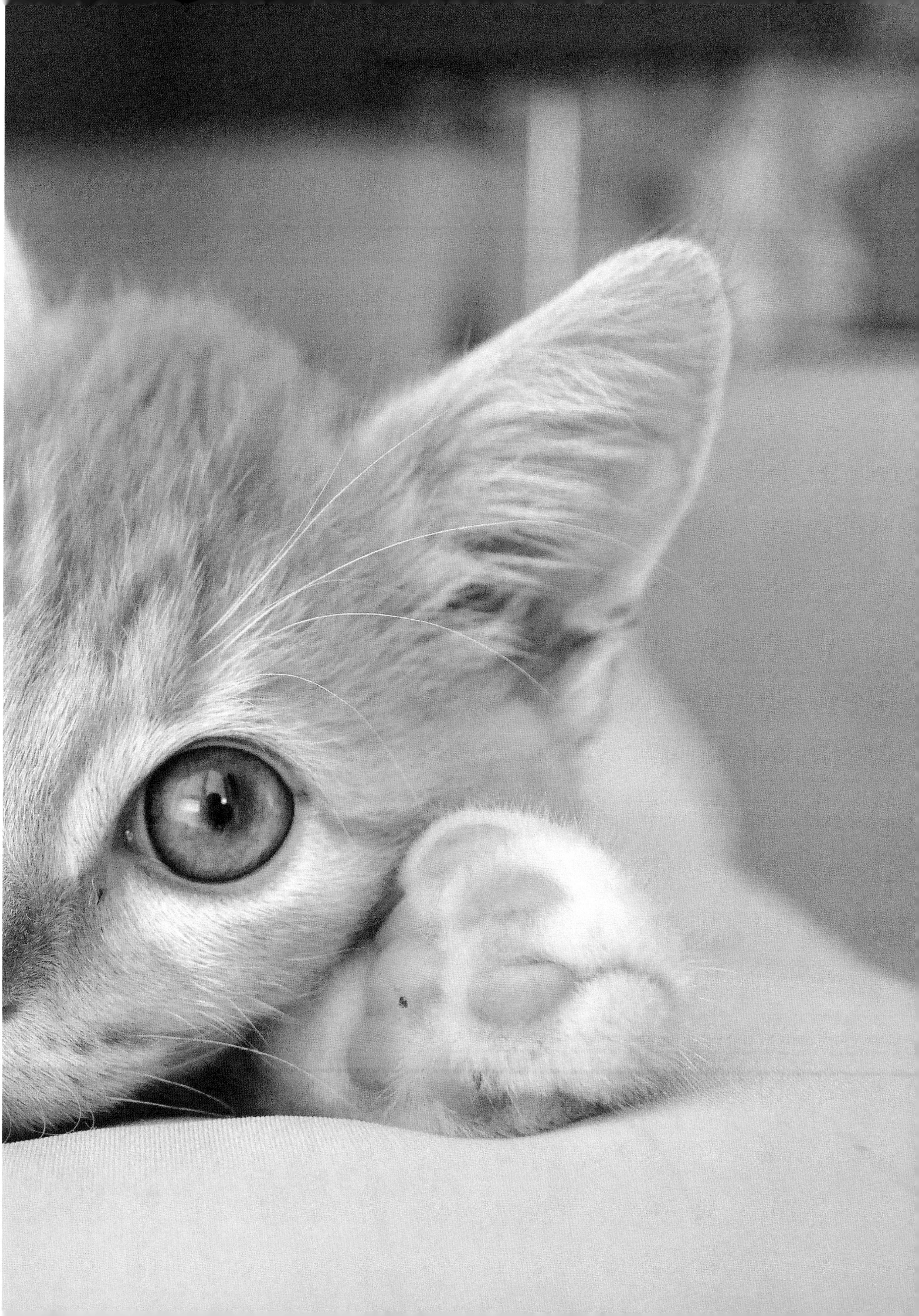

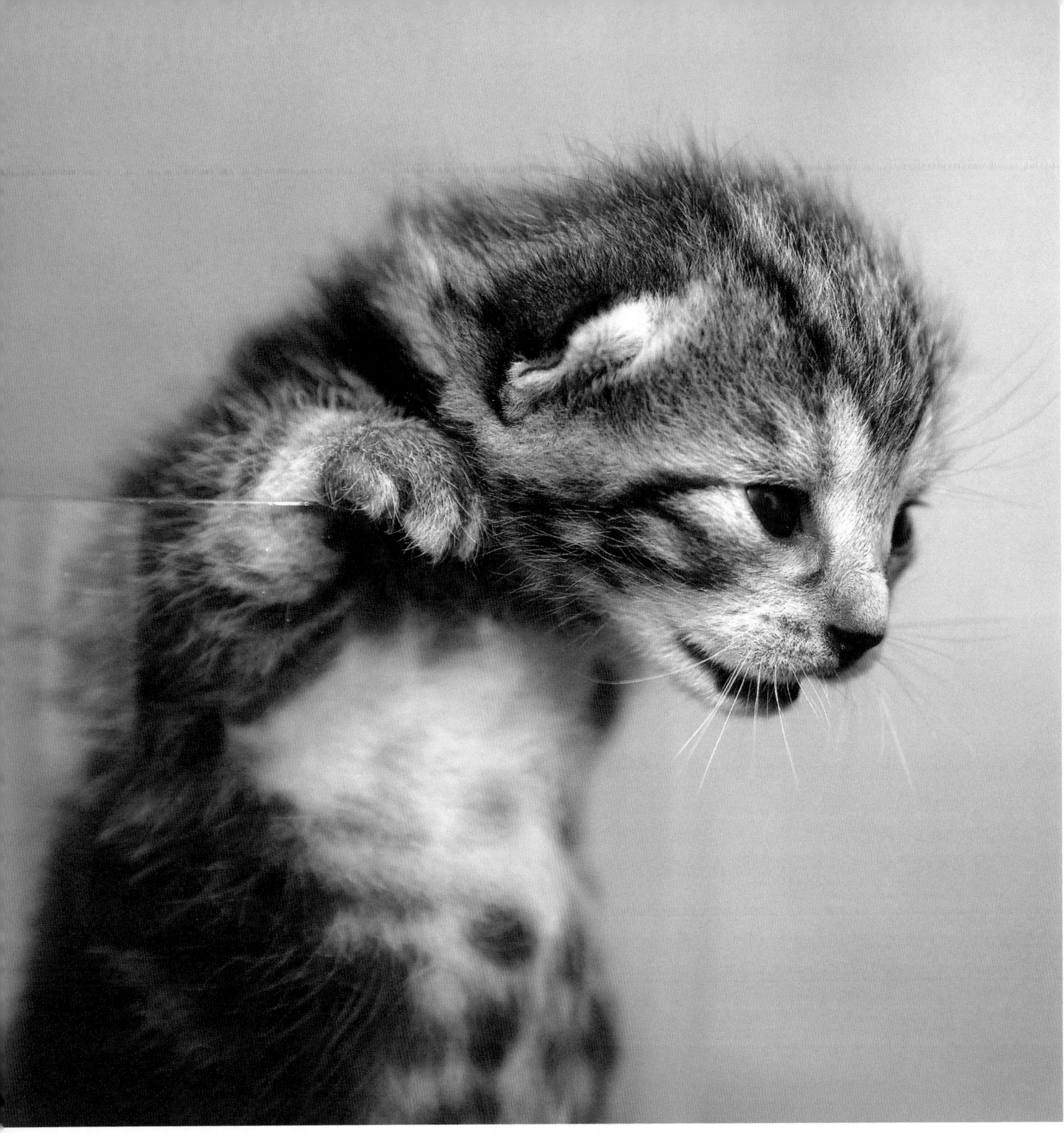

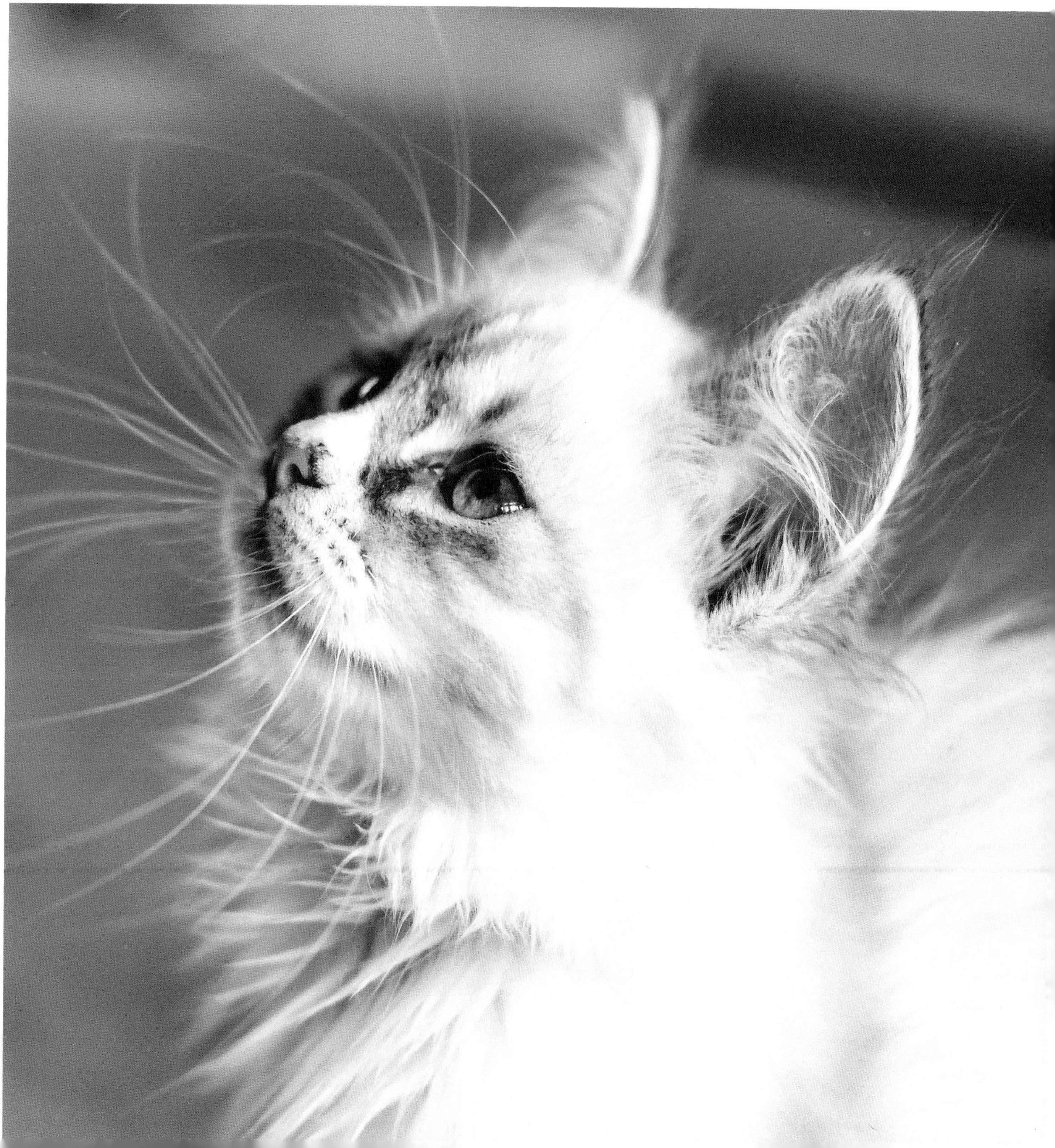

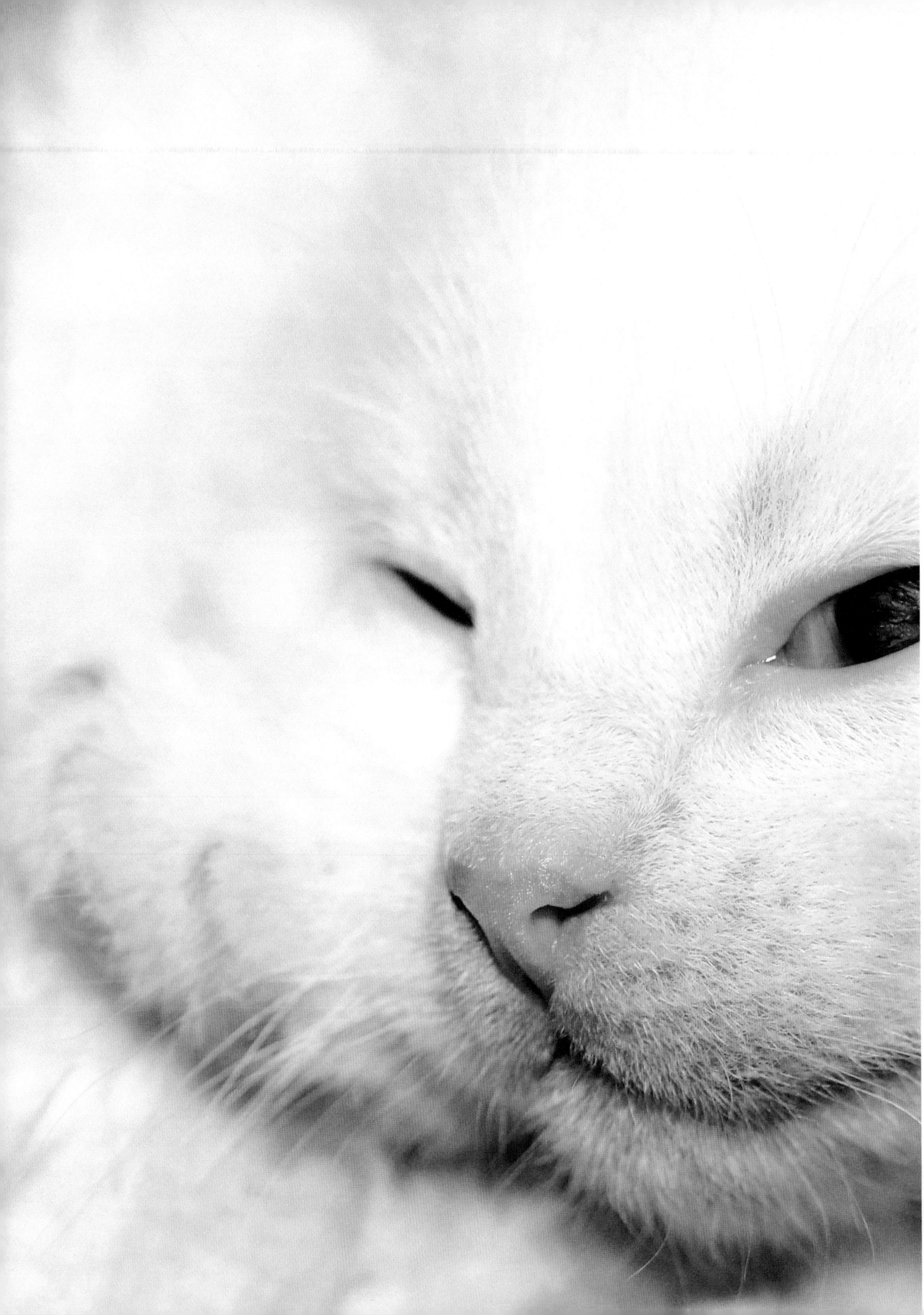

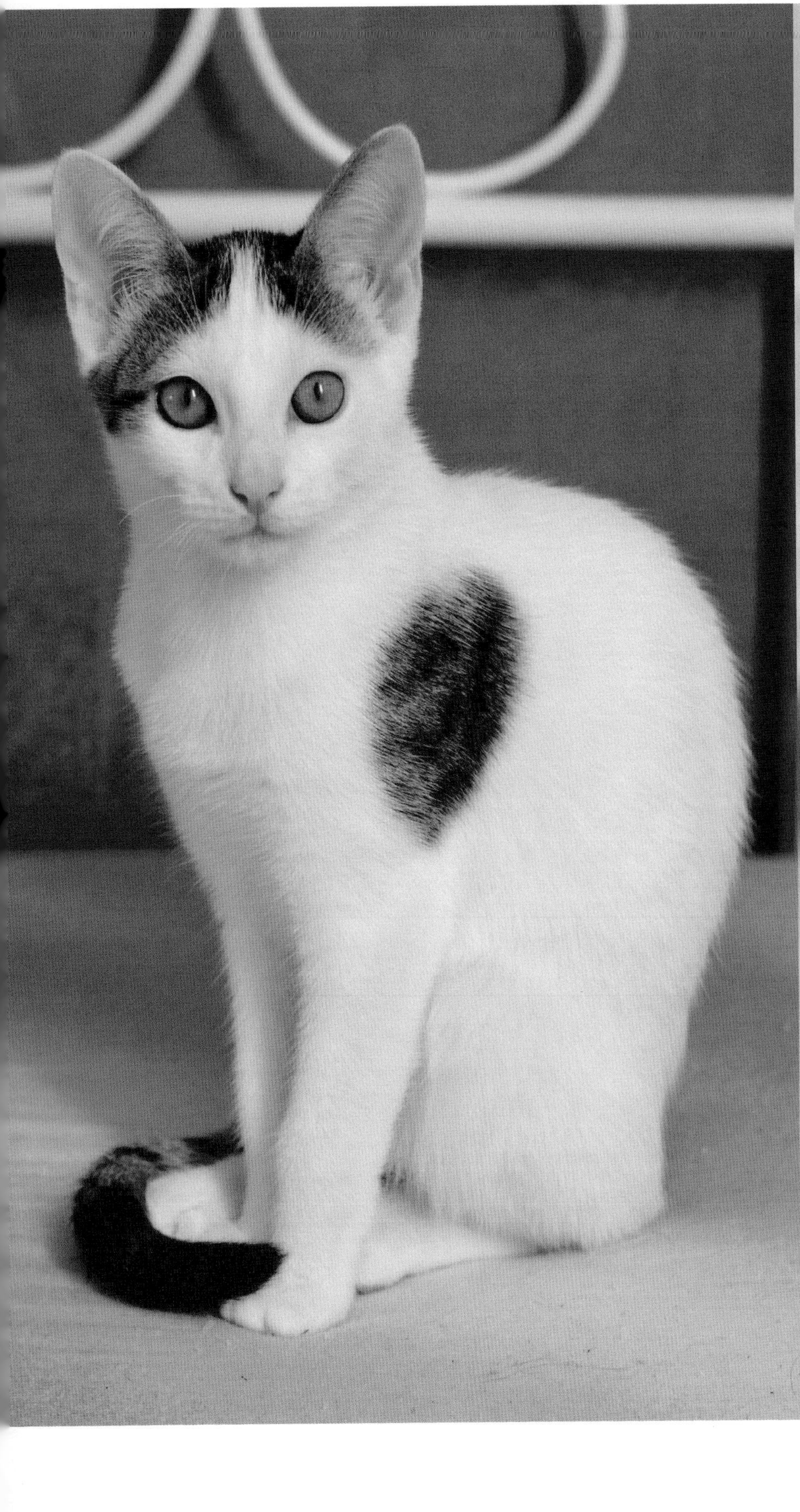
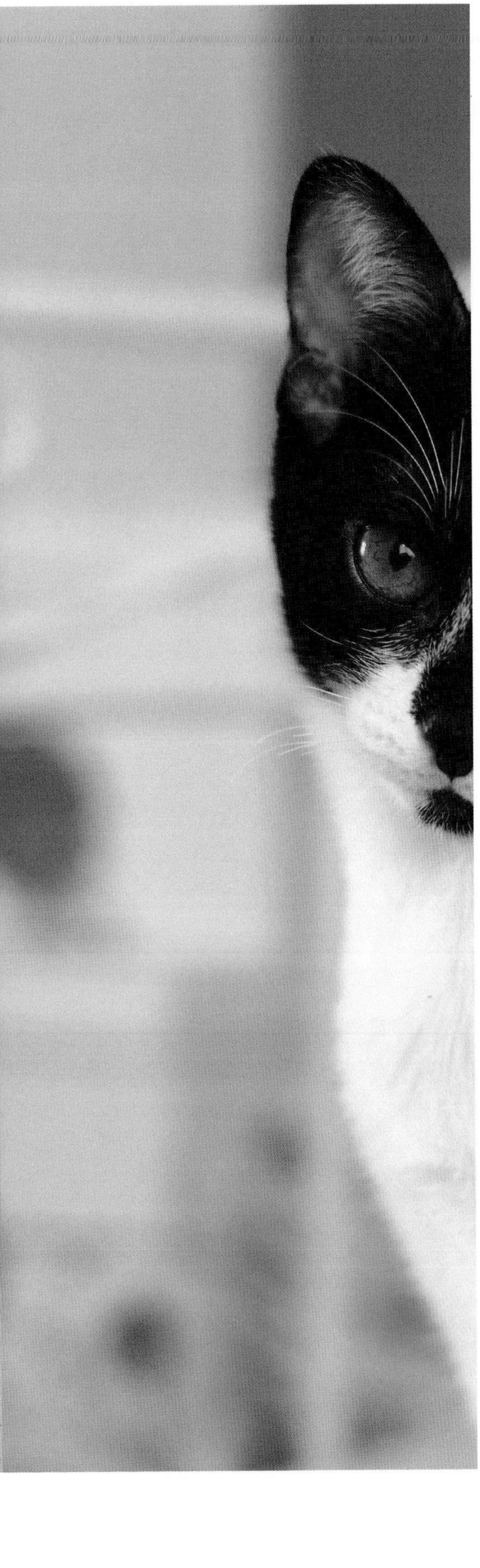

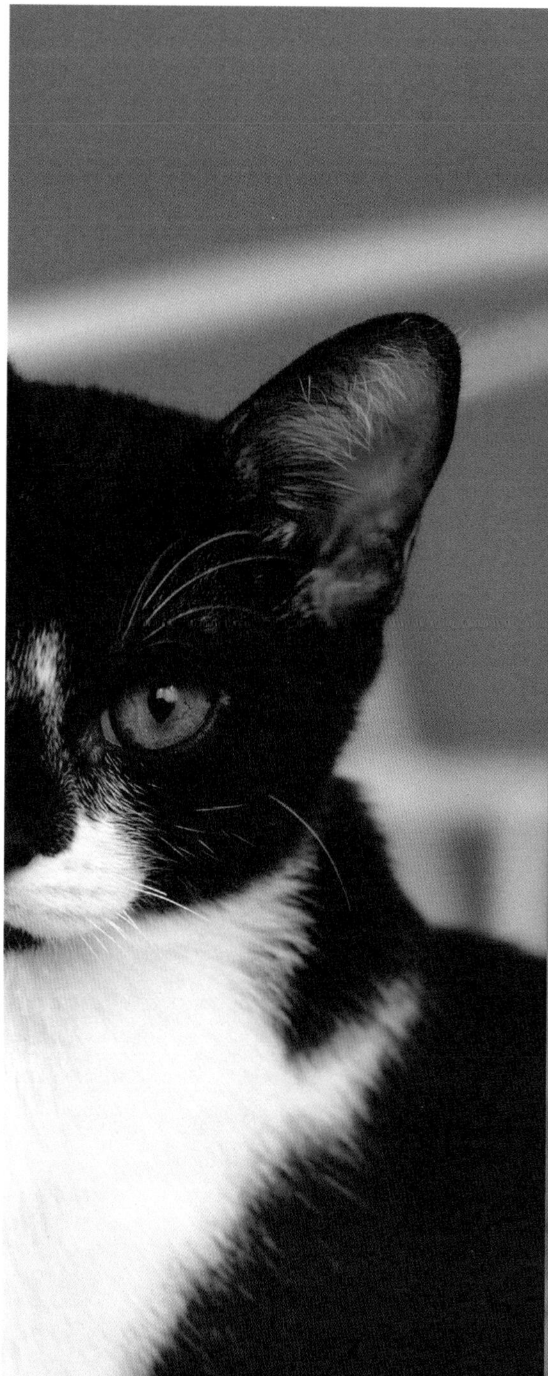
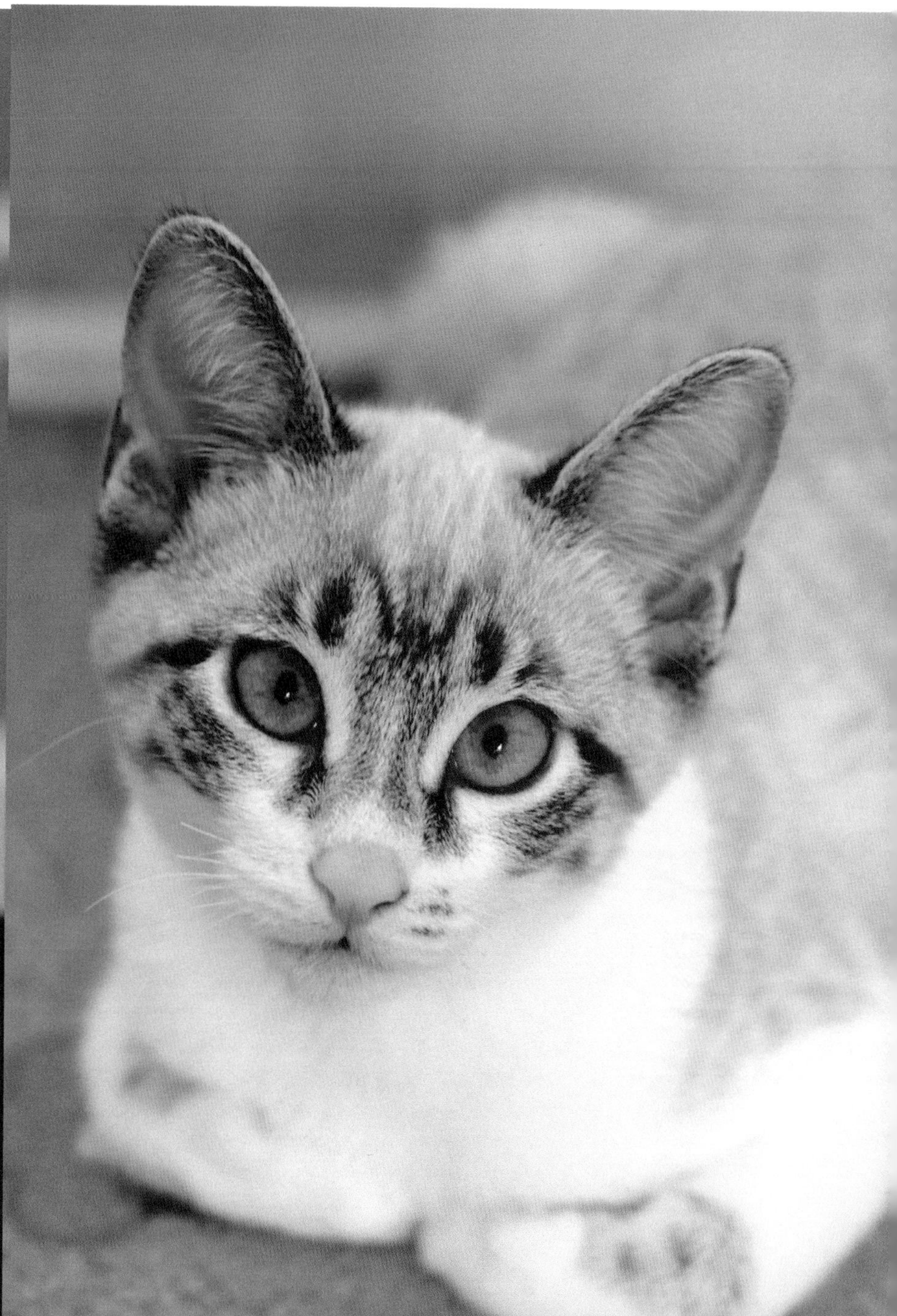

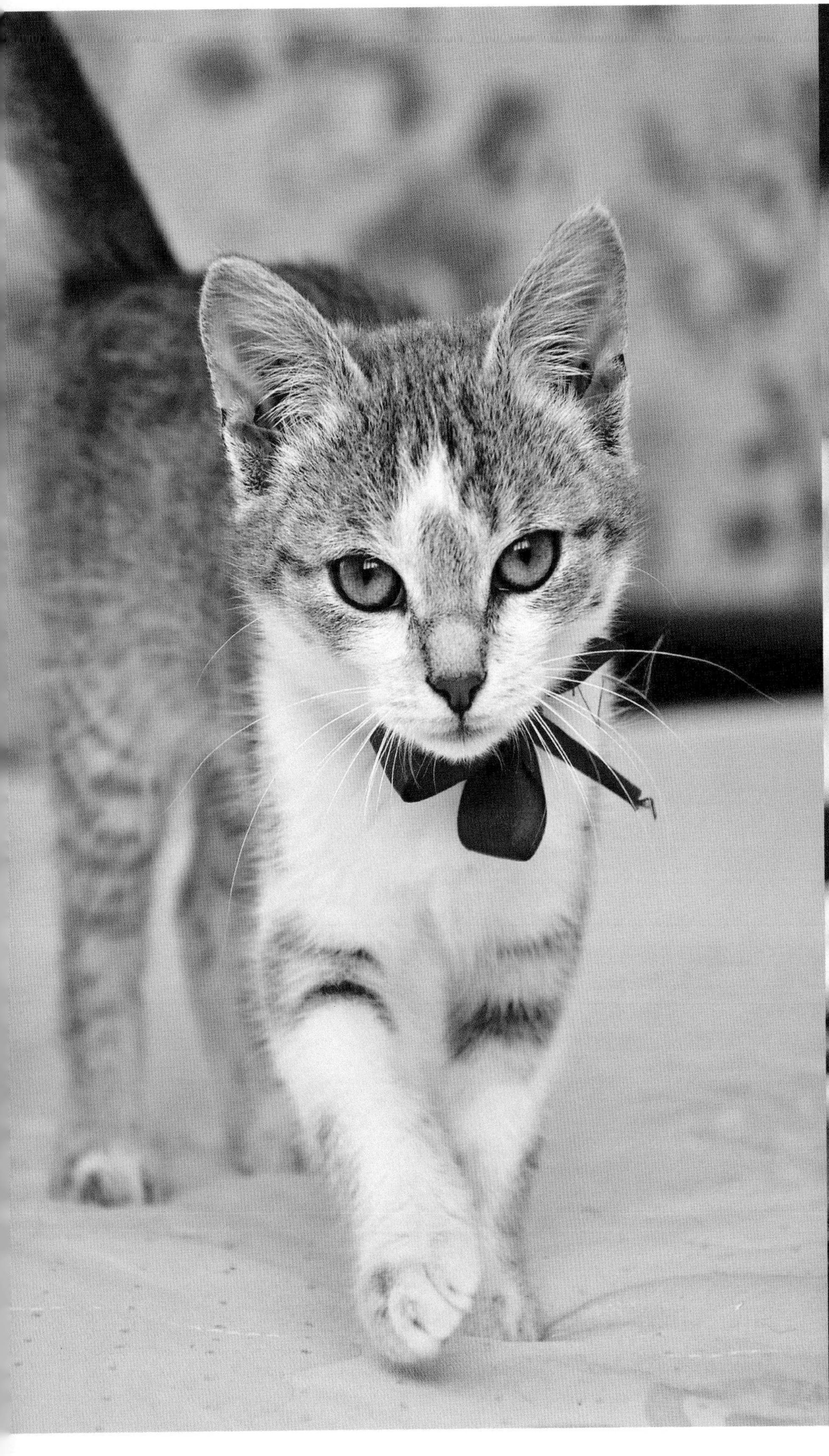
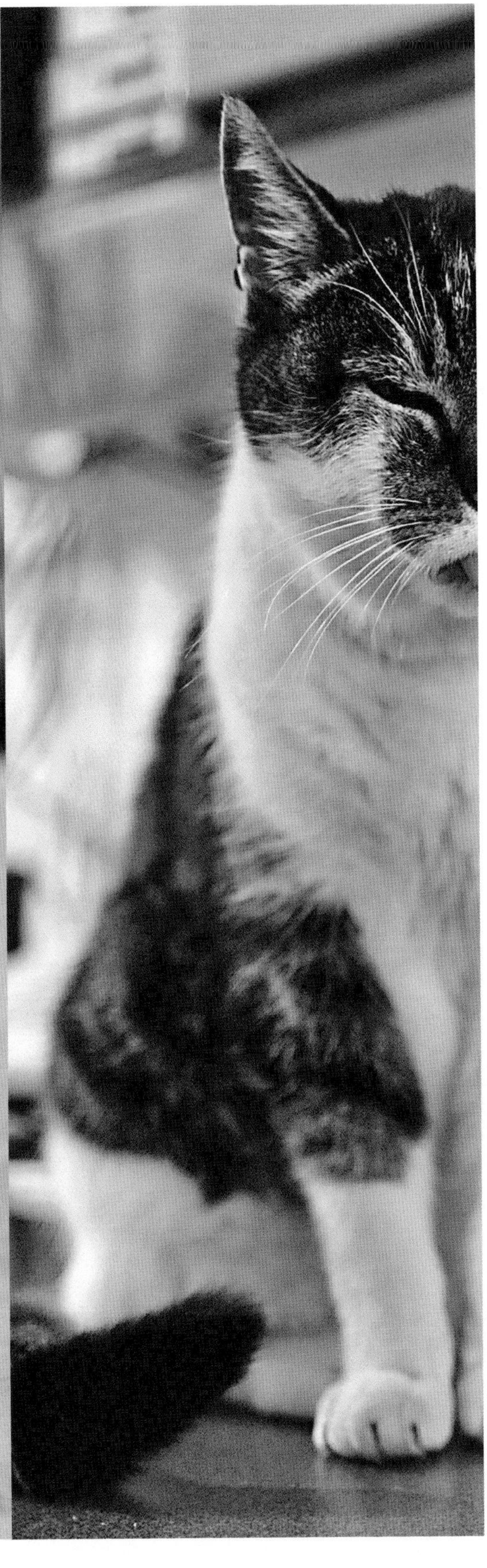

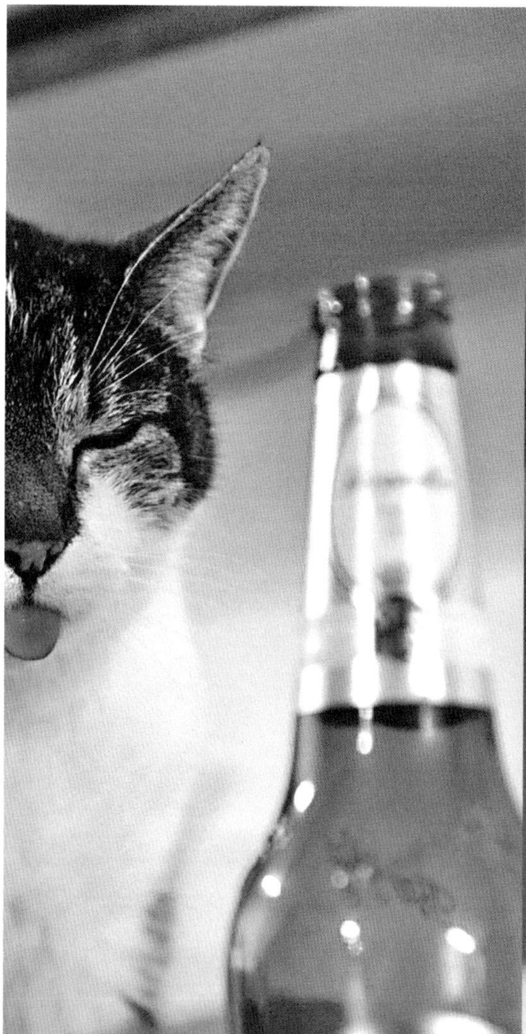

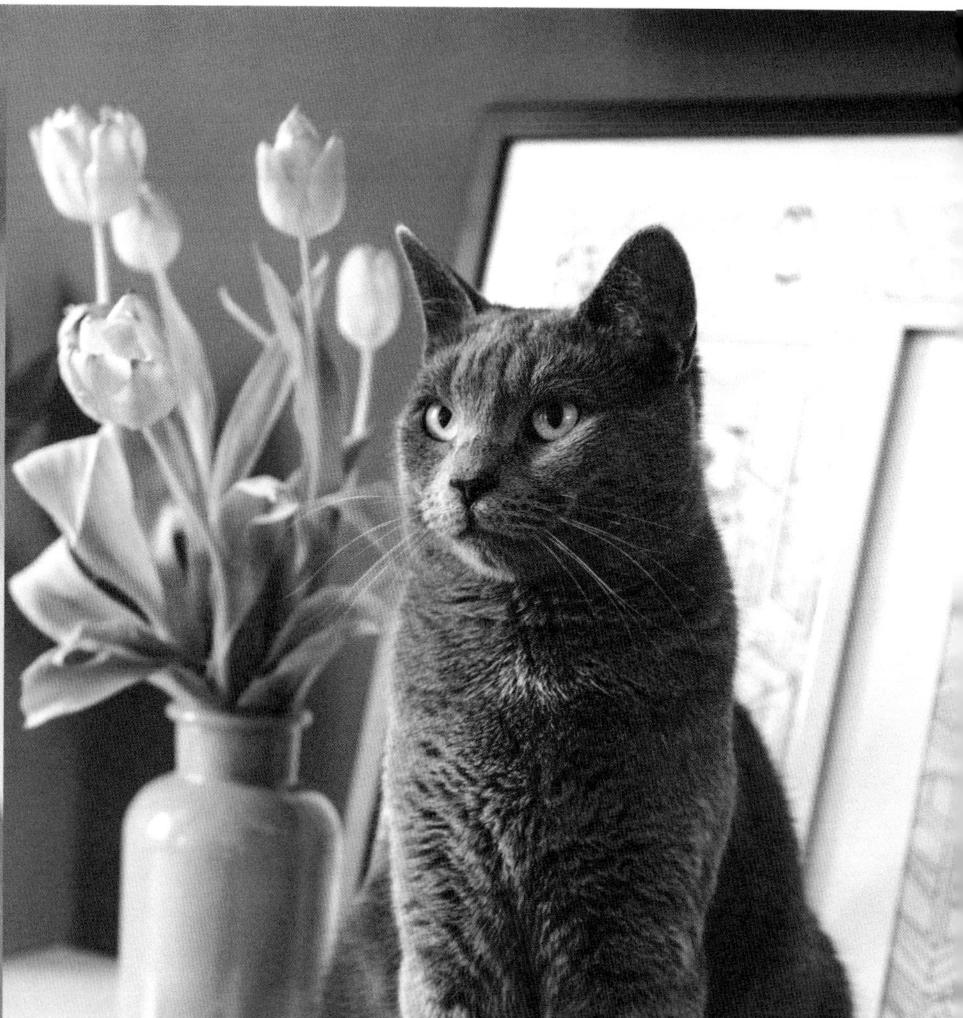

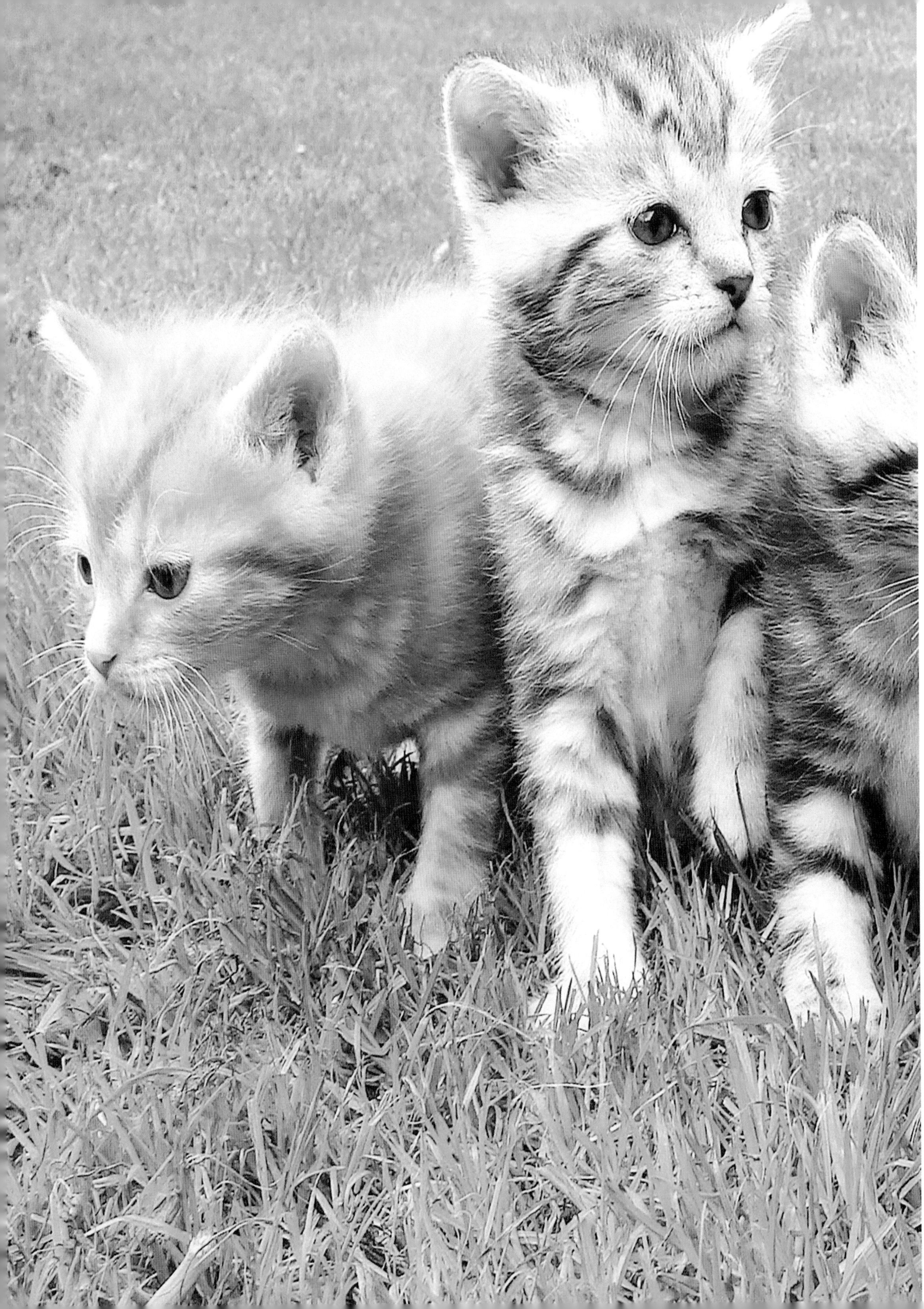

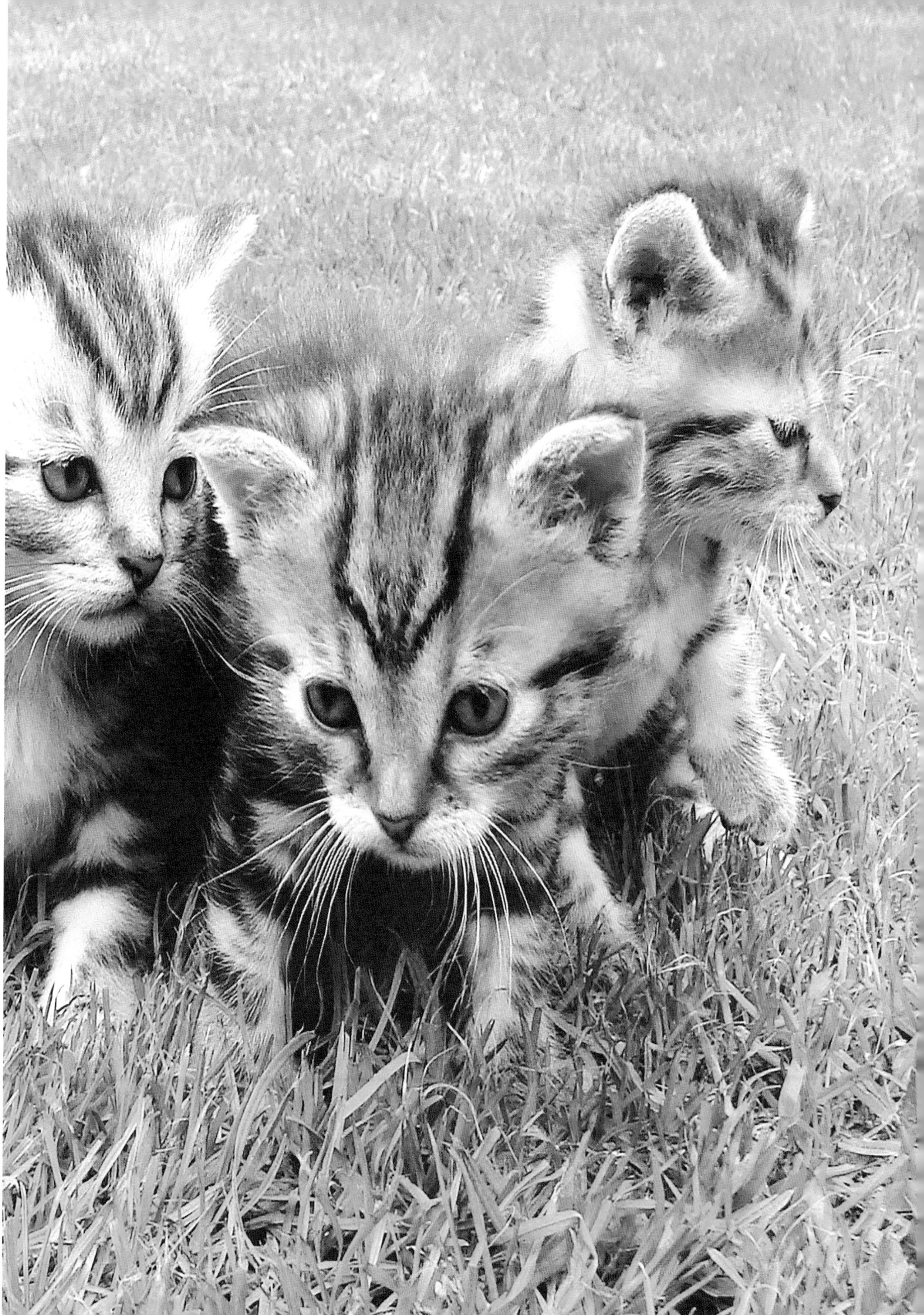

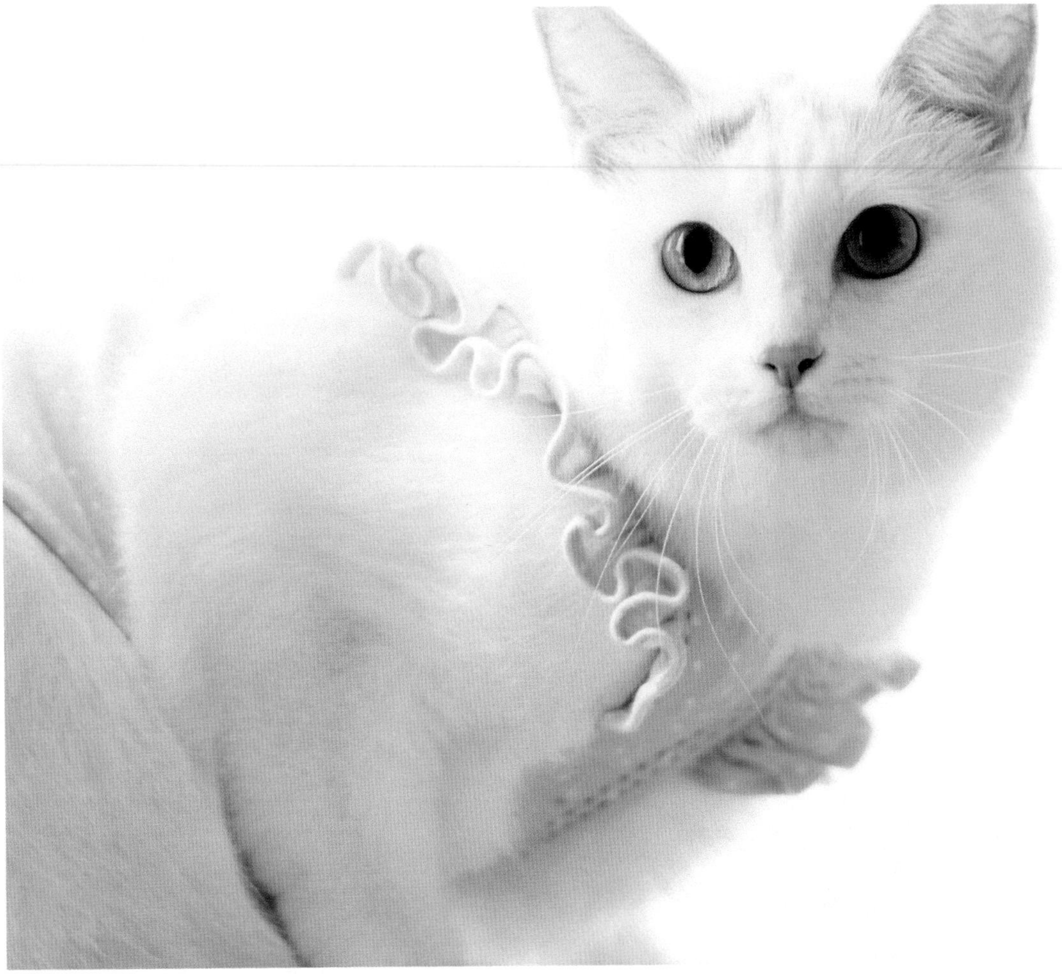

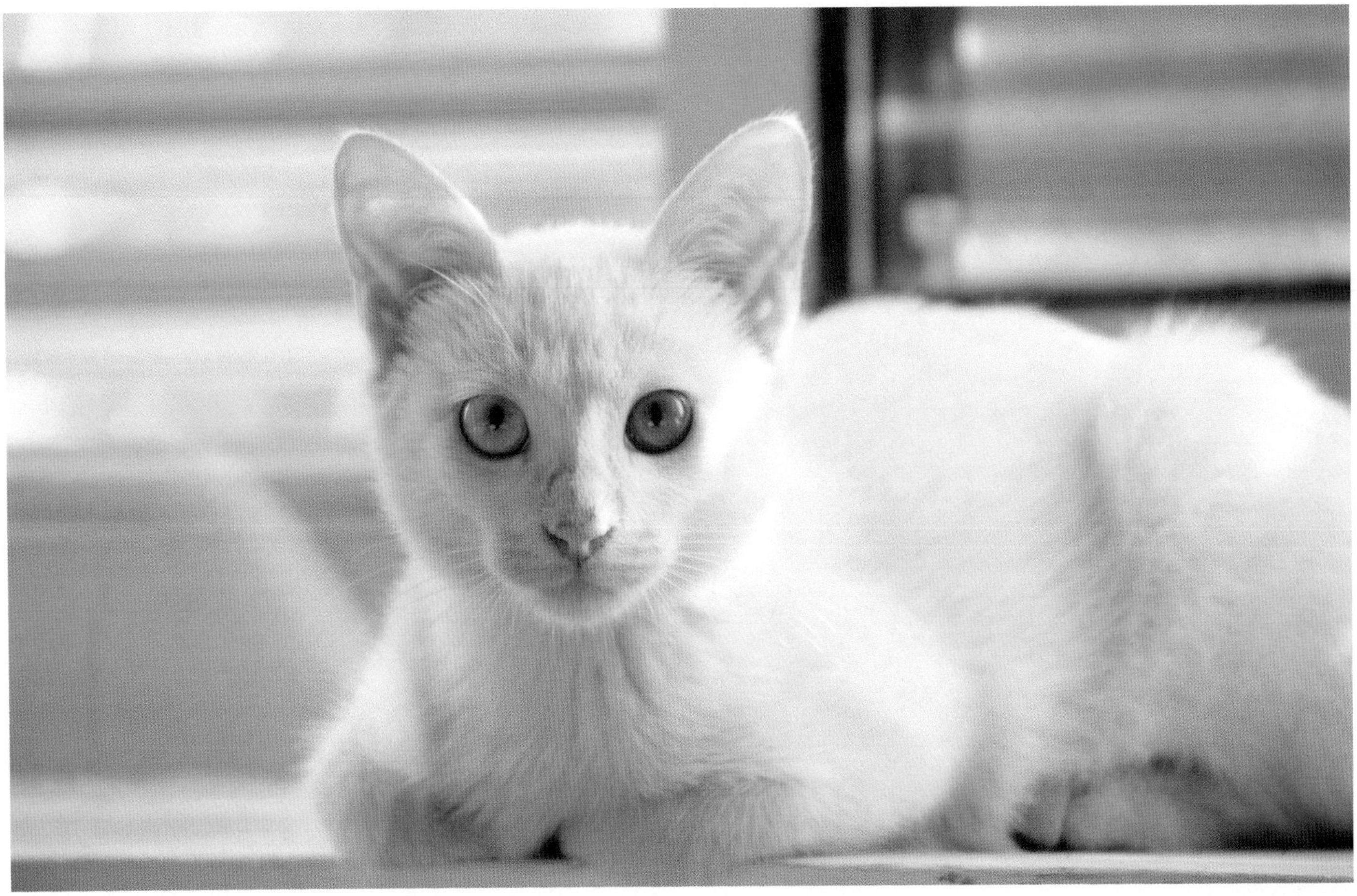

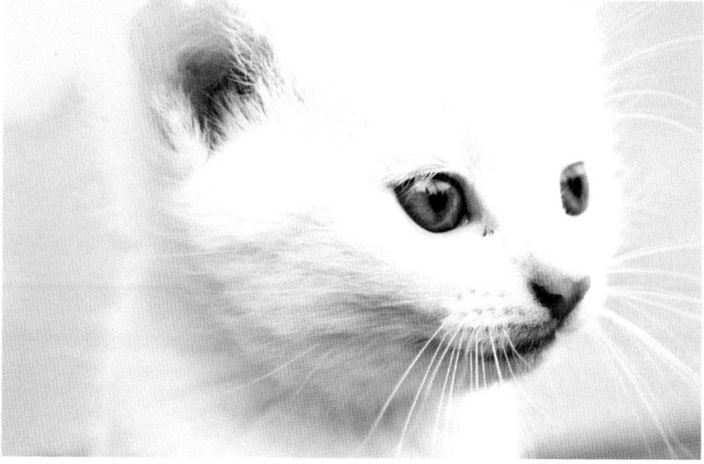
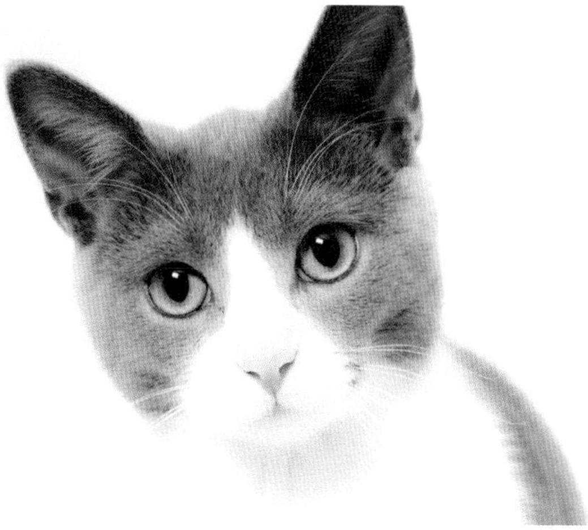
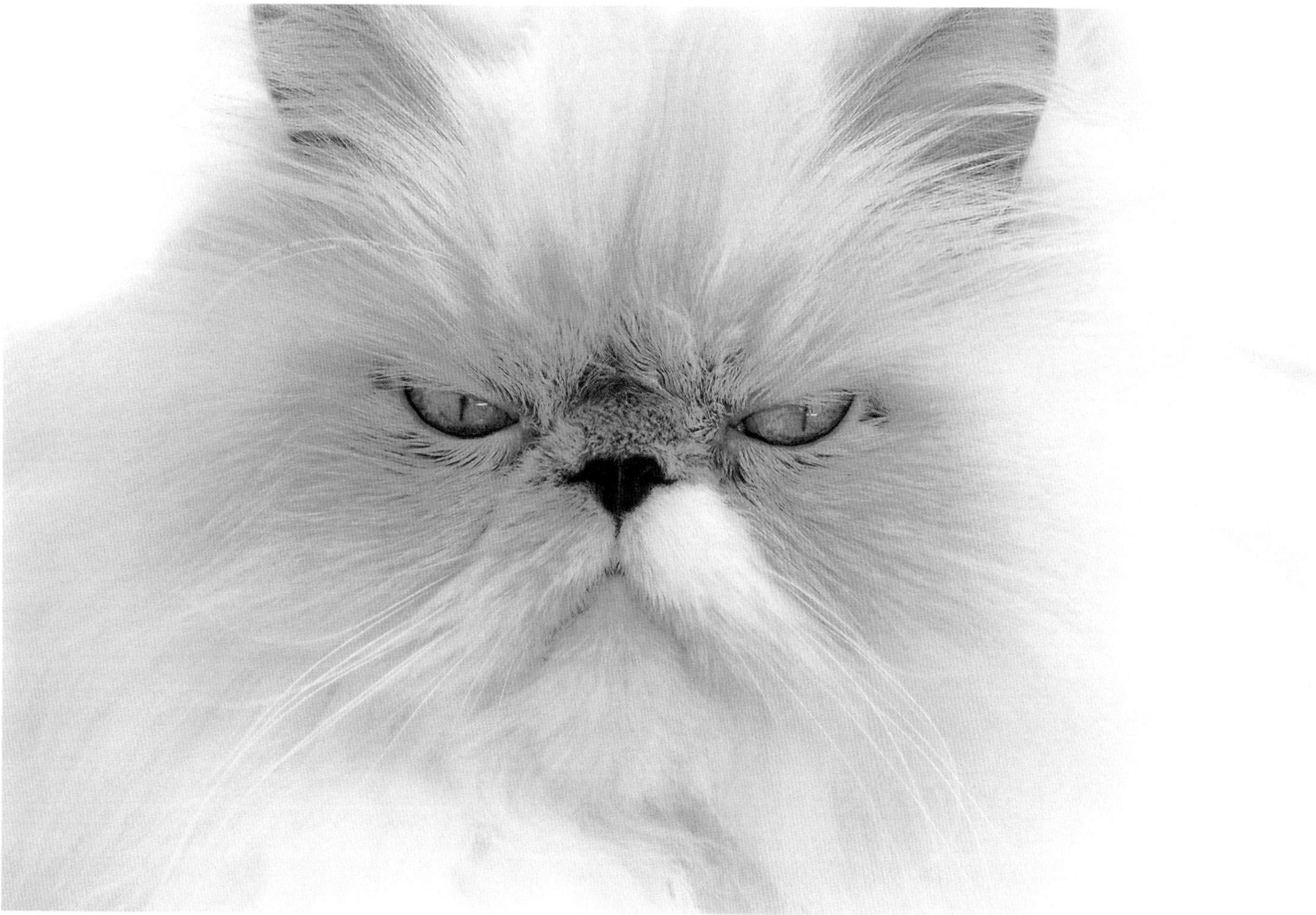
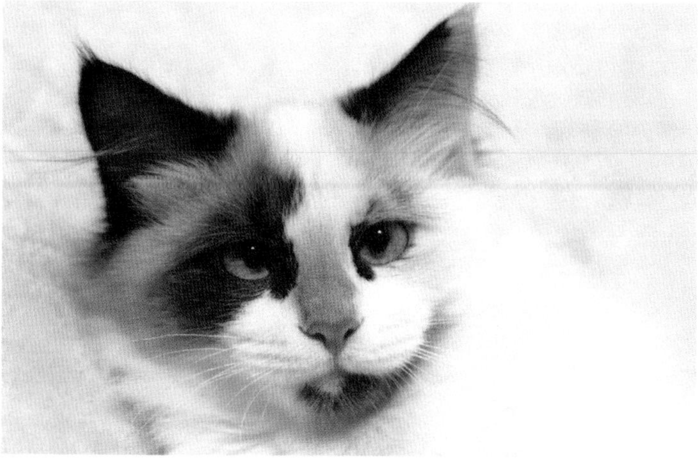
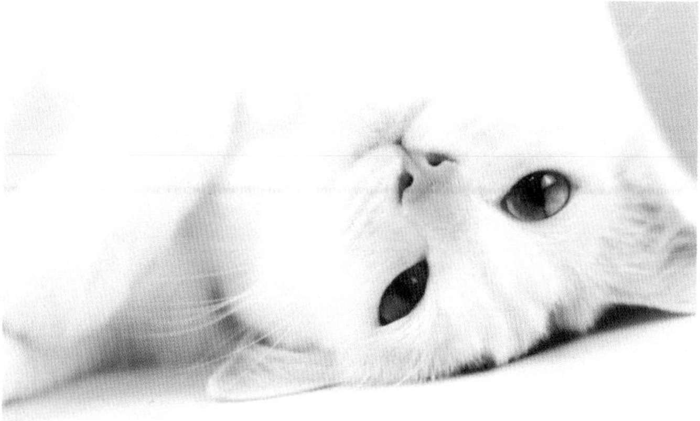

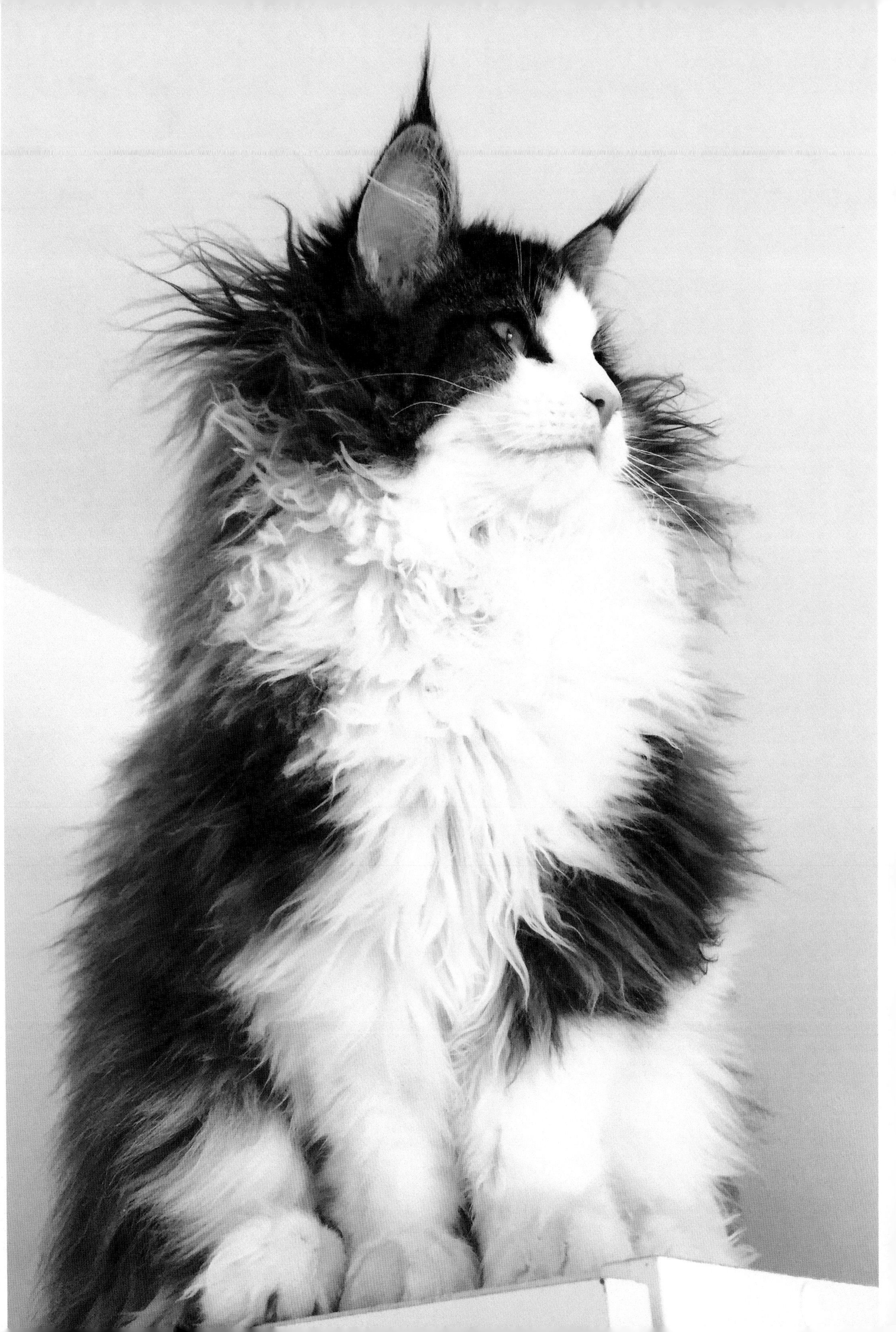

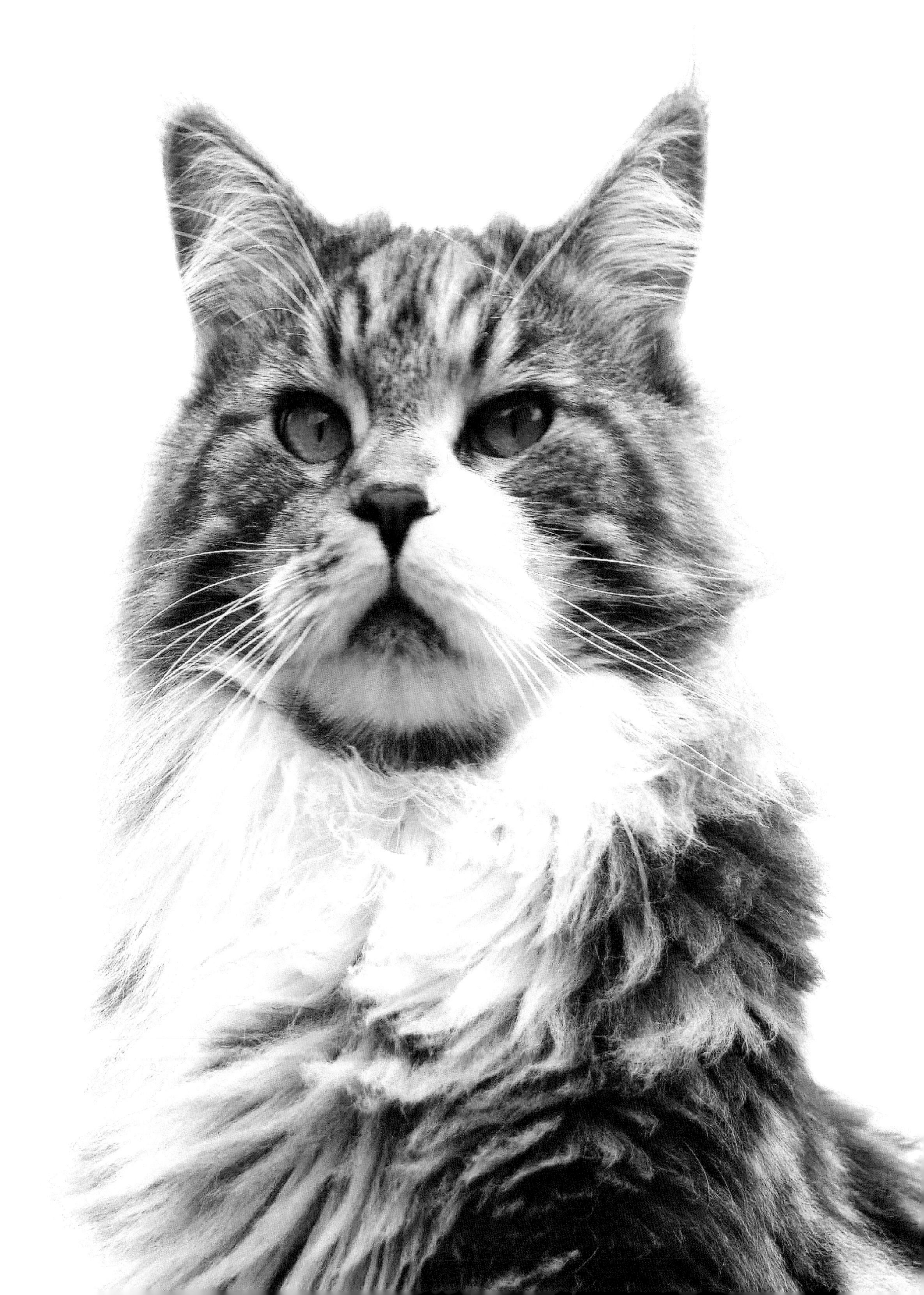

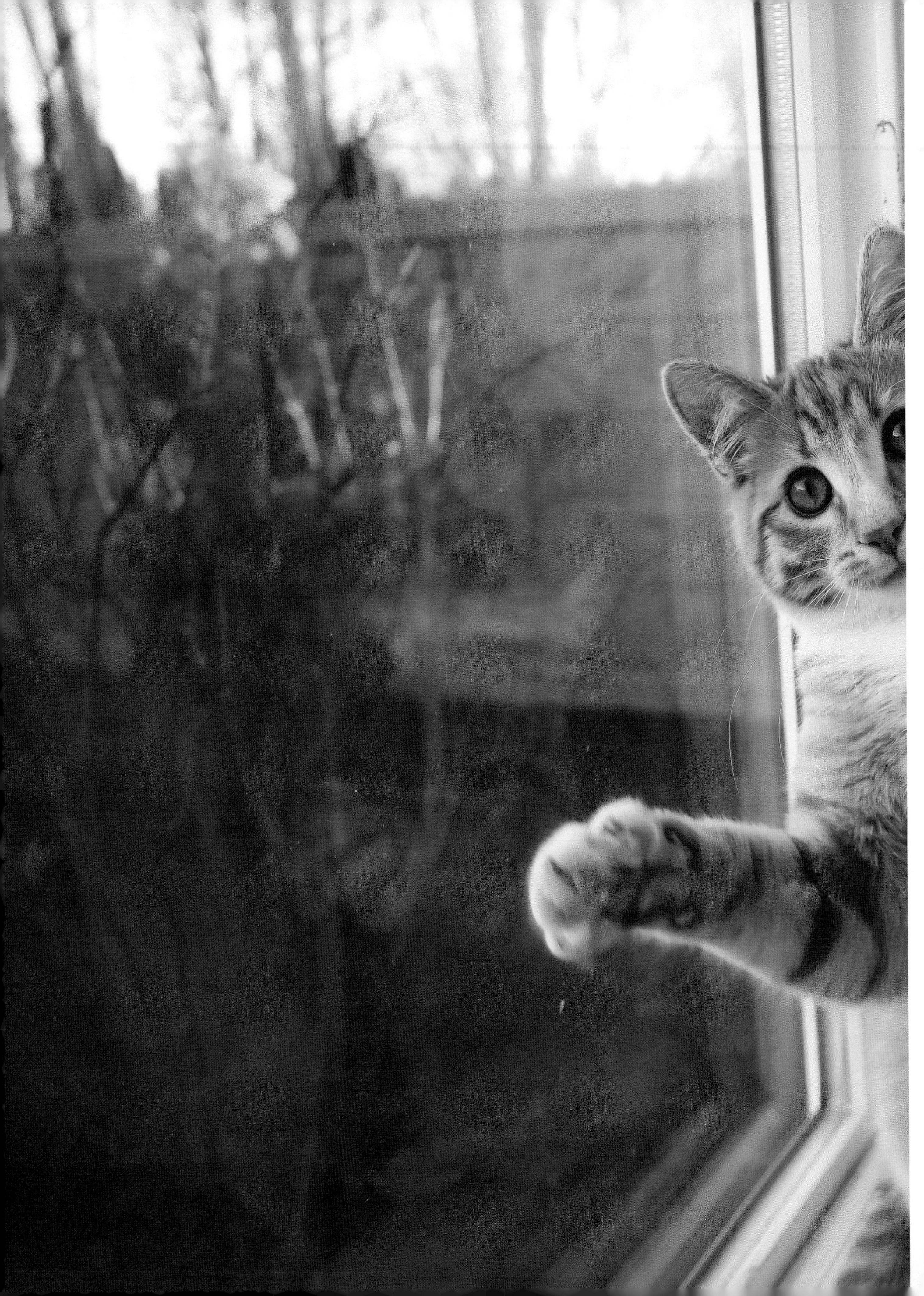

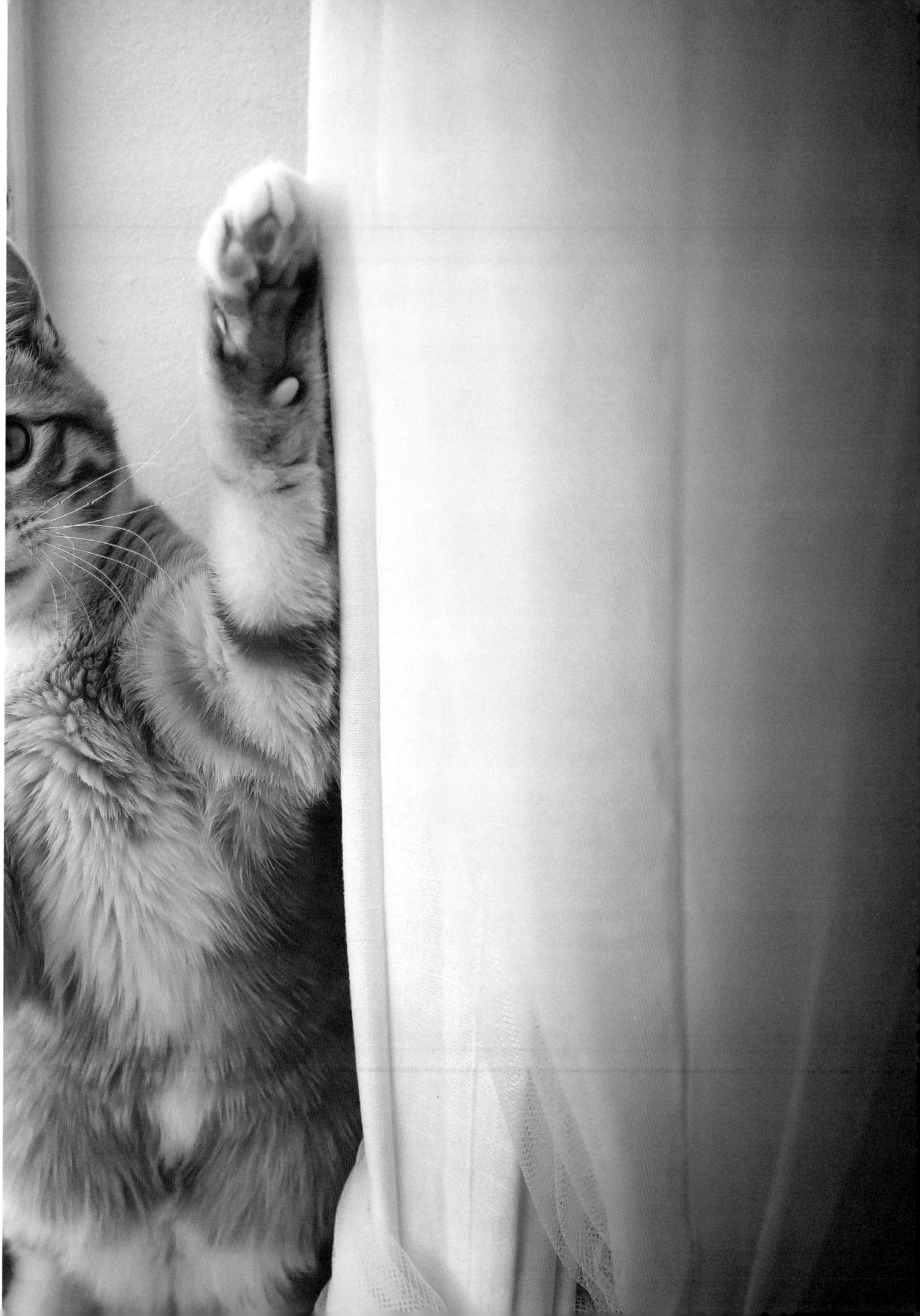

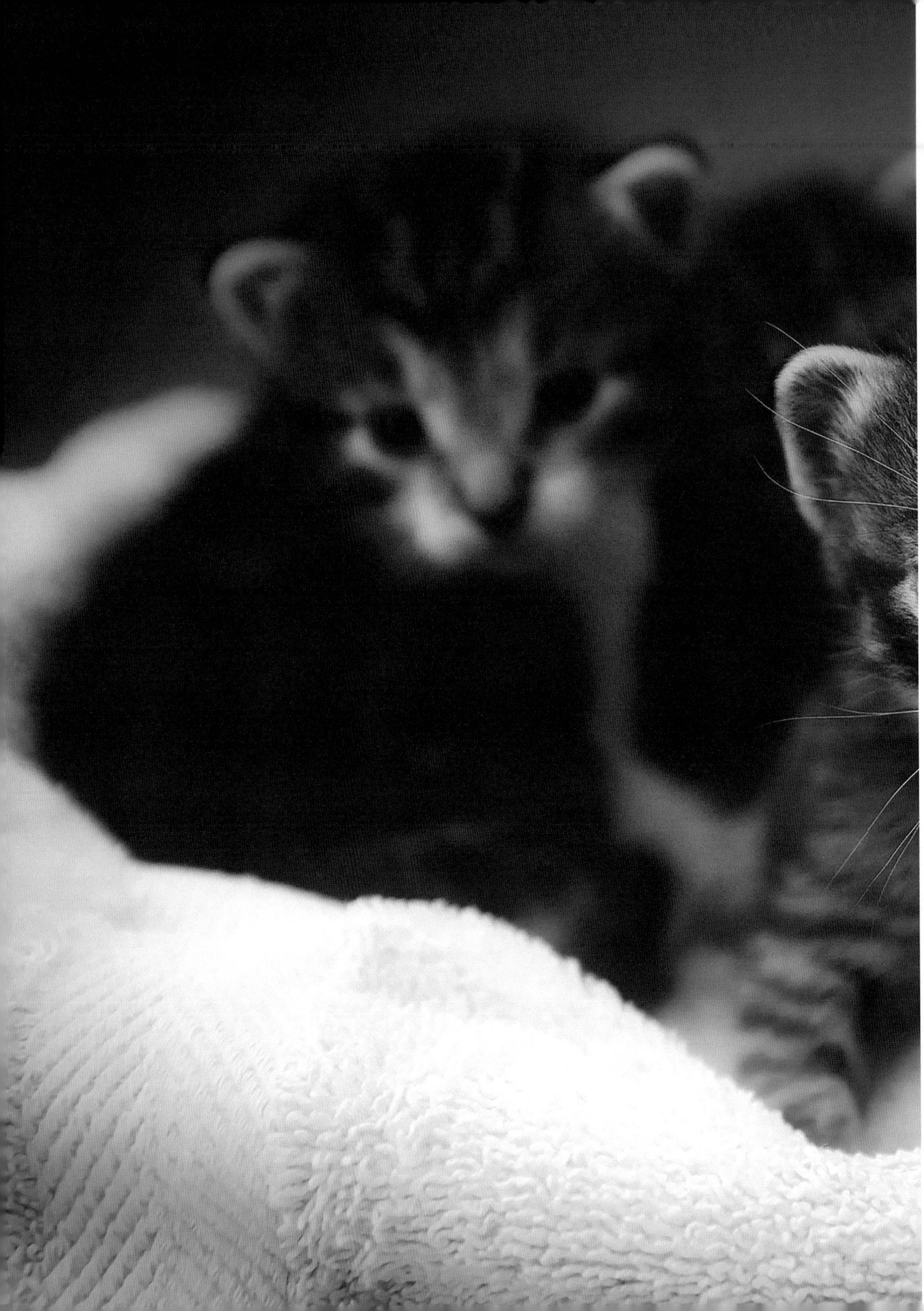

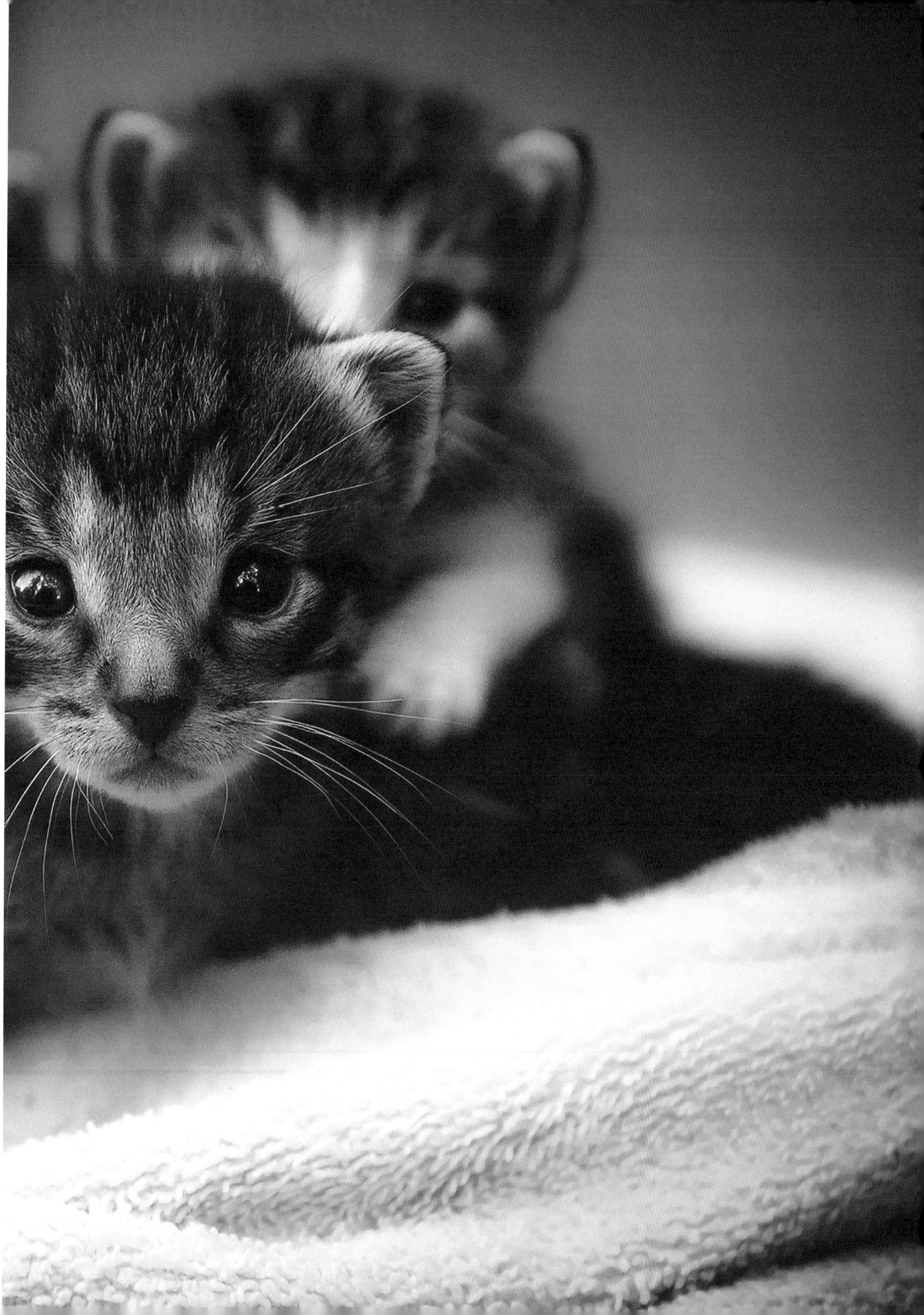

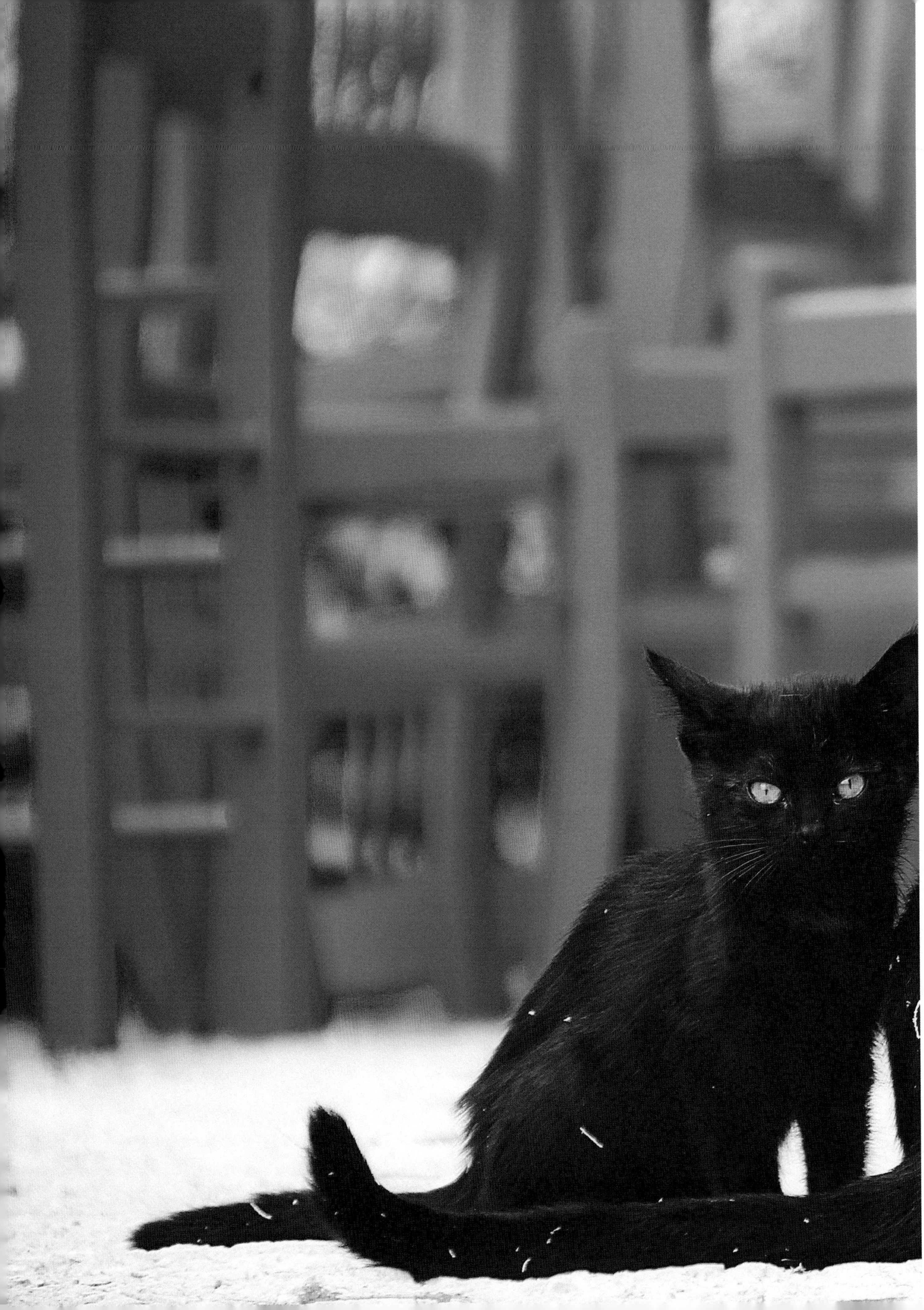

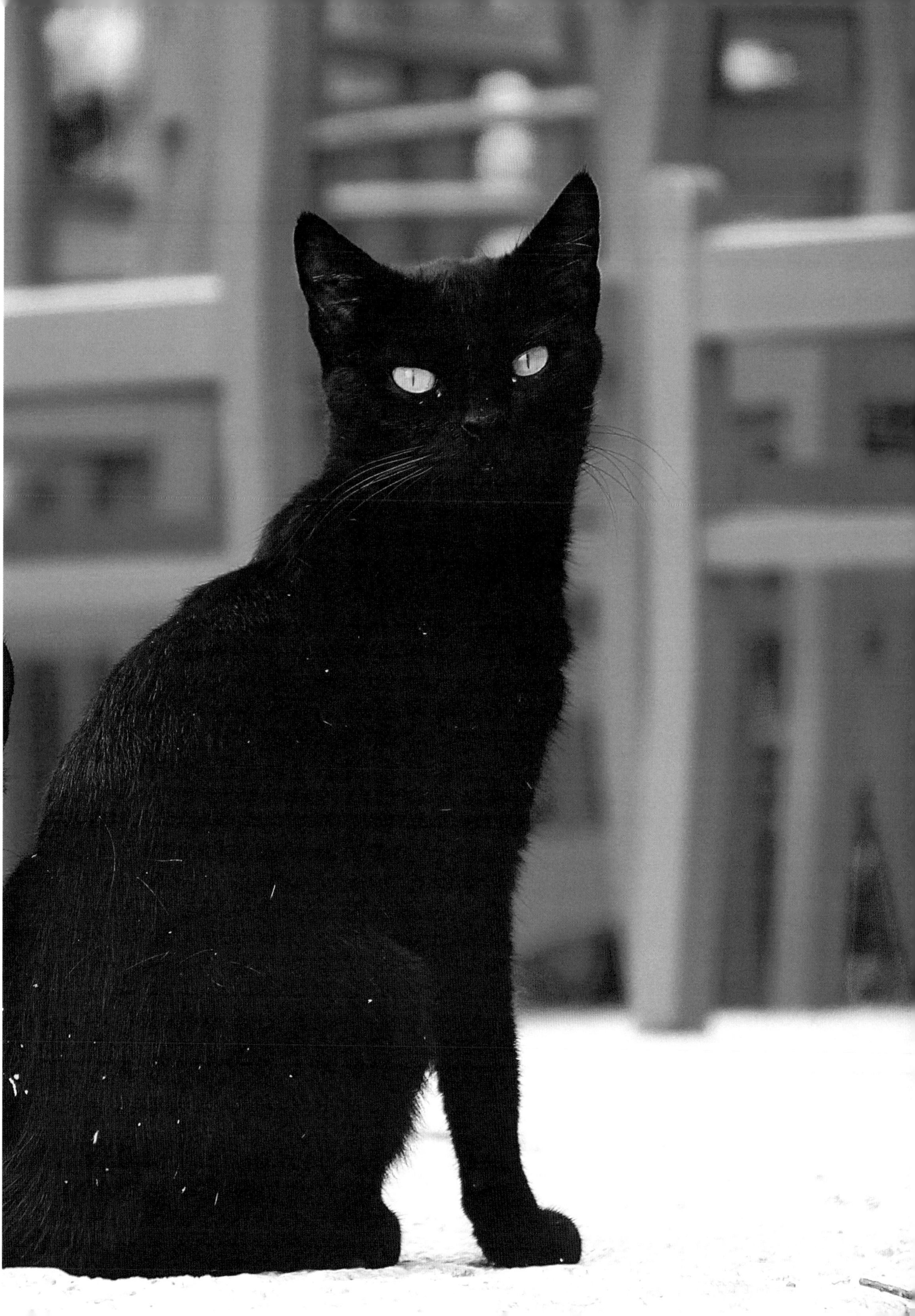

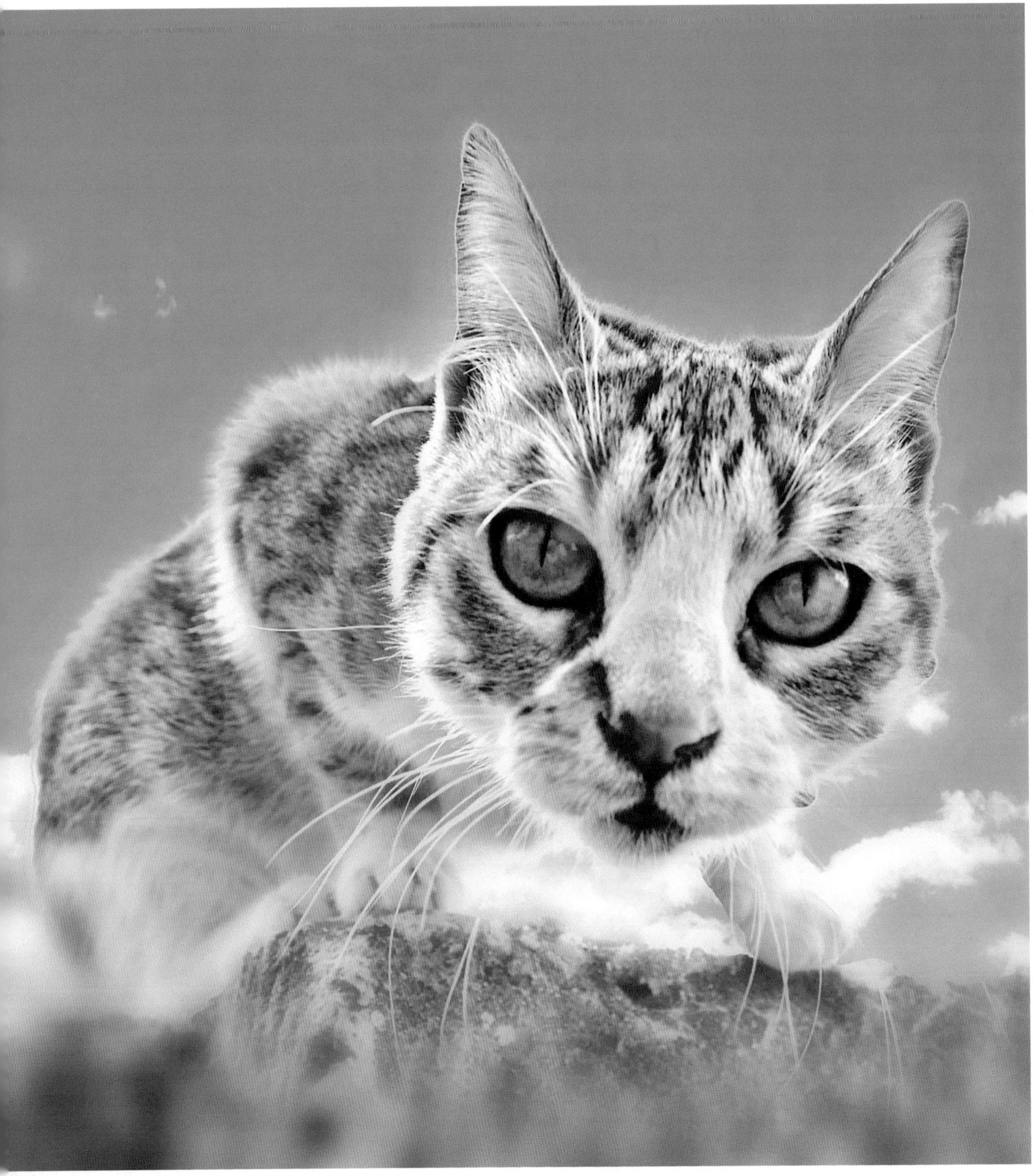

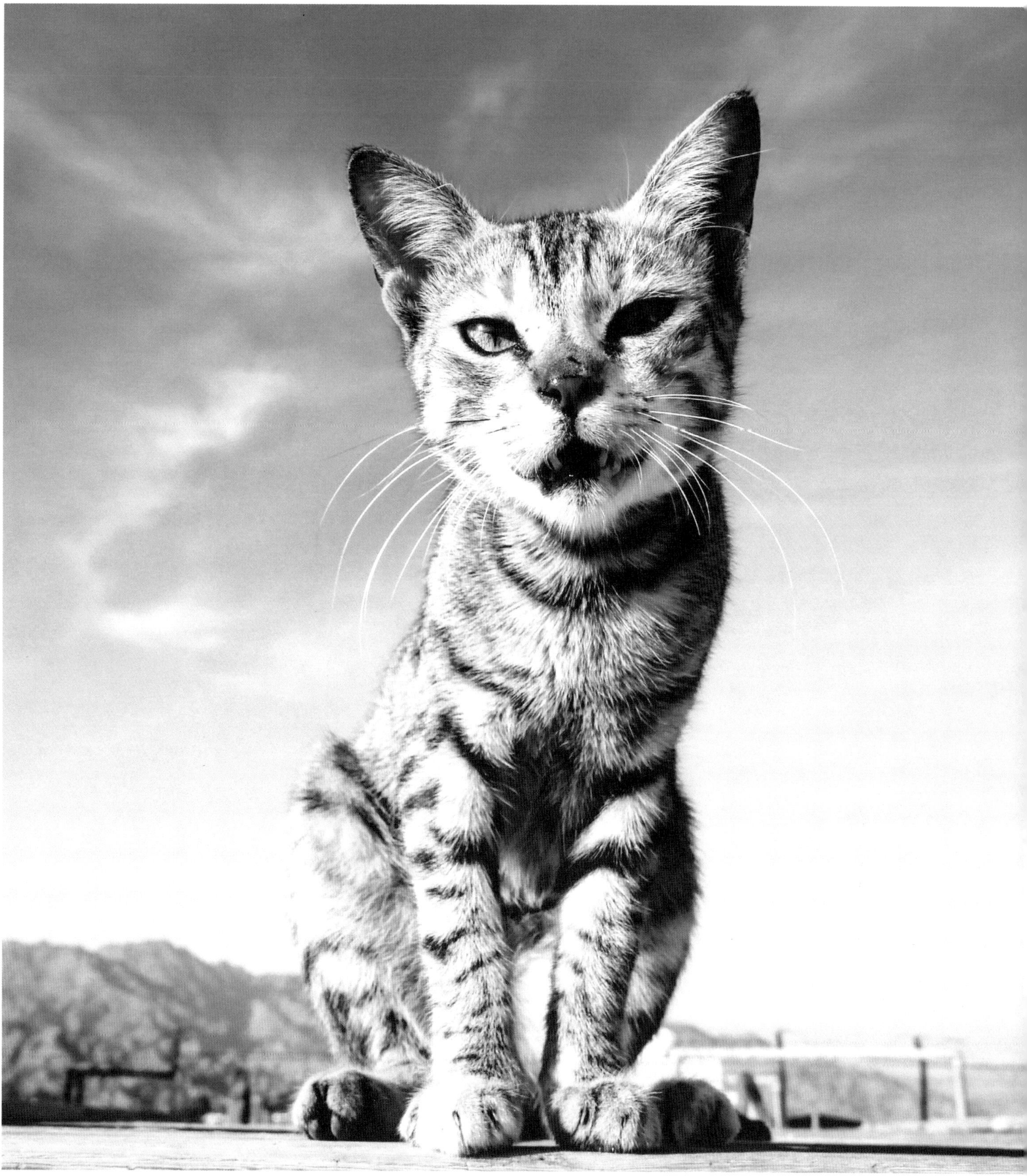

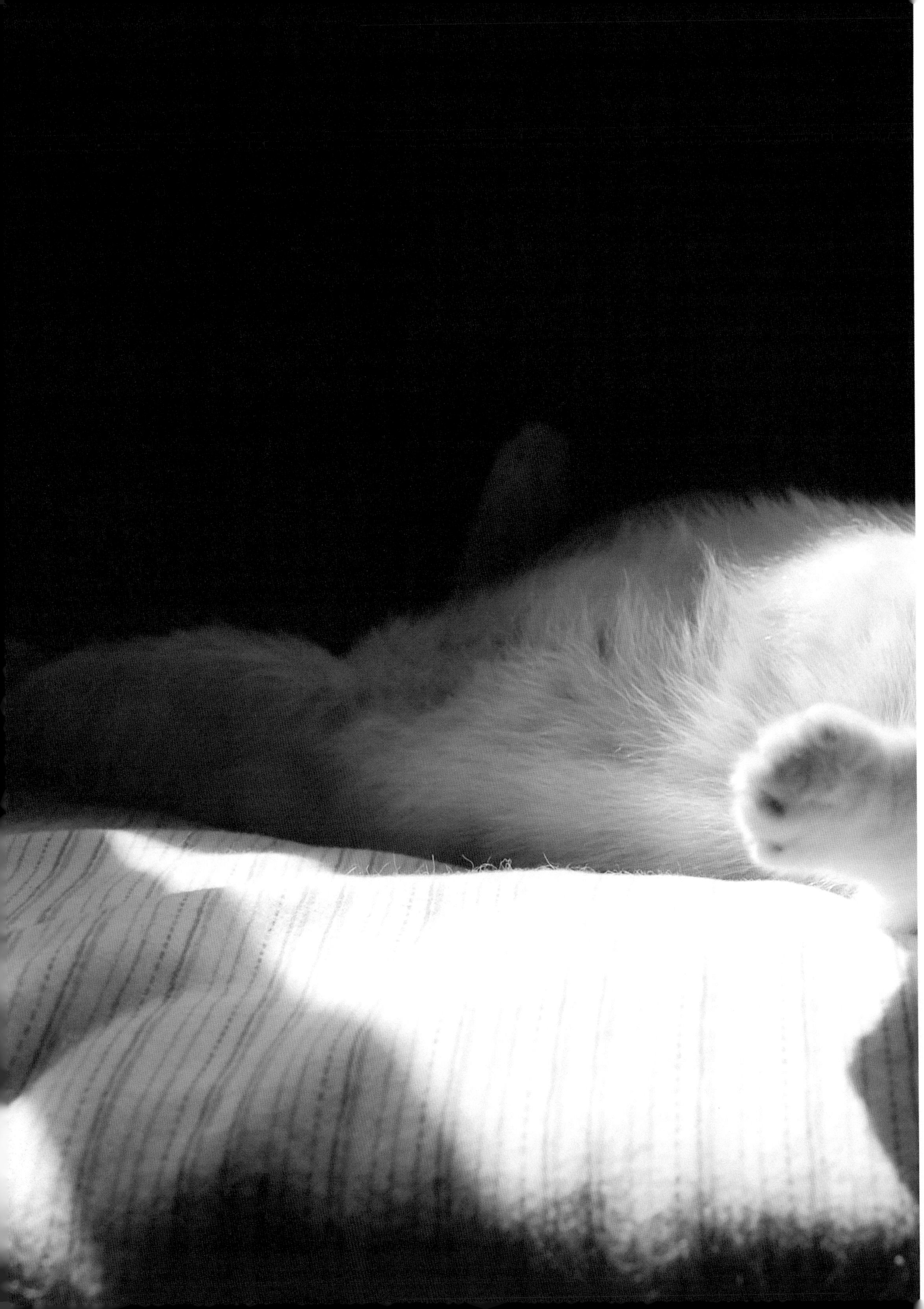

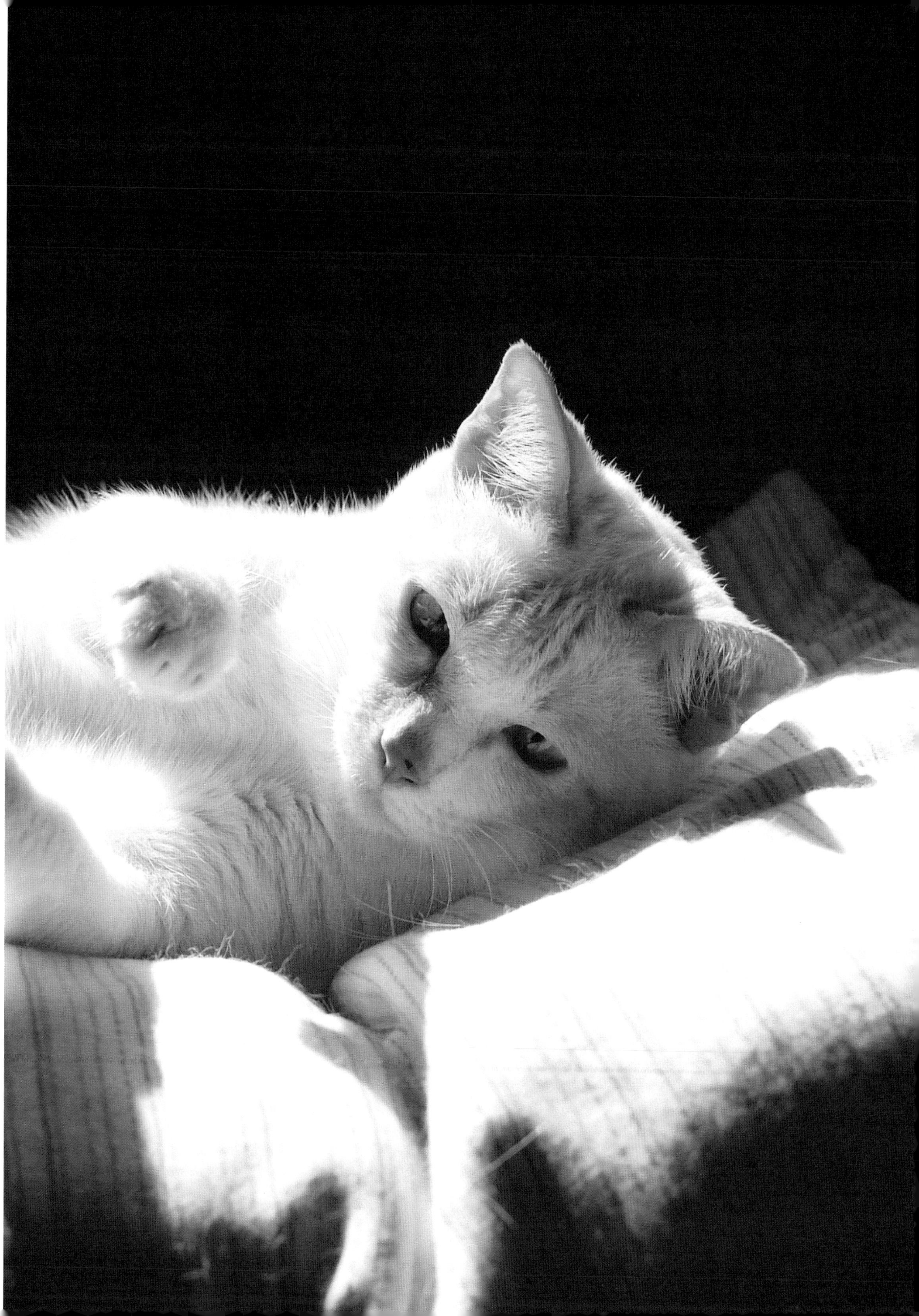

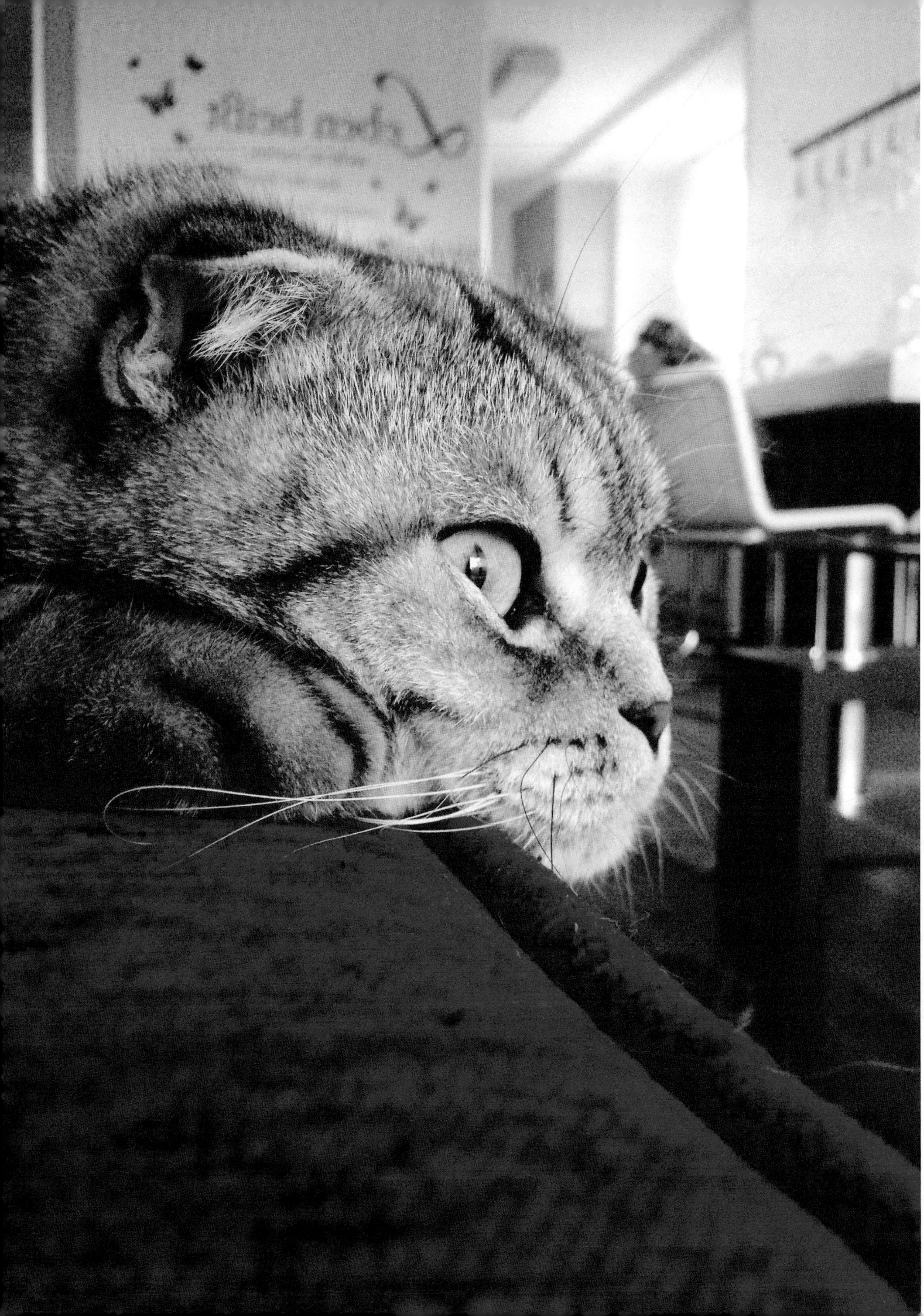

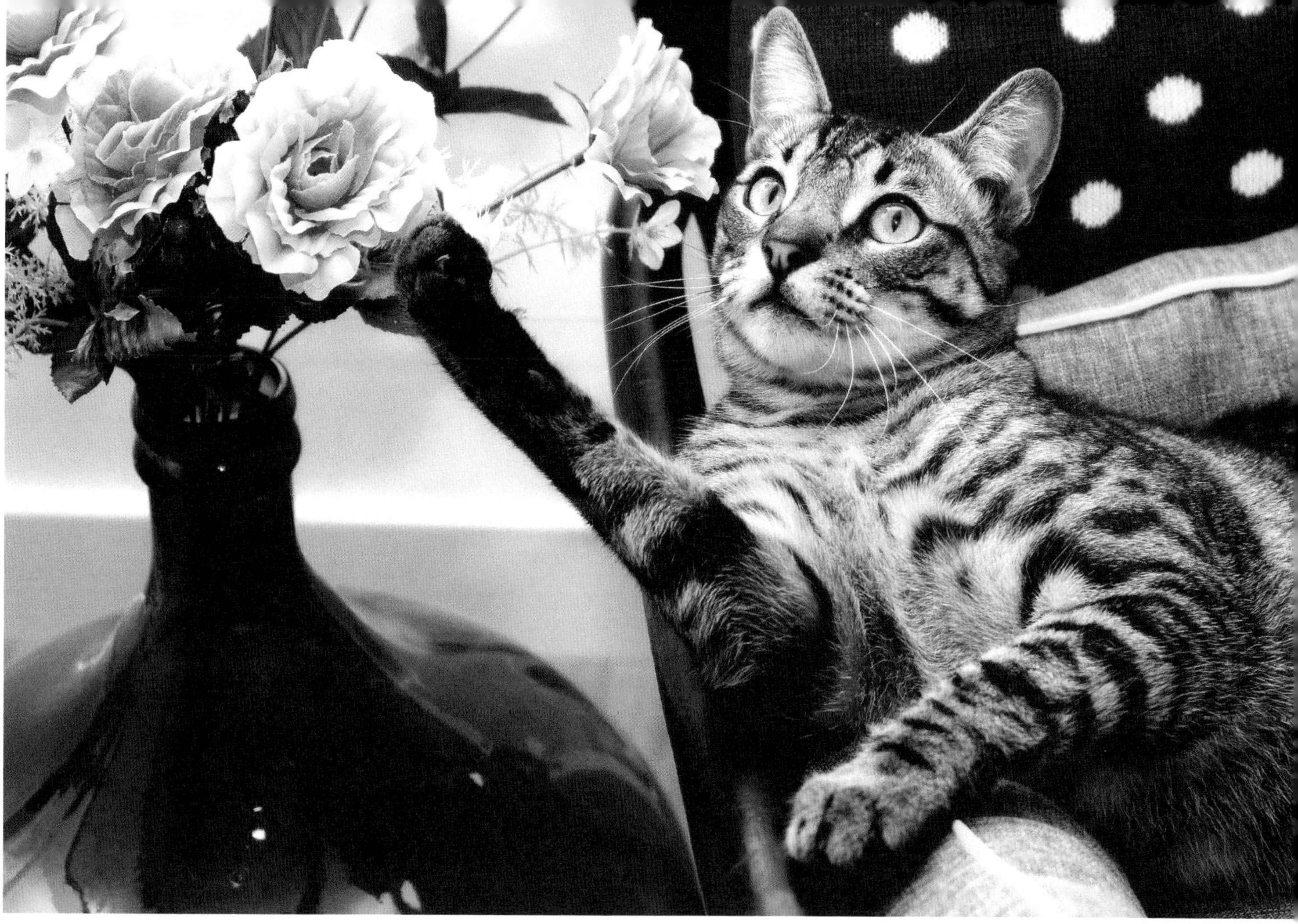

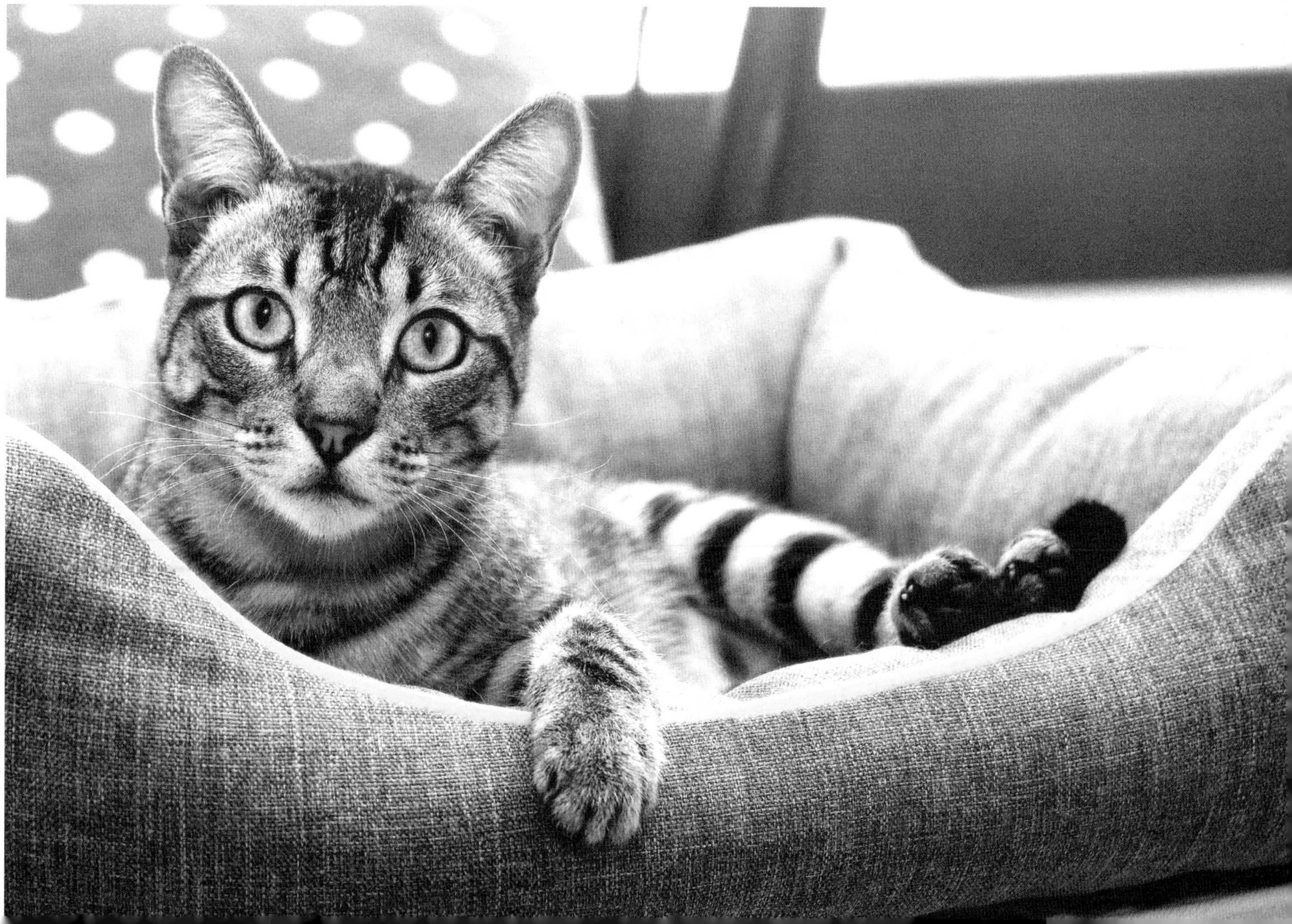

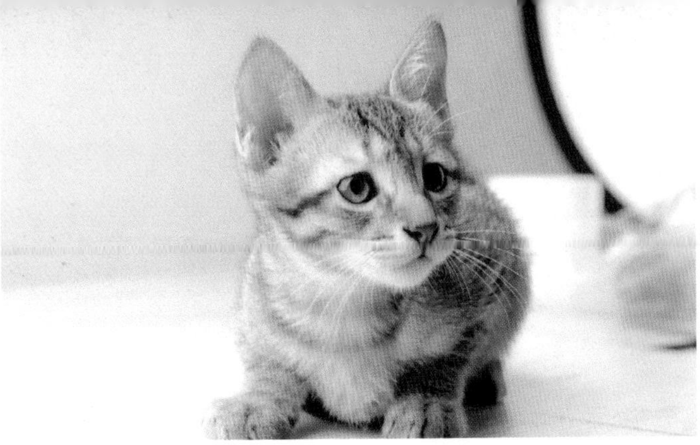
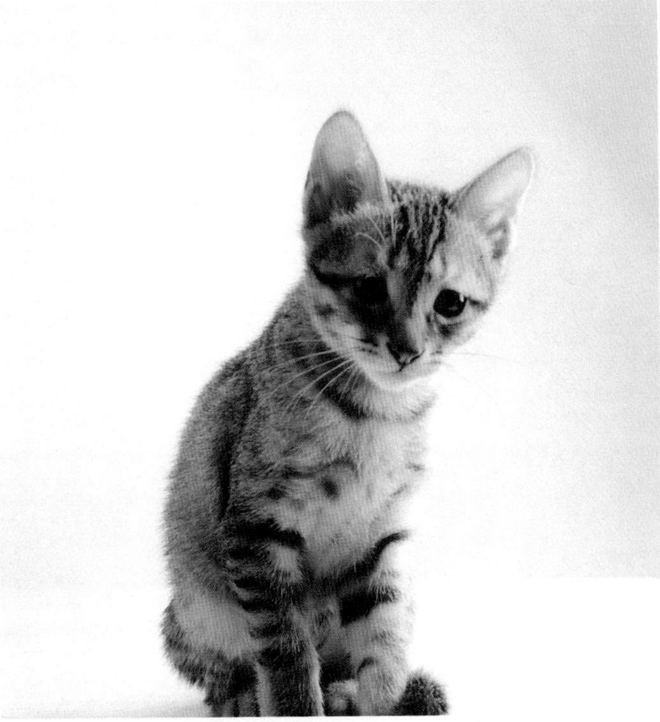
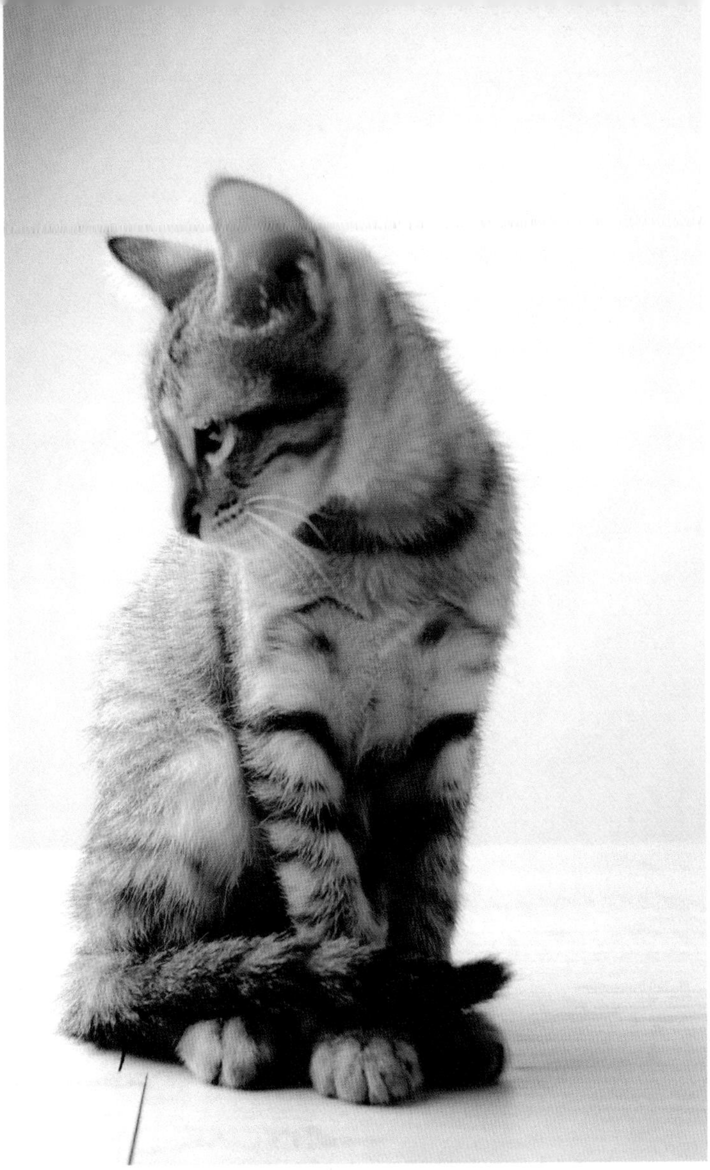
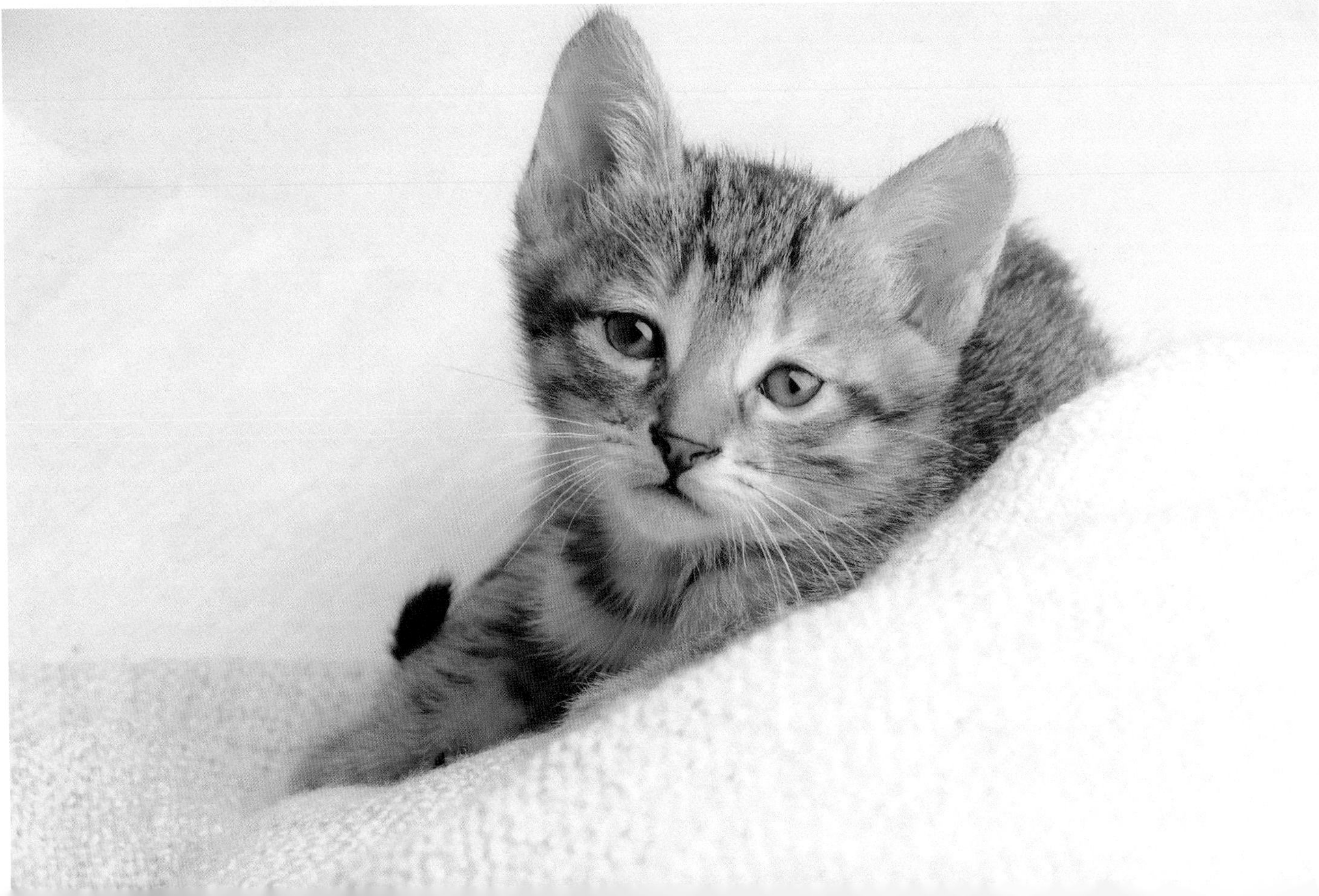

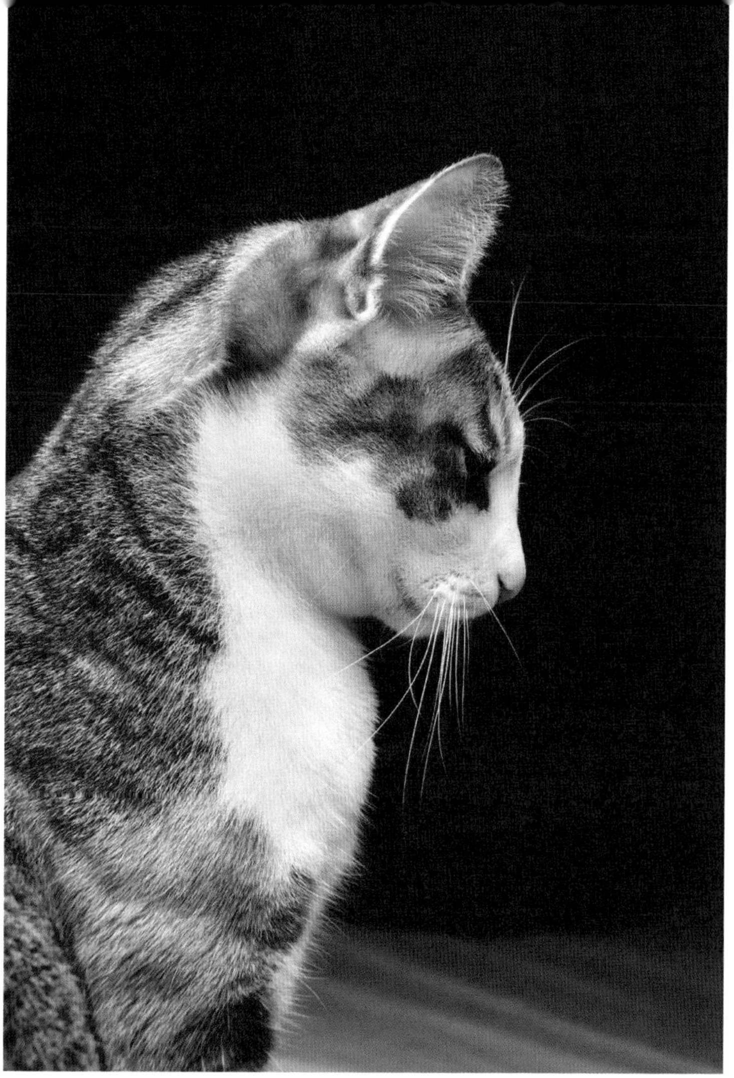
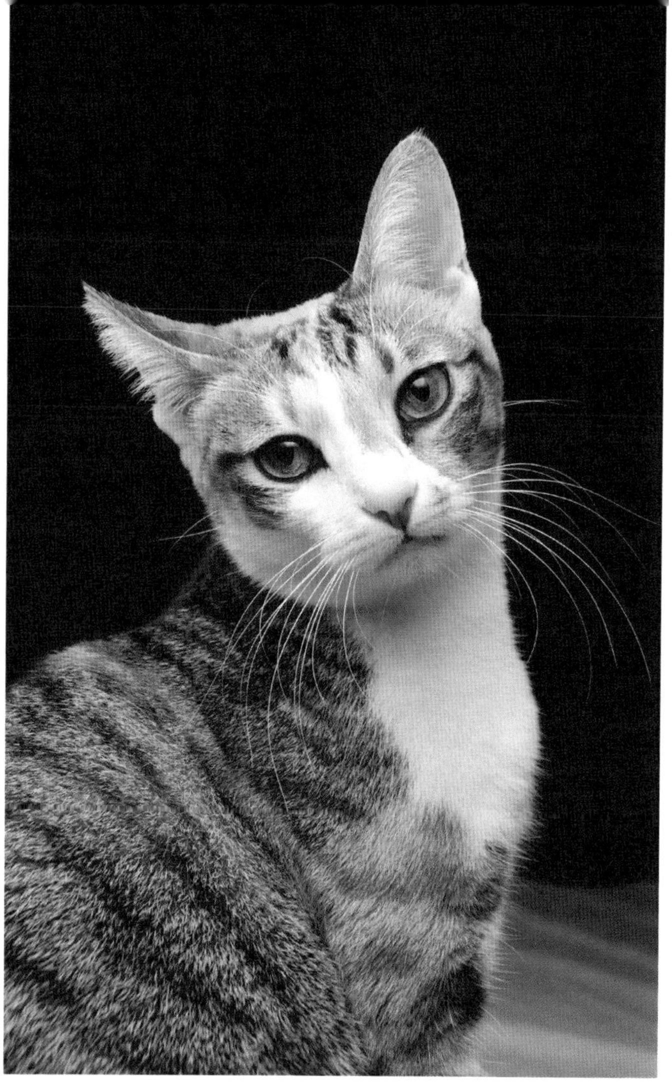
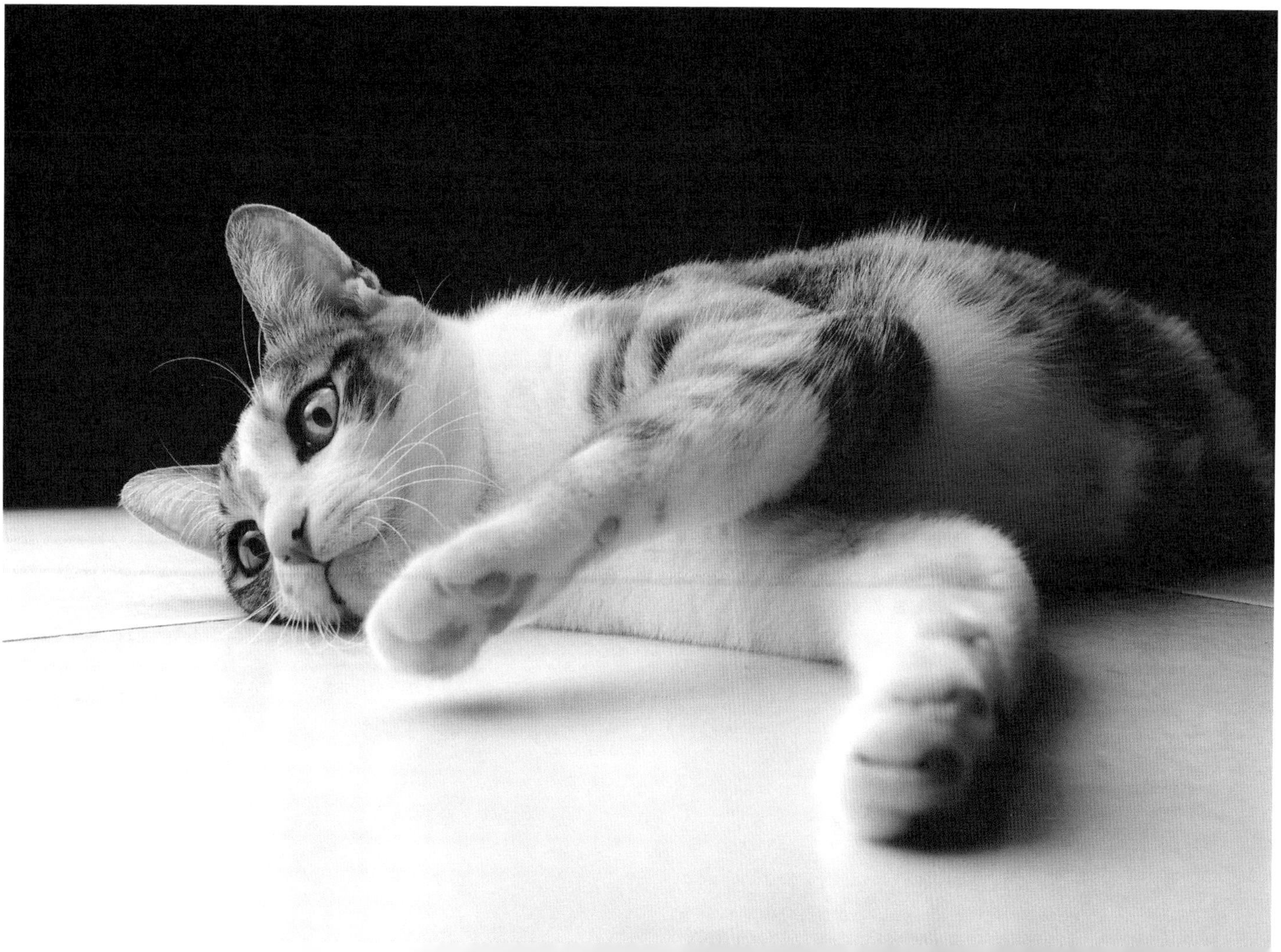

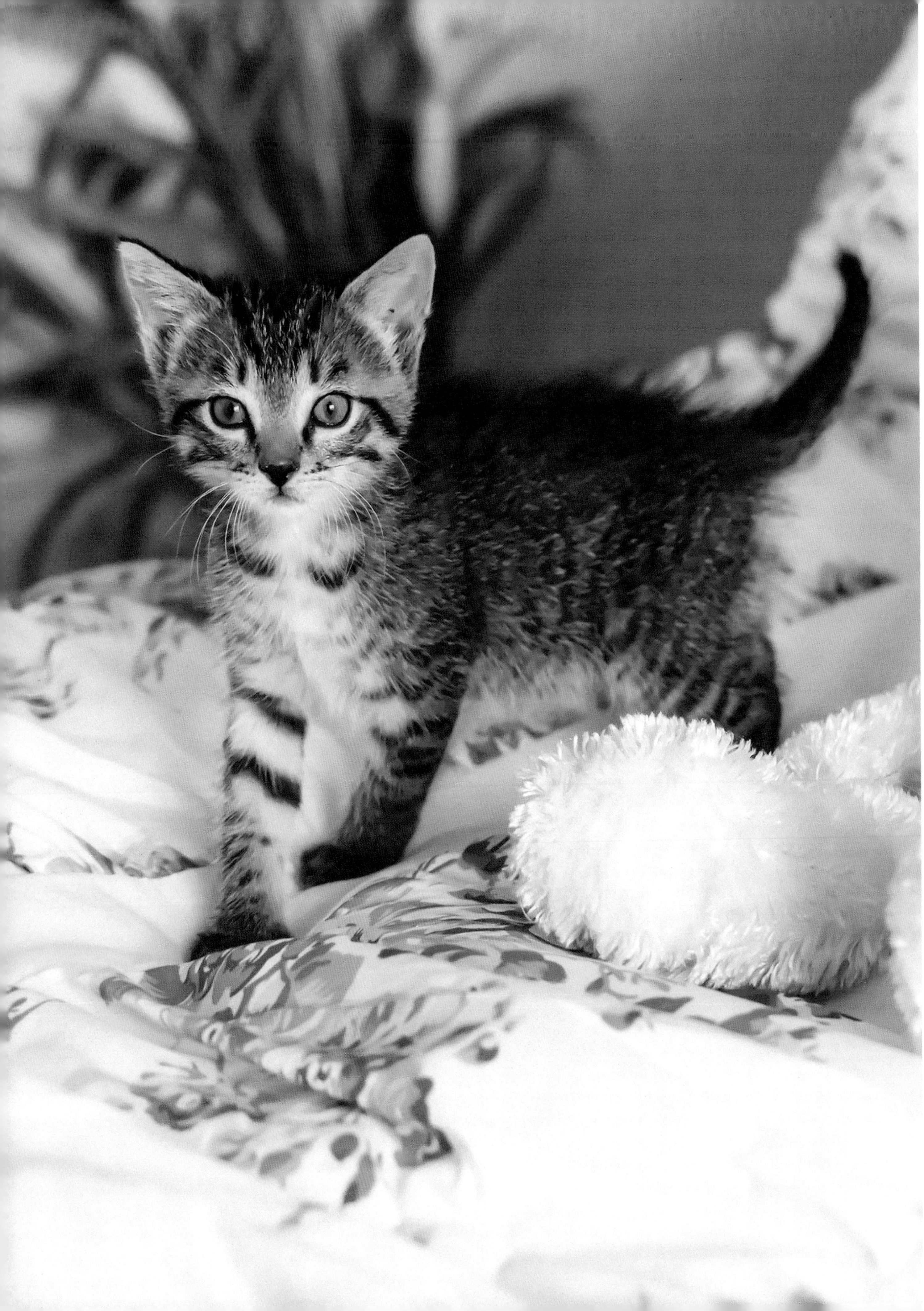

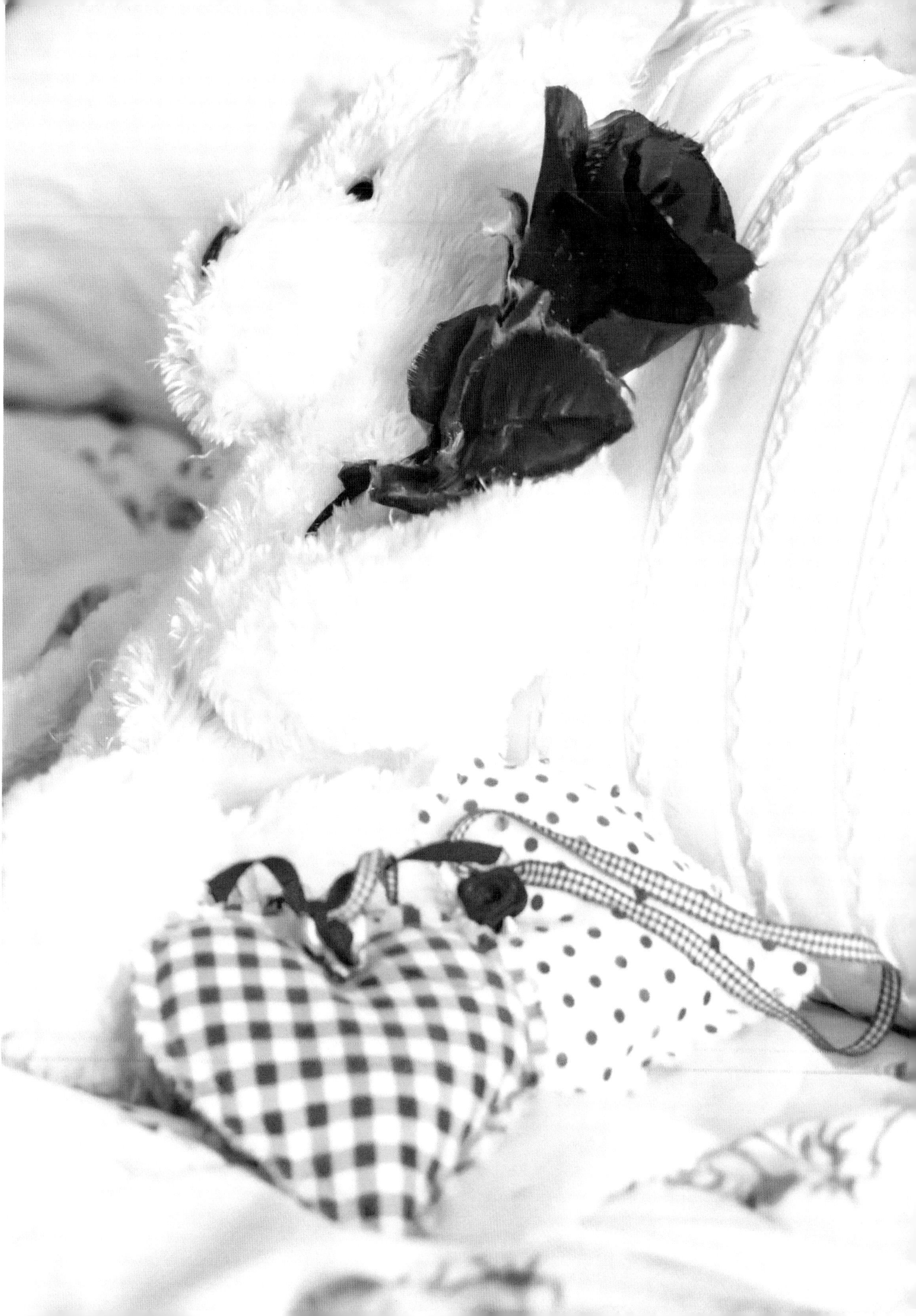

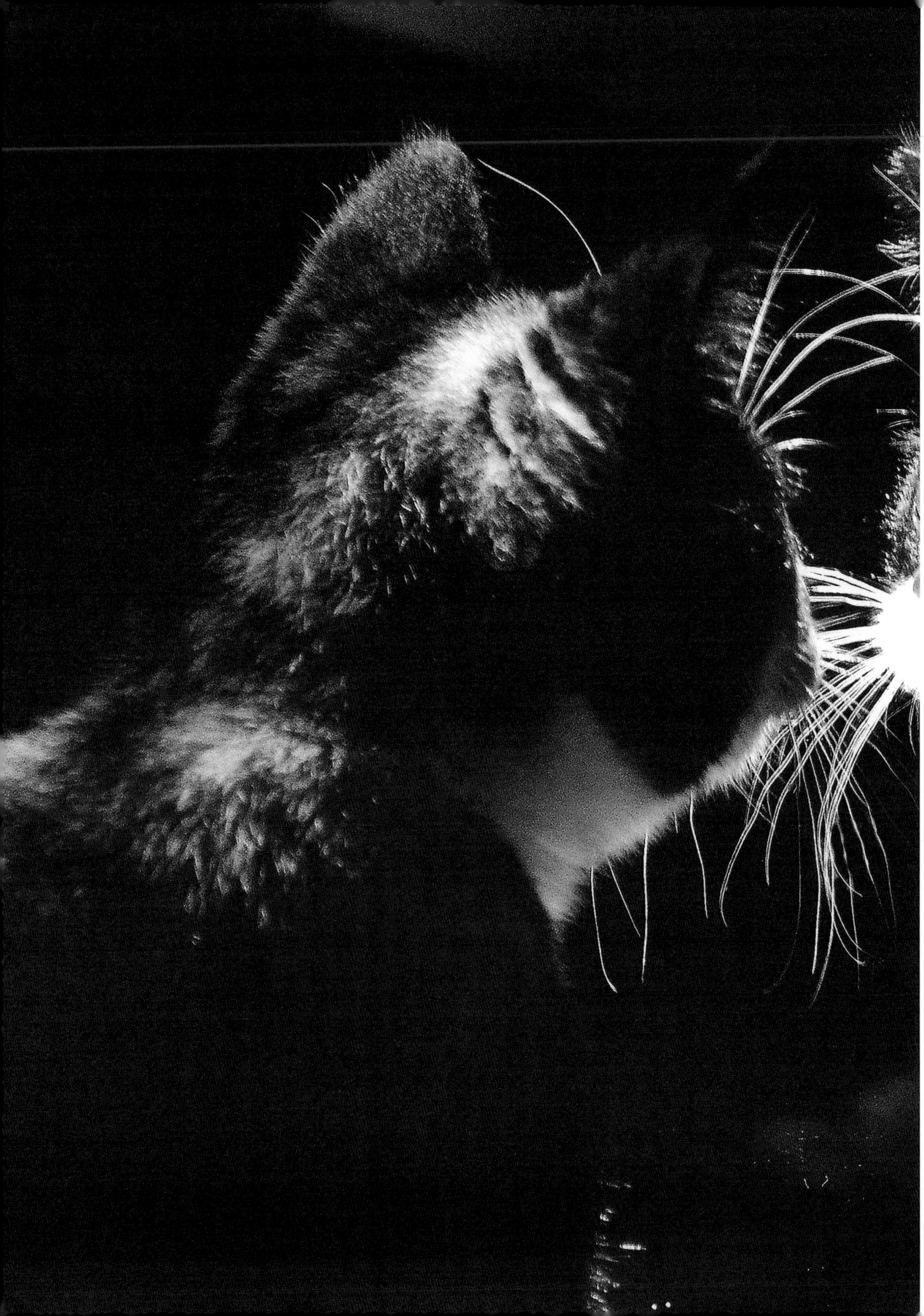

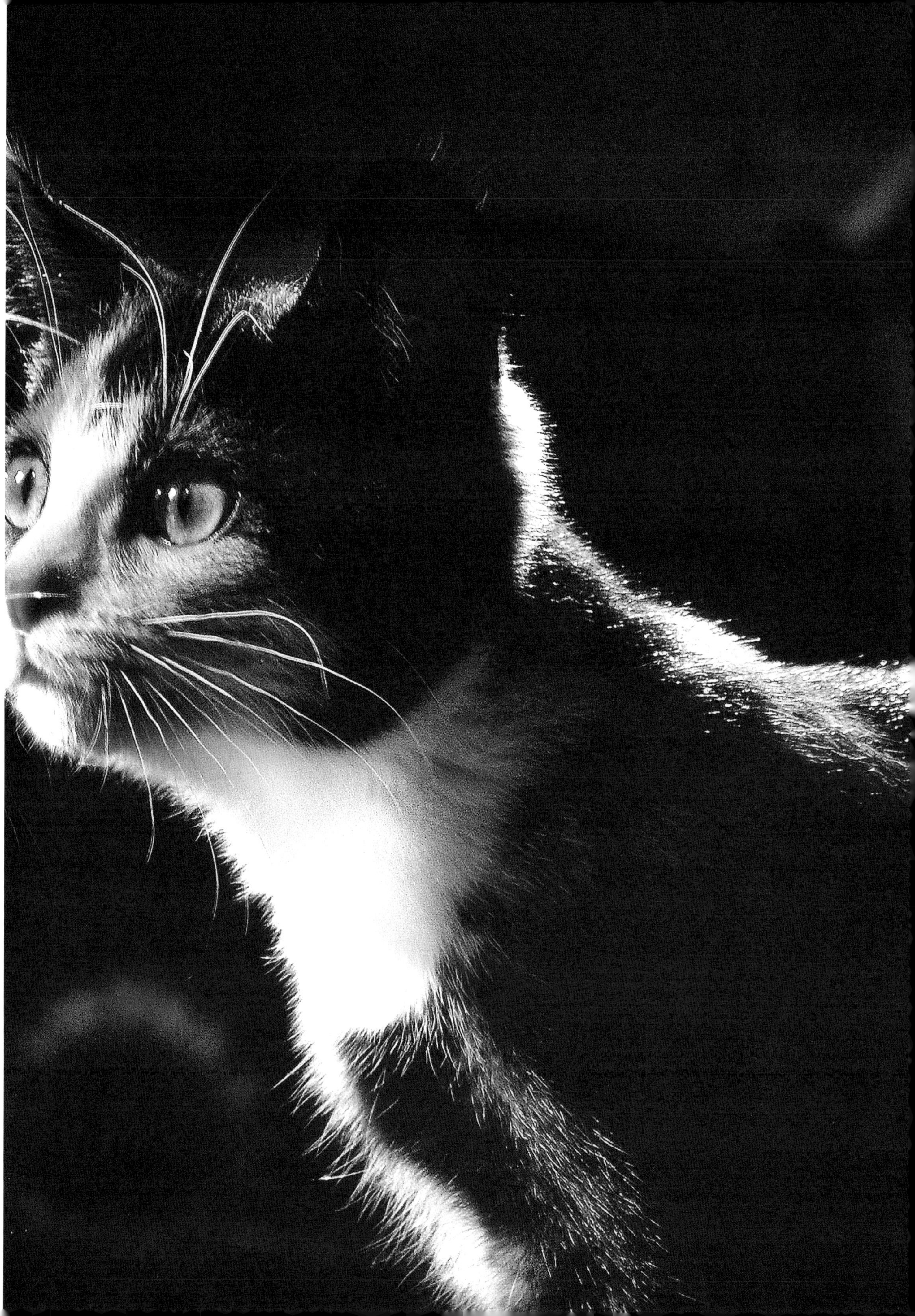

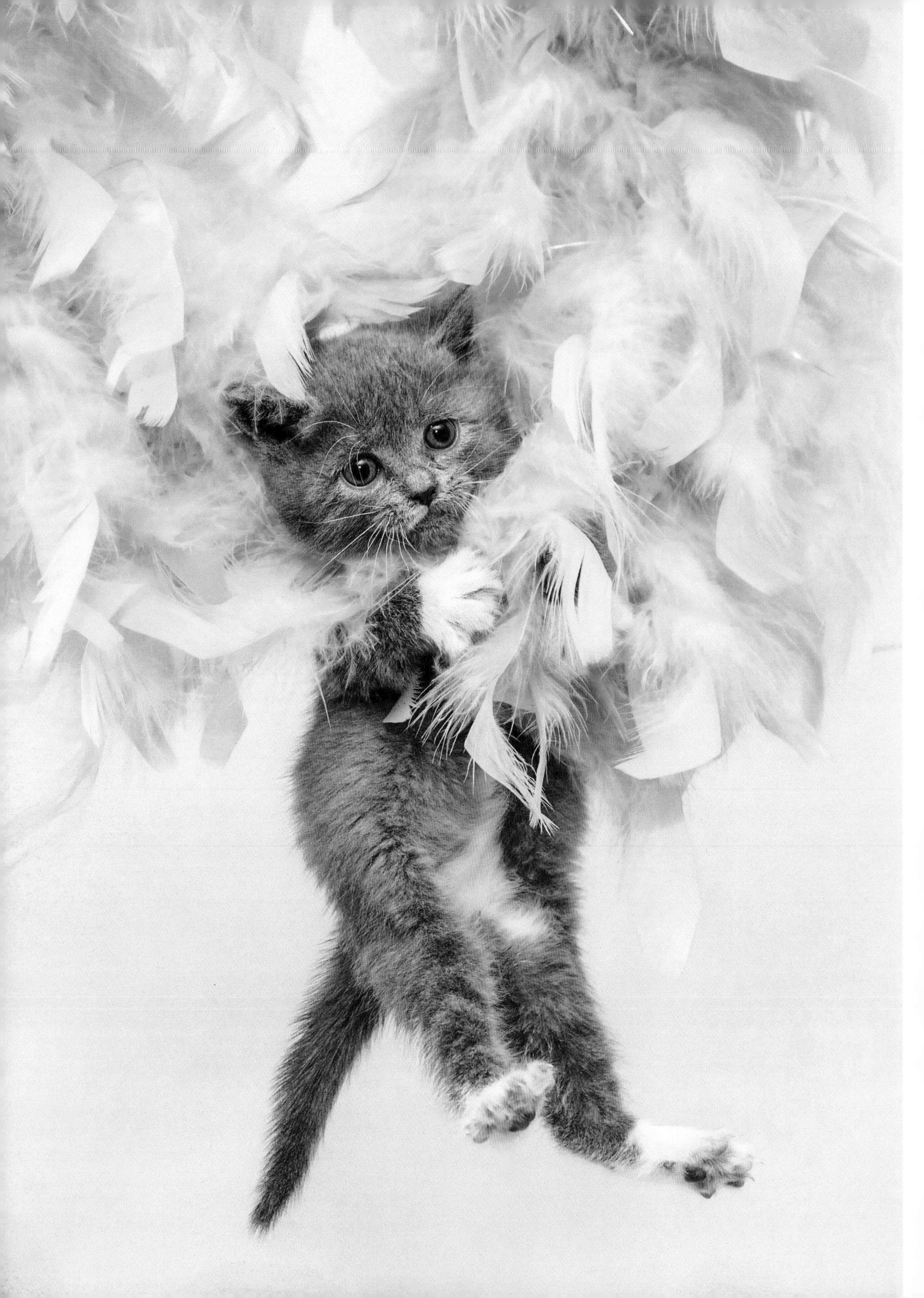

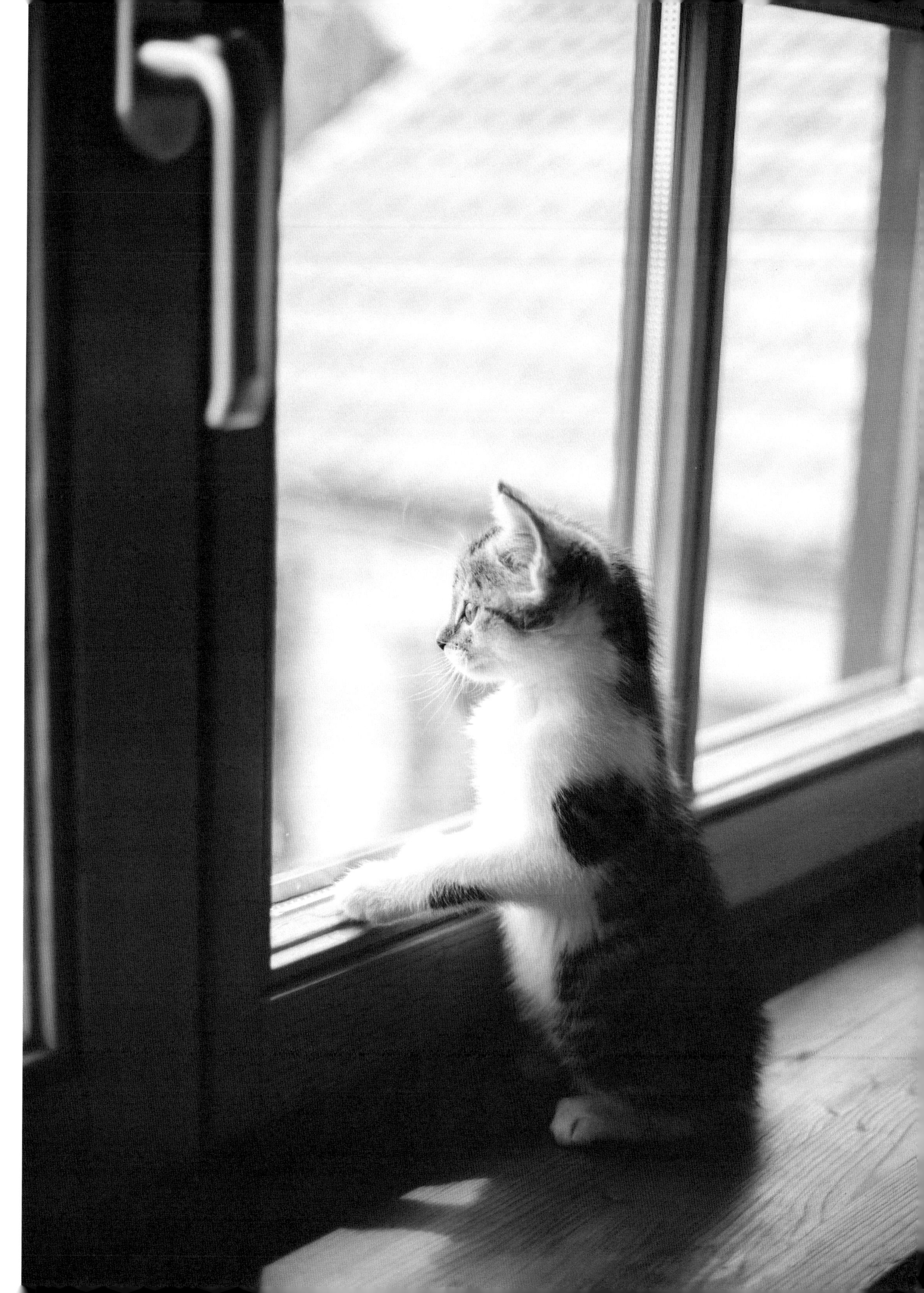

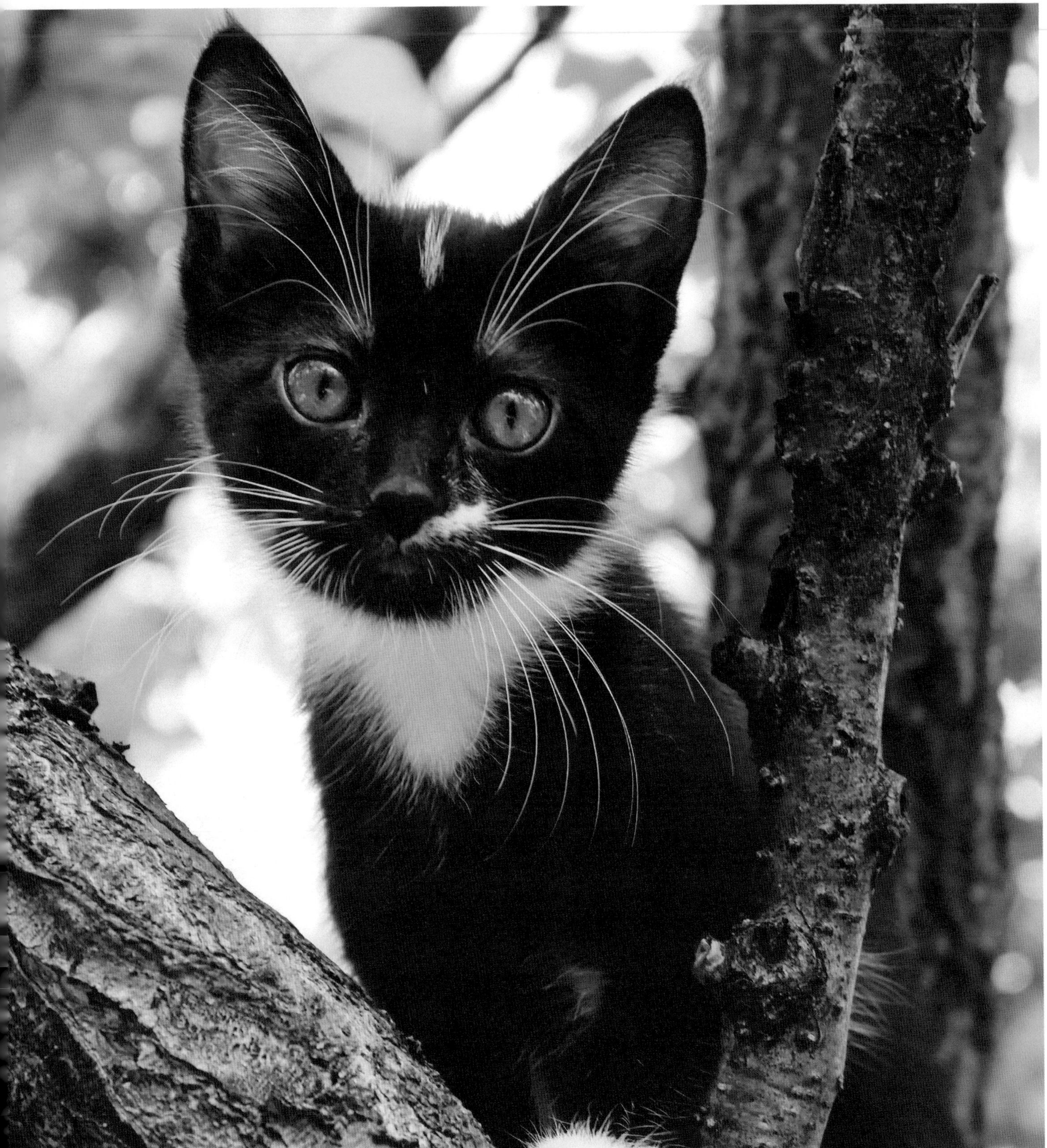

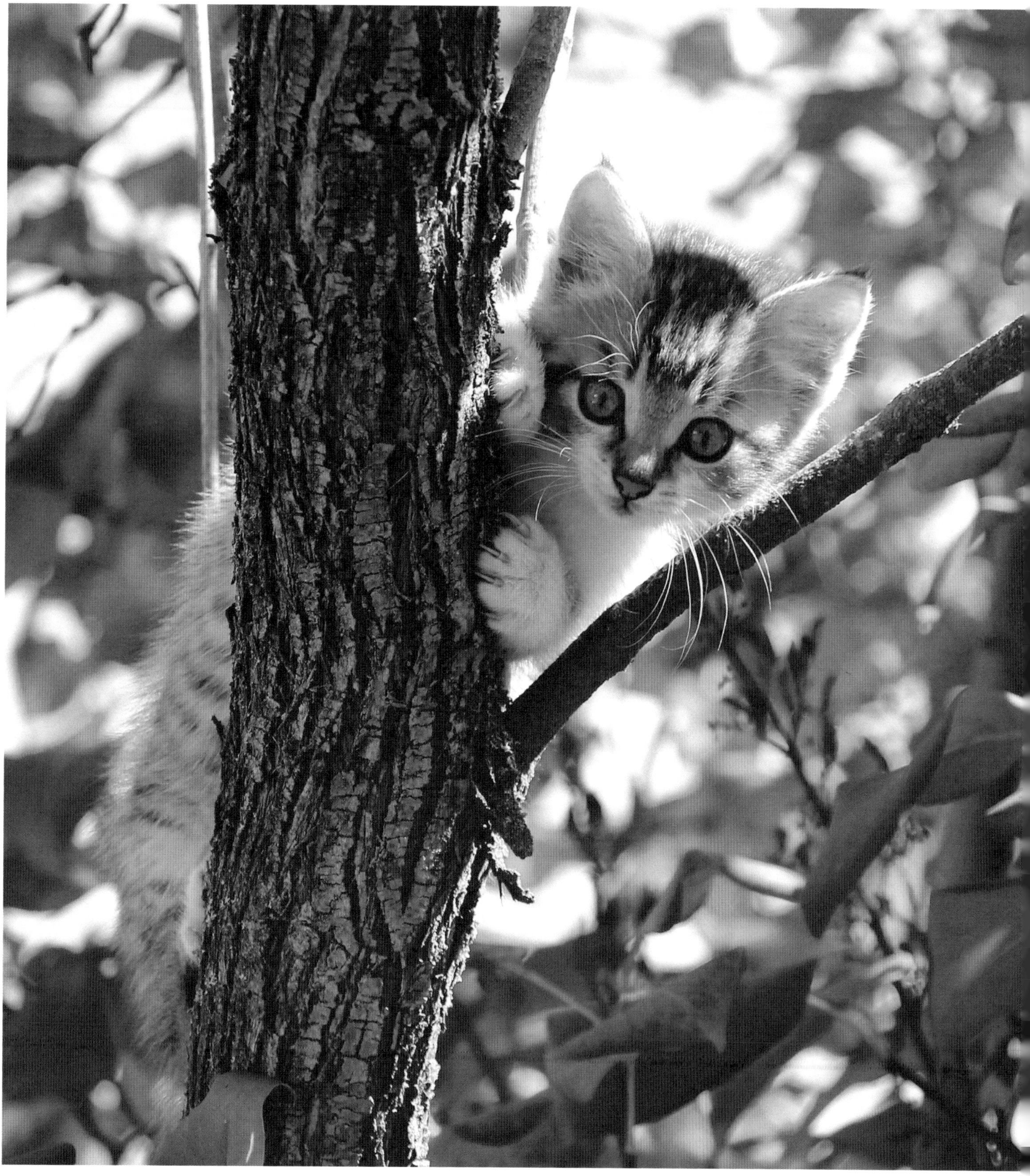

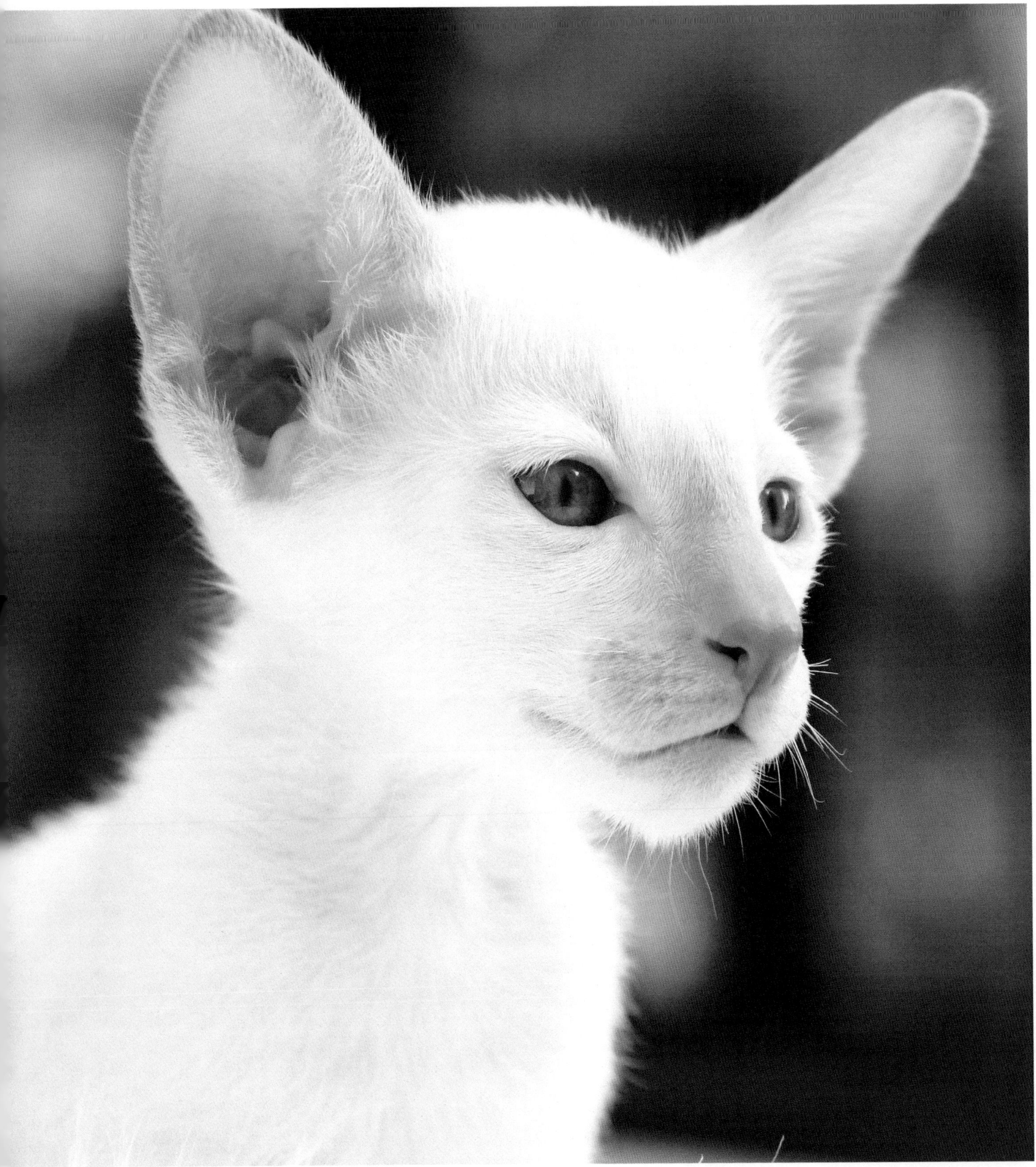

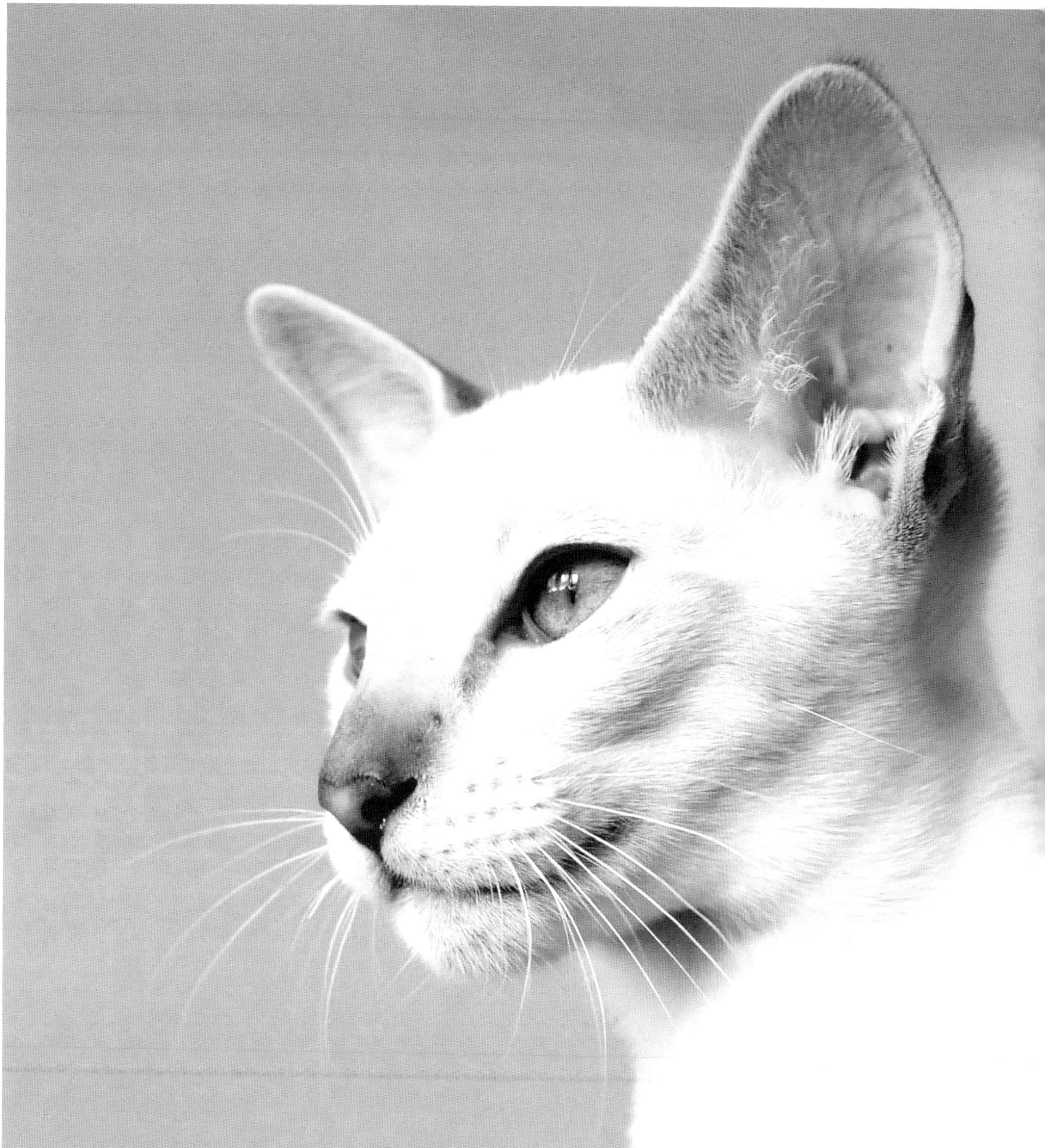

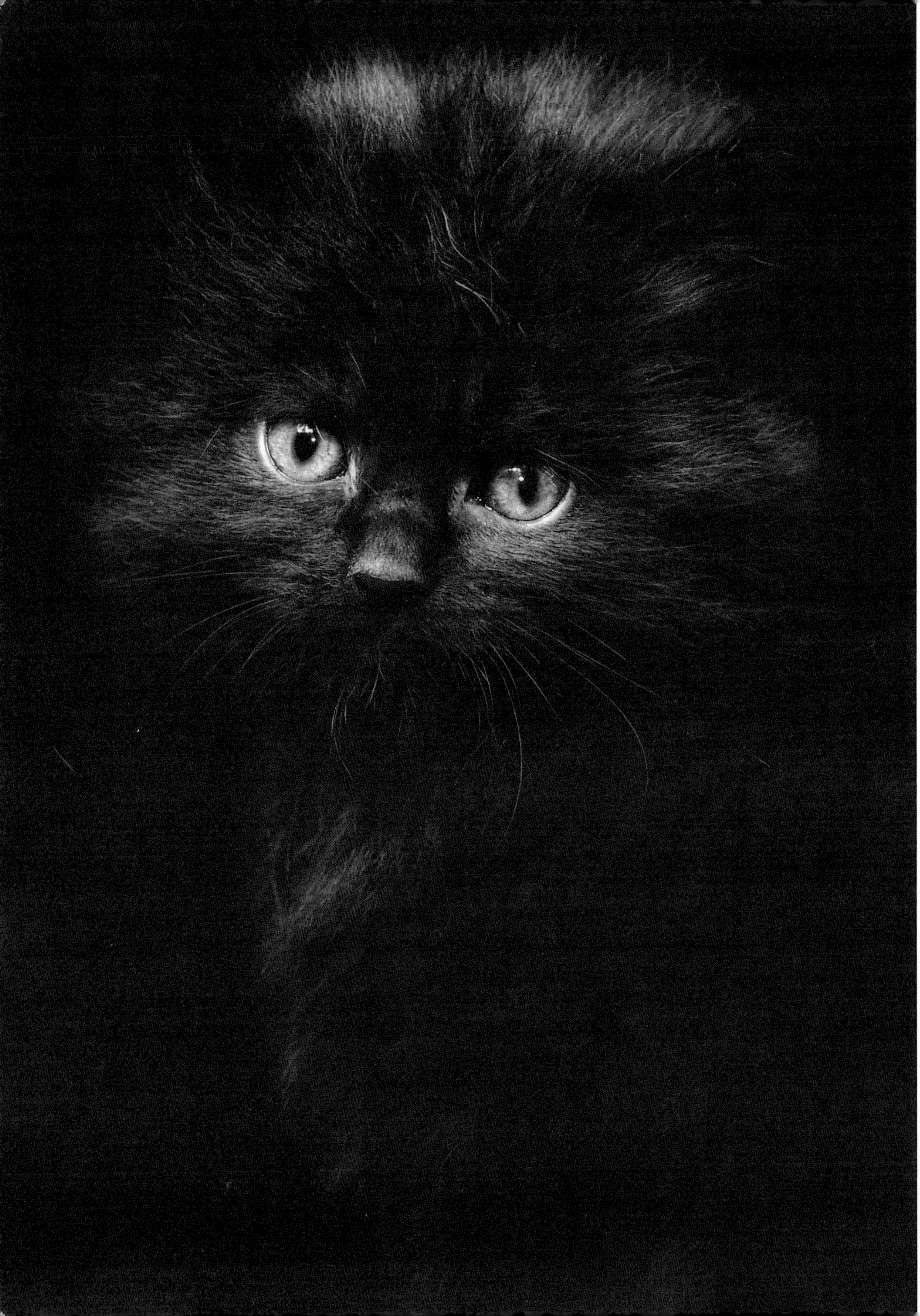

83108406R00058

Made in the USA
Columbia, SC
10 December 2017